Young and Defiant in Tehran

CONTEMPORARY ETHNOGRAPHY

Kirin Narayan and Paul Stoller, Series Editors

A complete list of books in the series is available from the publisher.

Young and Defiant in Tehran

SHAHRAM KHOSRAVI

PENN

University of Pennsylvania Press

Philadelphia

Published by
University of Pennsylvania Press
Philadelphia, Pennsylvania 19104-4112

Printed in the United States of America on acid-free paper

10 9 8 7 6 5 4 3 2 1

A Cataloging-in-Publication record is available from the Library of Congress

ISBN-13: 978-0-8122-4039-9
ISBN-10: 0-8122-4039-1

To two friends:

To Mansoor. A basiji *whose young body is devastated by chemical weapons in the Iran-Iran war. While I write these words—January 2007—he is suffering from irremediable and unbearable pain.*

*To lovely Behrooz. A fellow traveler (*hamsafar*). A dissident young man who disappeared without a trace when he tried to cross the border between Pakistan and India ilegally in November 1987.*

Contents

Note on Transliteration and Dates

The system of transliteration used in this book follows the style of the *International Journal of Middle East Studies.* Transliteration of Arabic words and words in Persian of Arabic origin follows the system used for Persian. All translations are by the author unless otherwise stated. In the text, dates are all Common Era unless they refer to Persian texts. In the text and bibliography, dates are given in the Iranian *shamsi* (solar) calendar and are followed by the corresponding Common Era date separated by a slash. Thus the year 2003 is 1382 *shamsi*.

Preface

It happened in Tajrish Square early one afternoon in September 1993. Tehran was burning under the summer sun. At this time of year, the daytime temperature can reach 45° C in the shade. Years later, in September 1998, I visited this place in north Tehran in the early afternoon on several September days in order to build up an image of the incident. Tajrish Square, a central business zone, is usually crammed with people and cars. On this day the hot sun had driven people away to look for the comfort of their air-conditioned homes. The lively square, like the rest of Tehran, was having its long, tedious daily siesta. Even the peddlers, who usually occupy the southern part of the square, had taken refuge in the calm neighboring gardens. A few taxis were parked in the shadow of large old planes and their drivers were taking a nap.

The teenage girl inserted a small coin into the telephone and dialed. Her friend was waiting outside the telephone booth. Both were dressed in robes, their hair was covered with chic scarves in bright colors. The girl in the telephone booth broke into laughter, causing her friend to laugh too. After a while, the girl waiting on the pavement saw a young armed man jump out of a car. She panicked when he approached the telephone booth. In the mechanical reaction Iranian women have developed since the Revolution whenever they face the moral police, she calmly but with shaking fingers pulled her scarf forward, hid some strands of hair under it, and knotted it more tightly under her chin. She tapped on the glass to warn her friend, who did not react but laughed even louder when she saw the man coming toward them. He passed the young girl on the pavement, pulled open the door of the booth, and asked to whom the girl was talking. She turned her back on him and said that was none of his business. The man snatched the receiver and loudly demanded to be told who was on the other end of the line. Silence. Upset, he accused the girl of talking to a man. He shouted at her to correct her veil and threatened her with arrest. She did not touch her scarf, which had slid backward so that a lot of her hair was unveiled. She told him to "get lost." He drew his pistol and pointed at her head. If she would not put her scarf straight he would shoot her, he said. She said that "he could do nothing." She was wrong. He fired. She fell. The bullet had shattered her skull.

The man was never held responsible and the case was dropped. Her defiance, her laugh at the young man who saw himself as the envoy of God on earth, evoke the political as well as the existential standpoint the Iranian younger generation is taking up. The image of the smoke of gunpowder rising like smog and the color of the fresh blood spattered on the glass inside the telephone booth have been with me throughout the writing of this book.

This tragic homicide scene, based on a short report in *Iran Times* (September 11, 1993), reveals the relationship between banality and brutality at work in Iran. The scene reflects many dimensions of my field of study. Like this book, the scene is about power relations, control over space, bodies, desires, and sexuality. The scene yields a glimpse of life in contemporary Iran, a glance at power and defiance. This is the story of a faceless generation whose voice is silenced. That is how I look at Tehran at the turn of the millennium.

I have nothing to say, only to show.

—*Walter Benjamin*

Introduction

This is a book about the situation of young people in Iran at the beginning of the third millennium. The book concerns the battle over the right to identity. On one side, there is the state's effort to construct a hegemonic identity for young people. On the other, there is the pervasive struggle by the young people to resist a subject position imposed on them from above. The book examines how young Tehranis struggle for subjectivity—in the sense of individual autonomy. It also deals with the generational divide in Iran between those who made the Revolution and those who reject it.

I intend to examine how transnational connections have been the catalysts for generation-based structured changes of lifestyle. How has the power built its social order? How do Iranian young people struggle to make sense of their lives? Concerned with such issues, the core of the book is the continuous struggle over power between the Iranian authorities and young people, and especially how this struggle manifests itself in spatial relations.

Spaces of Defiance

Domination is realized through arrangements of space. Space is fundamental in any exercise of power. Michel Foucault (1977) borrowed the model of the "Panopticon" as a metaphor for the spatial arrangements of surveillance that he saw as central to the way deviant individuals were disciplined.[1] Faced with the possibility that they are under constant surveillance and the threat of immediate punishment for wrongdoings, the observed discipline themselves.

But while spatial relations contribute to the creation of "docile subjects," space can also provide opportunities to contest power. Michel de Certeau (1984) describes two opposed forms of power in relation to spatial practices: "strategies" and "tactics." Strategies create and control specifically marked "places" by putting them under the control of the powerful state. Opposed to these are tactics that appear in situations which are not completely under control. Tactics produce spaces. Tactics rely on the use of time. Those who employ tactics are "always on the watch for opportunities that must be seized 'on the wing'" (de Certeau 1984: xix). Resistance builds on catching the elusive moment when it is possible to realize individual preferences, when individuals can challenge the rigid organization of place and turn it into a space for defiance. De Certeau argues that the oppressed cannot escape the system that has dominated them, but can continually manipulate events within the system in order to precipitate "fragmentary and fragile victories of the weak" (1984). These tactics are not necessarily political in the sense of organized and institutionalized political goals and actions, but are usually tricks and distortions that subvert the repressive order at an individual level. These "everyday practices" enable people to survive the oppressive structure of society and achieve limited practical kinds of autonomy. People create alternative spaces for social actions and ideas. In the context of this book, these include shopping malls in Tehran, basements (playing rock), coffee shops as meeting places for the young, the mountain retreats north of Tehran—all places that act as sites for the expression of alternative ideas, opinions, and even moralities.

Although this book is about resistance, it tries to go beyond what Scott (1985) calls the "everyday forms of resistance" to look at the pervasive dissatisfaction among Tehrani young people, who not only defy the authorities but also oppose the parental generation and question the very basis of the hegemonic social order. Individual acts of defiance and cultural escape are dominant aspects of young people's social life. Not necessarily part of organized acts of resistance, they can be seen as simple acts intended to challenge and provoke the representatives of the authorities. Given the long history of despotism, a culture of mistrust and hostility has developed between the central power and the Iranian people. A large part of what a scholar might classify as the "glorious resistance" of Iranians against the regime is a national habitus that goes back a long way in history. These forms of everyday "resistance" "require little or no coordination or planning; they often represent a form of individual self-help; and they typically avoid any direct symbolic confrontation with authority" (Scott 1985: 29).[2] This is seen ubiquitously among Iranians but is rarely referred to as *moqavemat* (resistance). Since many everyday activities among young people are classed as criminal by the Islamic state, even trivial acts such as dancing or wearing a T-shirt can be seen as "resistance." When Tehrani young people dance or mingle with the opposite sex at a party, they presumably do not consider whether they are resisting, doing *moqavemat*. Yet in acting as they do, they in effect reject the subject position the regime attempts to impose upon them, whether they intend to or not. I would like to make a distinction between resistance as a deliberate and organized response to state oppression (e.g., student movements) and the practice of defiance as a spontaneous, uncoordinated everyday challenging of the social order.

The ubiquity of resistance studies in anthropological research in the 1980s (see Brown 1996) has been criticized because of its failure to provide sufficiently detailed ethnography (Ortner 1995). Thin ethnography allows a homogenization and romanticization of the resisters and disregards aspects of gender, age, and class.[3] Moreover, as Ortner puts it, resisters "have their *own* politics" (Ortner: 1995: 177, emphasis original). Within resistance there are power relations based on class, gender, age, and ethnicity, which make relations between the dominant and the dominated more ambivalent and ambiguous.

Based on ethnography, this study looks at the cultural defiance of young Tehranis as constituting creative and transformative projects rather than merely being actions of opposition. How do oppressed young people create their own culture? How do gender, class, and age shape the framework of power along both a vertical axis (authorities versus youth; parents versus children) and a horizontal one (men versus women; poor versus rich; Tehranis versus non-Tehranis)? Young people defy the dominant order by, for example, engaging in global youth culture, but defiance is not solely restricted to this "new" arena of modernity. Youth's defiance has also grown out of tradition (Dirks et al. 1994: 20; 1994: 483). As I show in Chapter 6, along with taking part in "global youth cultures," young Tehranis utilize Sufism, and pre-Islamic Persian cultural forms to shape their defiance. Paradoxically, under the theocratic rule, a pre-Islamic Persian renaissance has emerged among young people, who use both the religious visions of the romanticized mysticism of Sufism and Zoroastrianism and the rituals of these movements (e.g., Chaharshanbeh souri) in order to reject the identity imposed from above.

The first two chapters of this study examine the efforts by the authorities to set up a social order based on a "caring" discourse, as well as on the social organization of power which produces the kinds of bodies, souls, and sexualities the regime desires.[4]

Generation

In anthropology, generation is a form of social identity alongside class, ethnicity, and gender. Rather than defining generation in relation to kinship or descent structures, anthropologists see generations as cohorts of people born in the same time period who have experienced the impact of common historical events and cultural forces (Lamb 2001). Generational identity is produced by common experience, which provides the stuff of a symbolic culture and leads disparate individuals to feel bonded to one another (Newman 1996: 376). Karl Mannheim in his classic essay "The Problem of Generations" (1952) asserts that a generation is a group of people who confront the same historical events. Not all members of a generation react to an event in the same way, but what makes a group a generation is its connection to that event and to shared historical and social experiences. Each generation thus differs from other generations. Developing Mannheim's theory, John Borneman asserts that generational disposition refers to the objective conditions and environment in which a generation lives and to which it reacts: "a generation is determined not only by the shared problems of the time, but by the responses to these shared problems" (Borneman 1992: 48). Each generation's experiences are categorized and periodized by the aesthetic and ideational frameworks set in relation to the policies of the state and other historical contingencies (285). Social and historical events and objective conditions become articulated in terms of generational consciousness. Furthermore, the social organization of any generation is built on the members' place in the social division of labor, their differential access to information, and their local, national, and transnational connections.

Generational consciousness is often seen as articulated in terms of youth culture and symbolism. By the creativity in social and symbolic practices and the selective use of global youth culture, Iranian young people construct individual as well as generational identity. In the influential youth studies of the "Birmingham School" of the 1970s and 1980s, youth culture has been approached as a class culture within the framework of hegemony and resistance (see Willis 1977; Hall and Jefferson 1983).[5] Youth culture, however, is both generational and class-based. It is generational in the sense that youth is a life stage within which a certain youth culture exists and in some way challenges the adult generation (Pais 2000), but also in the sense that each cohort of youth faces new circumstances. Youth culture in Tehran varies more with generation than with class. The authorities in Iran suppress young people whether they are from the upper middle or working class. The hegemonic order created by the parental generation has somehow caused a homogenization of the young people's demands. Youth culture does not idealize classlessness but puts the class background in the shadows. It can be defined as knowledge learned outside the established curricula of school or family (Thornton 1995). Heterotopias, like the Golestan shopping center and Tehran's many coffee shops, provide central spaces where this extra-curriculum is rehearsed, as we shall see further in Chapter 4.

Since 2001 a new emic generational classification has emerged in the public debates. The basis of this classification is the Revolution of 1979, and it does not match the analytical classification of generations. However, the young generation labels itself "the Third Generation" (*nasl-e sevoum*). The concept (elaborated in Chapter 5) refers to those who were born after the Revolution. They were what the clergy hoped would be "children of the Revolution," whom Ayatollah Khomeini called "an army of twenty million."

The First Generation made the Revolution. At the time of the Revolution they were in their twenties and older. They had spent their youth under the Shah's rule and had experience of pre-Revolutionary Iran. In the 1970s, thanks to the oil boom, they witnessed a relatively expansive economy and Westernizing urban life. They lived their youth in an Iran that was connected to the global village and aimed to be one of the most modern countries in the world. But what unites them as a generation is, perhaps, their experience of the Revolution. The Second Generation (to which I belong) was in its early teens at the time of the Revolution, born between 1965 and 1970. It has vague memories of the time prior to the Revolution. What unites them as a generation is spending their formative years during the eight-year war with Iraq between 1980 and 1988. This generation makes up a large part of the expatriates who left Iran in the 1980s. The Third Generation, who have just come of age, make up more than half the present population and have no memory of the Revolution. Unlike the First and Second Generations, the Third Generation has been totally formed under the rule of the Islamic regime. In their own words: "We are the product of the Islamic Republic."

Iran is one of the most youthful nations in the world. Iran's population increased drastically from almost 33 million in 1976 to more than 70 million in 2006. According to the 1996 national census, 68 percent of the total population are twenty-nine years old or younger. In other words, 68 percent were born after the Revolution (1979)—the Third Generation (see Table 1). The youth population in Iran is categorized as between fifteen and twenty-four. In 2006 this category made up almost 20 percent of the total population (Statistical Center of Iran 1385/2006). The huge demographic change over only two decades has caused huge social difficulties. Incapable of meeting the demands of young people and fueled by "moral panic" (Cohen 1972), the Islamic Republic views them as "a threat to the health and security" of the society. The young, associated with an "ethical crisis" (*bouhran-e akhlaqi*) in the society, are depicted as self-alienated, unauthentic, *bidard* (without pain), and *biarman* (without ideology). Utilizing a discourse corresponding to what Foucault would call "pastoral power" (Foucault 1983), the "caring" religious order characterizes young people as being particularly vulnerable to cultural threats from both within and without. As we shall see, much of the focus of the Islamic regime has been on how to protect them from moral hazards and to prevent them from becoming gateways for "cultural invasion" from the West. Accordingly, a large part of the youth culture has been redefined as crime. However, the Third Generation carry on their shoulders the social and economic burden of the Revolution for which their parental generation is responsible. As the statistics below show, it is within this generation that one finds a majority of the unemployed, the delinquents, and the mentally ill.

TABLE 1. POPULATION OF IRAN BY TEN-YEAR AGE GROUP, 1996 CENSUS

Age group	Number	Percent
0–9	14,644,869	24.4
10–14	9,080,676	15.1
15–24	12,337,529	20.5
25–34	8,689,220	14.5
35–44	6,383,865	10.6
45–54	3,542,118	5.9
55–64	2,749,674	4.6
65+	2,595,181	4.3
Not specified	32,356	0.1
Total	60,055,488	100

Source: Statistical Center of Iran, 1375/1996.

On the eve of the Revolution and during the war, the theocrats forbade contraceptives as well as abortion and encouraged people to have more children. The Revolution needed children. In the mid-1980s, the rate of population growth in Iran had reached 4 percent. With pragmatic new politicians after the war and after the death of Ayatollah Khomeini, the state launched a nationwide program to control the growth of the population. Accordingly, in the mid-1990s the rate fell to 1.5 percent. The earlier expansion has caused social crises, such as increasing unemployment, poverty, and criminality.

According to official sources, the unemployment rate in 2002 was 14.2 percent. In numbers, about 3.5 million of the active population—

between fifteen and sixty-four—are currently out of a job. The official sources indicated that between 50 and 60 percent of the job-seeking unemployed were young people between fifteen and twenty-four.[6] The same sources warned that in the mid-2000s at least 5.5 million high-school graduates will join the jobless population. The unemployment rate will subsequently rise to 24 percent.[7] Unofficial financial experts suggested that the real rate of unemployment in the country in 2002 was 20.2 percent and would reach 27 percent by 2004.[8] A study of the country's manpower indicates that an average of about 760,000 persons enter the labor market annually. To keep this already high average of unemployment static, there is a need for 760,000 new job opportunities per year. However, between 1991 and 1996 the Ministry of Cooperatives established only around 72,000 employment opportunities per year, not even 10 percent of what is needed.[9]

The need to contain the ever-increasing growth of unemployment has been a prime concern of the state since the mid-1990s. To control unemployment the country needs an annual economic growth rate of 6 percent, a remote possibility in the current situation. According to official sources inflation was 17 percent in 2002, and according to independent sources as high as 25 percent.[10] The petroleum-based economy of Iran, where the state still gets more than 80 percent of its revenue from petroleum, restricts the scope for development of the non-oil sectors. Moreover, the lack of foreign investment, as a result of political insecurity, the U.S. embargo since the Revolution, and the UN sanction for nuclear activities in 2006, leaves no hope of any improvement in the near future. Traditionally, higher education has always been seen as a way to make a career. For many young persons, however, higher education is an unrealizable dream. The annual number of applicants taking university entrance exams (*konkour*) is around 1.2 million, only 15 percent of whom are admitted to various higher education institutes and universities.[11] Furthermore, a university degree does not automatically guarantee employment. One of every 12 unemployed Iranians holds a university degree.[12] Unemployment and impoverishment have facilitated the growth of a series of social problems. Drug addiction has drastically increased in the 1990s. Iran's Welfare Organization and the United Nations Drug Control Program estimate that there are over 2 million addicts in Iran, more than 60 percent of them between twenty and forty.[13]

In a similar manner, criminality and prostitution have also increased. More than 650,000 persons are imprisoned every year in Iran;[14] 65 percent of those in prison are under forty.[15] Poverty is the preeminent reason behind the increasing criminality among young people. Robbery constitutes 47.4 percent of the offenses committed by male delinquents; "prostitution" is the most common among female delinquents.[16]

More optimistic young people seek remedy in emigration. All the young people I met in Iran saw emigration as a last resort. Everyone I came in contact with wanted to leave Iran for a better life abroad (*kharej*). According to the statistics from the Population Reference Bureau (2006) Iran is one of the five largest sources of immigrants. Almost 300,000 persons leave the country annually, the majority unemployed people with a university education.[17] Their reasons for leaving are not necessarily economic. While the best qualified (for instance, IT professionals) and the wealthiest easily find a relatively safe life in more developed countries, less privileged young men pay large amounts to human smugglers in the hope of seeking asylum in the West, joining the slavery-like underground labor market in Tokyo or Dubai.

Identifying themselves as victims of the Revolution and calling themselves a "burned generation" (*nasl-e sokhte*), they blame not only the official ideologies but also the cultural norms of their parental generation. "The Third Generation" is producing a social movement of change that permeates different layers of Iranian society. One way to approach the social world of young Tehranis is to focus on the local debate on "modernity."

Tradition and Modernity

The generational conflict and the tension between young people and the Iranian state are articulated partly in terms of the dichotomy between *sonat* (tradition) and *tajadud* (modernity). This dichotomy is expressed both temporally, in terms of generational gaps, and spatially. Places are classified as traditional or modern, representing the dichotomy between local and global influences. Instances of this are Shahrak-e Gharb versus Javadieh (in Chapter 3) and the Golestan shopping center versus the bazaar (in Chapter 4). Before going further, I want to point out that this book is not about modernity per se but rather about the local "debates *about* modernity" (Appadurai and Breckenridge 1995: 16).

Such discourses of "tradition" and "modernity" have played a crucial role in the configuration of contemporary social patterns in Iran, and have blueprinted two major social movements in the Iran of modern times, the Constitutional Revolution (1905–1911) and the Islamic Revolution (1979). A similar split is now characterizing the youth movement in Iran.

Explicit attempts to struggle both for "modernity" and for the revitalization of "tradition" have been made in Iranian political and social domains since the early twentieth century. Although these ideologies have precursors that can be traced back several centuries, they received an impetus in the mid-1920s, when the systematic modernization of Iran and the construction of a nation-state was started by Reza Shah Pahlavi (r. 1925–1941). Following the kemalist model in Turkey, Reza Shah attempted to transform Iran rapidly into a secular, industrialized, modern country. His first steps were to replace the Islamic law, *sharia*, with the Swiss Civil Code, and to "emancipate" women by removing their veils by force. Modernization accelerated during his son's rule (1941–1979), thanks to the oil boom and the dramatically increased revenues it brought for the government. Western lifestyles and culture became more noticeable among the urban-based upper and middle classes after the Shah's modernization program. In other words, "modernization" became synonymous with accepting Western habits, which were seen to be based on mass consumption. Thus, the marketing and consumption of Western goods became salient features of "modern" Iran. Questions concerning the disjunction with the old patterns of life have been raised with increased intensity in the last few decades, due to the intensification and proliferation of transnational connections and the increased mobility of cultural products and meanings. The project of a rapid Westernization of Iran in the 1970s was followed by a wave of "Islamization" in the 1980s, a vast effort to revive "Islamic tradition."

The collective life-changes are followed by the development of a "split loyalty," on the one hand to Iranian "traditional" patterns of life and on the other hand to "Western modernity." The difficulty Iranians have had in adapting to "modernity" has been diagnosed as "cultural schizophrenia" (Shayegan 1992) or the "social malady" of "Weststruckness" (*gharbzadegi*) (Al-e Ahmad 1982). Many analysts see the 1979 Revolution as a reaction to this "social malaise" represented in Iranian modernity, all emblems of "Western" and non-Islamic culture, popular culture, and the consumption of Western goods among young people.

The conceptual dichotomy between *sonat* and *tajadud* is heavily gendered. In Iran and other Islamic countries, the most characteristic distinction is the way it is reflected in the duality of veiling/unveiling and thus explicitly imprinted on women's bodies and voices (Milani 1992: 32–39; see also Najmabadi 2005). Iranian women have been seen as the hallmark of efforts toward *tajadud* since the Constitutional Revolution in the early twentieth century. "Compulsory unveiling" (*kashf-e hejab*) in 1936 was the focal point of the modernization project, started by Reza Shah Pahlavi. Barely a half-century later the Islamic Republic's search for "authentic" culture began with veiling the women and pushing them back into the patriarchal private spaces.

While veiled women have been seen as a touchstone of *sonat*, unveiled ones personify the *tajadud*. In this book, I shall use the dialectics of veiling and unveiling to approach questions on the disjunction or conjunction of "tradition" and "modernity" in Iran. The veil in its general meaning is not only an expression of sex segregation per se but also an indication of de-individualization, concealment, and a walled (untransparent) society (see Chapter 2). Societal veiledness negates the presence of voiced individuals. It connotes a normative modesty, the silence and absence mainly of women but also of men (as I develop in Chapter 2). Unveiledness indicates self-assertion and characterizes all who oppose normative modesty.

This book has two goals: to explore the contexts out of which the current cultural politics has emerged and to provide an ethnographical description of the practices of everyday life, with which young Tehranis demonstrate defiance against the official culture and construct their own culture. Hopefully I shall contribute also to a scanter but optimistically growing number of urban anthropologies of Iran and ethnographical works on contemporary Iranian urban life.

Fieldwork

Doing urban anthropology in general and studying youth in particular in Iran indeed meant starting from scratch. In Iran anthropology has preeminently been interpreted and practiced as nomadic studies.[18] The handful of anthropological studies of urban life (here I refer only to works done in English) in Iran are based mainly on ethnographical inquiries prior to the Revolution.[19] However, a few major academic works on the urban life of young people in Tehran have recently been published, Yaghmaian (2002), Shirali (2001), Varzi (2006), Amir-Ebrahimi (1999), and Adelkhah (2000).

In search of a suitable field location for my study, I was looking for centers of young defiance. Shortly after my arrival in Tehran I found that the young people I was looking for were those referred to as *bidard*, *biarman*, and *gharbzadeh* (Weststruck). As I discuss in Chaper 3, *dard* (pain) is a significant feature in how young people are represented. *Dard* is associated with inner purity (*safa-ye baten*), conscience, and responsibility. *Bidard* (without pain, painfree) is, accordingly, associated with ignorance and frivolity. They were concentrated in a modern middle-class affluent neighborhood called Shahrak-e Gharb, a center for production, reproduction, and spreading of Western youth culture in Iran. These young people were viewed by the authorities, the parental generation, and experts as "nonrepresentative" or "atypical" of Iranian youth (I elaborate in more detail in Chapter 3). The local construction of a Westernized youth identity opposed to the native youth identity attracted me to this neighborhood and its young people. Hence, persons in my study were selected not as being representative and typical middle-class young people, but as being part of a specific youth culture.

Although I conducted my fieldwork mainly in this "modern" middle-class neighborhood, my study also includes young Tehranis from other parts of Tehran, particularly from poor neighborhoods in South Tehran. Throughout the fieldwork I worked with 46 young Tehranis, 15 of them south Tehrani with a working-class background. Of the 46, only 11 were female. For the obvious reason of Iranian gender segregation, I had restricted access to female informants. In most cases, the young women I interacted with were girlfriends or sisters of my male informants. Moreover, the tacit ethical codes in Iran for communication between the sexes impeded talking with girls about a range of topics, particularly sexual ones. My informants were all between eighteen and twenty-five years old. I also obtained valuable information from older people around, usually their siblings or parents. I was curious to know what non-Tehrani young people in the periphery thought about their Tehrani contemporaries, and generally wanted to explore Iranian youth culture. So, in addition to the first group, I interviewed 12 young men and women in Isfahan. I came to know many of my informants quite well, others not so well. I interviewed some only once, others several times. Although I met the majority of them regularly, only two turned into what could be called "key informants." Simon and Dara became good friends from an early stage of my fieldwork.

There is a strong emphasis on "locale-centered ethnography" in this book. My choice is based on ethical and political considerations—to protect people involved in the study. The ethnography, therefore, moves through a spatial arrangement of power in the first two chapters; spaces in Shahrak-e Gharb in Chapter 3; the Golestan shopping center in Chapter 4; cinematic spaces in Chapter 5; heterotopias of everyday life in Chapter 6.

The fieldwork was a combination of "appointment" anthropology (Luhrmann 1996: vii) and conventional participant observation. There was not a fixed group of young people for me to join. Therefore I met my informants individually. I spent many mornings meeting officials or interviewing film-makers, musicians, and journalists. Other days I used the mornings reading through documents and publications in libraries or visiting "Houses of Culture" to make a note of their activities. In the afternoon and early evening I hung around with my informants in the Golestan shopping center or elsewhere in Shahrak-e Gharb. In the late evening I socialized with Dara or Simon, who did not like each other, so it had to be with one at a time. We met in more intimate milieus, usually in their homes but also at my apartment. Sometimes we went to the

cinema or a concert. Only four of the Tehrani young people in my
study belonged to the *basij* (volunteer militia). As I explore in more detail later on, several reasons contributed to makeing the presence of
young *basijis* so small in my study. It was preeminently a matter of access. As guardians of Islamic values and norms, *basijis* stood opposed to
the majority of young people in this study. My Iranian background
robbed me of the chance to position myself in the field as an anthropologist first and an Iranian second.[20] Furthermore, regular contact
with *basijis* would definitely damage my other informants' confidence
in me.

Despite my background as an Iranian, this book is not "anthropology
at home," either spatially or temporally. Both Tehran and the Third
Generation were unfamiliar for me. Writing about Tehrani young people and their cultural identity after more than a decade of being outside Iran put me in relation to a different generation from my own as
well as in a city I never had visited before. However, as an Iranian, I enjoyed privileged access to certain kinds of knowledge, though I had an
in-and-out experience during the fieldwork.

The fact that I grew up in Iran often faced me with the question as to
when exactly my fieldwork began. Did I really start my fieldwork in May
1999? If I include all the knowledge, experiences, and emotions of the
first two decades of my life before I left Iran, my fieldwork started long
before I became an anthropologist. However, since the official start of
my fieldwork in May 1999 I have spent eight months in Tehran, followed by regular visits once or twice a year, usually lasting not more
than a month. Although my most recent research visit was in Summer
2006, I have followed, or rather been followed by, information and new
data through all the links that connect me to Tehran, not least through
digital networks. In Stockholm, the Internet offered a way for me to re-
fresh my information, to get access to public debates (newspapers,
youth radio channels, youth magazines) and public as well as private
homepages and blogs written by young people. My cyber-ethnography
even included long talks with young Tehranis in chat rooms. Sometimes
I had access to more information about things happening in Tehran
through the Internet than Dara, who was living in Tehran.

The Structure of the Book

The first two chapters provide an anthropology of societal order; the
rest of the book is concerned with the anthropology of change. Chapter 1 explores the structure of authority and social control. I analyze the
processes used by the "caring" Islamic state in order to guard the
"health and purity" of the society. I shall argue that, alongside the overt

modes of disciplining—the metaphoric "panopticon," education, media, and punishment—the social order is based on the "pastoral modality of power," paternalistic care. As has been mentioned, in the Iranian case this is formulated as the principle of mutual discipline, *amr-e be ma'rouf va nahi az monkar* (the promotion of virtue and the rejection of vice. The anxieties felt by the Iranian authorities are expressed through campaigns that mainly target the younger generation and their lifestyle and have led to the criminalization of a large part of youth culture, under the label *jorm-e farhangi* (cultural crime).

Chapter 2 examines the ways the religious authorities have sought to anchor an Islamic order of things in the bodies and subjectivities of individuals. While Chapter 1 deals with the structure of authority, Chapter 2 examines its aesthetics. I look at the aesthetic notions of the authorities themselves and how they are implemented by the practices of social control. "The aestheticization of modesty," as I call it, is manipulated through three schemes: a Revolutionary romanticization of poverty; the practice of veiling; and the emotionalization of politics. I show how theocratic aesthetics view "pain" (*dard*) and "suffering" (*ranj*) as hallmarks of dignity and purity. Accordingly, "*bidard*-ness" is seen as a sign of immorality and an anti-Revolutionary stance.

Chapter 3 provides the reader with a sense of the spatial layout of the setting of my fieldwork, Shahrak-e Gharb. The chapter begins with a brief illustration of the urban milieu of Tehran. It continues with a presentation of how people in Tehran perceive the city, how it is structured by the dichotomies of poor/rich, modern/traditional, and local/global. With reference to a "distinct" mentality, social organization, and neighborhood identity, the young people of Shahrak-e Gharb try to dissociate themselves from the wider society, through claims on culturalized lifestyle choices, such as "being modern," individual autonomy, secularism, and globalism. This chapter shows how geographic indications reveal a status hierarchy in the city as a whole (north versus south Tehran), but also inside the Shahrak-e Gharb neighborhood.

Chapter 4 takes us to the Golestan shopping center. I argue that the center is, above all, a space of "imagination." It is also a site where the knowledge of "how to be modern" is communicated. I demonstrate that the production of modern identity in the Golestan shopping center is formed in opposition to the "traditional" marketplace, the bazaar. For young people, the bazaar is synonymous with a traditional lifestyle that is seen as reactionary and allied with the Islamic regime. Chapter 5 takes as its subject the Third Generation and the generational conflict that characterizes Iranian society today. The chapter also examines the parental generation's views on the Third Generation. Chapter 6 is a collection of narratives of defiance. It illustrates the tactical ploys used by youths to negotiate hegemonic social order. Rarely planning and organizing "resistance" in a collectively structured and reflected way, young people utilize any opportunity that arises to assert their autonomy.

In the Conclusion I discuss how the predicament of young people is related to imagination and modernity. I underscore the significance of access to the means of imagination (read means of modernity) for young Tehranis' struggle for subjectivity.

Chapter 1
Cultural Crimes

> There is not a single topic in human life for which Islam has not provided
> instruction and established norms.
>
> —*Ayatollah Khomeini*

I start with myself.

One cold night in late autumn 1984 I was arrested by *basijis.* I was eighteen years old and in the last year of high school. Early that night a
friend of mine had called me and asked me if I could take him somewhere in my car. Later on, we were driving with another friend of ours
toward Julfa, the Armenian district in Isfahan. He had arranged a party
for the weekend and wanted to buy illicit home-made *aragh* (Iranian
vodka) and wine from an Armenian acquaintance, who was known in Isfahan for his good-quality *aragh* and wine. After the Islamic state pro-
hibited alcoholic beverages, a lucrative underground market for
home-made products emerged, particularly in the Armenian minority.
I parked the car in Khaghani Street, the main street of Julfa. We waited
in silence. It was getting dark. After a long and anxious wait the Armenian man appeared and my friend followed him into a narrow alleyway.
After a few minutes my friend jumped into the car with a dark bag in
his hand and I put the car in gear. At the end of the street, just as we
were leaving the Armenian neighborhood, a *basiji* patrol on a motorcycle stopped us. They had apparently followed us. We were sent to the
nearby mosque and from there to the office of the Central Committee
(*komiteh markazi*). After a night in prison we were sent to the Revolutionary Court, which was located in a several-story luxury house, apparently confiscated by the Islamic state. The three of us sat opposite the
judge (*qazi*), a middle-aged cleric, surrounded by several uniformed
young men. He looked at some papers, probably a report on us. He
raised his head and looked at us in silence. Then he sentenced us to
flogging for "cultural crime," thirty lashes each. The whole process

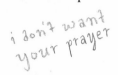

lasted less than half an hour. For some reason we were not punished publicly (which is usually the case). We were led to a little room on the roof of the building. One at a time we were taken inside the room for the ritual. I was the last. While waiting my turn, I heard the screams and bellows of my friends. In the room I was placed on a metal bed with no mattress. My hands were stretched out and tied to the bars of the bed. The guard asked me kindly if I needed some piece of clothing to put in my mouth in order to prevent damage to my teeth (to avoid grinding the teeth together). I said yes and absurdly thanked him (perhaps for his concern for my teeth!). I was wearing a shirt and jeans. The guard did not insist on stripping me and the ritual began with reciting the phrase "Besm ella ahe rahmaane rahim" (In the name of Allah the beneficent the merciful)—an important phrase each Muslim should say at the beginning of every good work. Only the first five or six strokes hurt. I did not feel the rest. For many years to come red lines remained on my back to testify to how the new social order had been embodied.

*   *   *

Seventeen years later, in the summer of 2001, I found myself in the most agonizing part of my fieldwork. By then at the stage of choosing a topic for my study, I knew that it would become an ethnography of suffering and anguish. What I witnessed during July and August 2001, however, exceeded the scope of my imagination. More than 200 young people were publicly flogged in Tehran in only a few weeks. As a traditional Islamic punishment, public flogging appeared in the early days of the Revolution but was gradually carried out more discreetly away from the public gaze. At the end of July 2001, however, conservative forces controlling the judiciary started a fresh wave of public flogging, as a response to the reelection of the reform-minded but powerless President Mohammad Khatami the month before. Khatami had enjoyed a triumphant victory based on the support of young followers, but remained ineffective against the powerful conservative forces inside and outside the state. Simon said:

We chose Khatami and they [the conservative judiciary] are punishing us for that.

Public flogging is usually inflicted on young people. The victims are men, and occasionally women, who have been accused of different kinds of "cultural crime." Common charges are alcohol consumption or extramarital sex. In the recent wave of flogging, the youngest victim was a fourteen-year-old boy charged with "harassing girls" in front of a girls' high school. He received ten lashes. A young man of nineteen was given ten strokes for playing "illicit music" loudly in his car. For alcohol consumption, the number of lashes goes up to 80. More than 100 lashes may be given in the case of "sexual crimes." There were young people who got 180 lashes.[1]

For me, as an anthropologist, attending the flogging was an ethical dilemma. To watch seemed important to my fieldwork. I decided to attend only some floggings and to follow others indirectly through the media. In Tehran the ceremony of flogging is usually performed in the afternoon and on a main square. All traffic in and around the square is halted. A large number of *basijis* are present to counter possible protests. At each ceremony, between two and twelve persons are flogged. Before the eyes of some several hundred people, the young people are in turn stripped and fastened standing to a post or sometimes to a pick-up. Their arms are stretched out and tied with ropes. The policemen who carry out the punishment usually use a cable. The mass of spectators, almost all men, watch silently. I was stunned each time I saw the whips waving slowly backward in the air and then flying forward forcefully to hit a teenager's back, lacerating his skin and injuring the flesh. When the whip hits the back, its top rotates before slapping hard the smooth skin along the side of his body.

"Cultural crime" (*jorm-e farhangi*) appeared in the post-revolutionary Penal Law as a new term for breaking Islamic rules. Such crimes are seen as violations of the "collective sentiments" of the Muslim community and result in different kinds of sanction, mostly in the form of physical punishment. The Islamic regime underscores the category of age, more than class or ethnicity, as a societal factor which causes differences in participation in crime. In Islam the self is thought of as split in a conflict between reason (*aql*) and passion (*nafs*). The former directs one toward God and a harmonious life, while the latter represents Satanic forces (*sheytani*). Although all individuals possess both, the capacity to develop reason is seen as stronger in adult men, whilst the impulse toward passion is held to be stronger in women and young people. Youth are all passion (*nafs*) and therefore have an inclination to crime. In the post-revolutionary Islamic order the collective cultural experience that youth represent is seen as a central intersection of culture and crime. The anxieties of the theocracy are expressed through "moral panics," which have led in practice to the criminalization of a large part of youth culture.

However, the range of what can be included in the notion "cultural crime" has shrunk since the early 1980s. What in the 1980s was punishable as a cultural crime had turned in the late 1990s into a daily scene on the Tehran streets. In the early 1980s, a young man would frequently be warned and "corrected" by the Islamic club or moral police for wearing a short-sleeved shirt or clothes of a "delightful color," or for talking to a *namahram* (unrelated) girl. In the late 1990s, the atmosphere was considerably more relaxed, particularly after Mohammad Khatami won the presidential election in 1997. Nevertheless, a new wave of harassment and terror was launched in the summer of 2002, when special black-uniformed police units equipped with black four-wheel-drive vehicles appeared in numerous northern and eastern districts of Tehran. More violent than before, these units have begun a war against such *fesad-e akhlaqi* (ethical corruption) as *aloudegi-ye souti* (sound pollution), loud music in cars and "depraved" private parties in Tehran.[2] The anti-"cultural crimes" policies grew tougher after the victory of President Mahmoud Ahmadinejad in 2005.

After the Revolution the Iranian clerics embarked on a comprehensive project to desecularize the judicial system, which had been affected by seven decades of Western-inspired modernization. They also had to mold it to fit a centralized theocracy,[3] which implied fundamentally transforming the principles of Shiite law. Central legislation by the state replaced the ad hoc legal interpretation carried out by Islamic jurists (see Arjomand 1989). Clerics, however, occupied powerful positions in the legal system. In the Islamic judicial system, ethical and moral regulations replaced the civil code of law in all spheres, including criminal justice. New criminal laws were introduced to enforce Islamic morality and values. The transformation of society into an *ummat* (Islamic community) was followed by a reduction of the individual's status from a legal subject as a citizen to a "servant of God." The new legal system as adjusted for "God's servants" is based on criminalization of sins. By making an increasing number of moral offenses criminal, legal reform has progressively reduced the autonomy of the individual (see Sanadjian 1996). When *shariat* (the Persian version of Arabic *sharia*) was extended to cover public law, the distinction between the illegal, the immoral, and the sinful disappeared. Thus, crime, vice, and sin become synonymous.

The Islamic Penal Code divides punishments into three categories: *hodud, qessas,* and *taazir. Hodud* is for crimes that endanger the moral order, such as adultery or drinking alcohol. Punishment of *hodud* is mandatory and is prescribed by the Qur'an. *Qessas* is for crimes against the person, for instance, homicide, punishments for which are mentioned in the Qur'an and *hadiths.* Finally, *taazir* is for all crimes for which there are no specified penalties in the Qur'an or *hadiths.* Thus, *taazir,* the criminalization of acts and the punishment given for them, is left to the discretion of the judge (see Bassiouni 1982). Islam views *taazir* as subject to rehabilitative and corrective punishment. Public flogging not only punishes the sinner/criminal with severe physical pain, but is also a "tangible preventive measure."[4]

The 18th Chapter: Crimes Against Chastity and Public Ethics
Article 638: Anybody who demonstrates unlawful [*haram*] conduct in public places will be sentenced to prison for between ten days and two months or to up to 74 lashes. And if his or her conduct is not punishable but nonetheless harms public chastity s/he is sentenced to prison between ten days and two months or to up to 70 lashes.
(a) Unveiled women who appear in public places and in the public's sight unveiled will be sentenced to prison for ten days to two months, or a fine.

Article 640: The following persons will be sentenced to prison from three months to one year and to a fine of 1,500,000 Rial to 6,000,000 Rial and to up to 74 lashes:
(1) anybody who trades, distributes, or demonstrates in public paintings, drawings, text, pictures, publications, signs, films, cassettes, or anything else that harms public chastity and ethics.
Anybody who personally or through somebody else imports or exports, rents, or is the intermediary in the trading of the above-mentioned goods.[5]

Occidentophobia

Since popular culture is seen as a manifestation of "Weststruckness," it has been regarded as the main source of cultural crimes. Mojtaba Navab-Safavi, a radical Islamist operating in the 1940s and 1950s, identified Western imports such as the cinema and romantic novels and music as a "melting furnace, which melts away all the wholesome values and virtues of a Muslim society. . . . Moviehouses, theaters, novels, and popular songs must be completely removed and their middlemen punished" (Navab-Safavi 1357/1987: 4, 11, quoted in Naficy 1992: 179–80). After the Revolution, all forms of modern popular culture were banned and the entire industry of popular culture went underground or into exile. Los Angeles, with a huge concentration of Iranian pop artists, has been turned into a site for the production of the Iranian popular culture (see Kelley and Friedlander 1993; Naficy 1993). *Irangelesi* is the common term used to refer to this culture.

During the Revolution all emblems of Western popular culture were attacked as symptoms of impurity. Cinemas, nightclubs, discos, luxury restaurants, liquor stores, bars, music studios, malls were burned down or closed. In the opinion of Ayatollah Khomeini, the Pahlavis had tyrannized people by corrupting their minds: "Spreading the means of pleasure, and preoccupying people with unveiling, European clothes, cinema, theater, music, and dance" (Khomeini 1323/1944, quoted in

Paidar 1995: 121). The first major event of symbolic importance to the
Islamic Revolution happened when Cinema Rex in Abadan was burned
down on August 10, 1978, and over 300 persons were killed inside it.
Less than a year later as many as 180 cinemas had been burned, demolished, or shut down (Naficy 1992: 183).[6]

It was even worse in the case of music. All popular music, foreign or
Iranian, was banned. At first, only military and revolutionary songs were
allowed, but later on the clergy began to tolerate classic Western and
Iranian. Classic Persian music is usually associated with spirituality and
Sufism and is even referred to as "authentic music" (*musiqi-ye asil*). Popular Iranian music, in contrast, is seen as a "light" (*sabouk*) and "superficial" (*sathi*) imitation of Western pop music. Popular music is seen as
harmful primarily for its hybridity and inauthenticity, and second for its
relation to sexuality and immodesty. In the late 1990s a so-called Islamic
popular music (*mosiqi-ye pop-e eslami*) was introduced to combat influences from Irangelesi culture.

A prevalent opinion among young Tehranis is that after the end of
the war the authorities needed a new enemy. This enemy has been
found in what the Islamic state has labeled the project of "cultural invasion" (*tahajom-e farhangi*). The invasion is perceived to be conducted by
the Great Satan, that is, the U.S., and its "indigenous agents," in order
to demoralize young Iranians. Although "cultural invasion" has been a
key term in the revolutionary discourse since the early 1980s, the political significance of the notion increased considerably after the war.
Later, in the second half of the 1990s, it became the main political tool
of the conservative forces. The propaganda of the state claims that a
"cultural invasion" is more dangerous than military ones are. Mesbah
Yazdi, the spokesman of the hard-liners, sees continuity between the
military war and the cultural war:

We should believe that the previous war [Iran-Iraq war] is taking place today in
the cultural sphere. If we had been defeated in that war, we might have lost ter-
ritory, but if we are defeated in this war, it will mean the loss of our religion and
faith and domination by the enemy's corrupted culture.[7]

The youth are believed to be the main target of the invasion, the
weak point of the *ummat*. The minister of education, Mohammad Ali
Najafi, claimed, "It is our duty to combat the invasion of our culture
that threatens the juvenile population. We should create a safety shield
to protect our youth from all evil plots and conspiracies."[8]

The authorities see a link between the strategy for "cultural invasion"
and the strategy the Christians used in Andalusia in the late fifteenth
century. In summer 2002, deputy commander of the *basij*, Brigadier-
General Gholam Hossein Kolouli Dezfuli, declared in relation to this:

Christians were consistently defeated in their campaign to avoid the infiltration of Islam into Europe. Later on, they thought of a remedy and concluded that they had to make soldiers forget their beliefs. Therefore, they distributed plenty of alcoholic beverages among the people, free of charge. On the other hand, they had the Muslims entrapped by beautiful Western women to corrupt the combatants of Islam and stop the spread of Islam into Europe. I think our Islamic Revolution was a similar case. Since the triumph of the Revolution in 1979, they have undertaken ceaseless efforts to avoid infiltration of our Revolution but they failed. Now, they are in the process of repeating the Andalusian experience in our country.[9]

The genealogy of the notion of "cultural invasion" (*tahajom-e farhangi*) in the Iranian context led to a discourse of authenticity, which dominated the political culture of the 1960s and 1970s and emphasized authenticity and the idea of "returning to our roots." This discourse was promoted by several influential intellectuals, such as Ahmad Fardid, Ali Shariati, Jalal Al-e Ahmad, Daryush Shayegan, and Ehsan Naraghi. It mobilized an ideology of nativism (see Boroujerdi 1996), a yearning for a "purity," which supposedly had been demolished by Westernization.

The most prominent and influential work in this tradition was undoubtedly Jalal Al-e Ahmad's *Gharbzadegi*. Published in the early 1960s, *Gharbzadegi* has been praised as a pioneering work in defense of cultural authenticity (*esalat-e farhangi*), and has deeply affected the cultural debate and politics in Iran. In this polemical essay, Al-e Ahmad rigorously criticized the Shah's policy of modernization (Westernization) and the tendency for mimicry among Iranians. *Gharbzadegi* as a notion is still used as a political tool by the Islamic authorities to oppress opposition. Al-e Ahmad borrowed it from another Iranian intellectual, Ahmad Fardid, who had translated the term as *dysiplexia* (Gheissari 1998: 89). In Greek "dysis" means "West" and "plexia" means to be afflicted, as in "apoplexy." The concept has been translated into English as "Westoxication," "Weststruckness," or being "plagued by the West" (the title used in the English translation). However, Al-e Ahmad defines *gharbzadegi* as an illness. *Gharbzadegi* is a metaphor for "cultural disease."

I speak of being afflicted with "westitis" the way I would speak of being afflicted with cholera. If this is not palatable, let us say it is akin to being stricken by heat or by cold. But it is not that either. It is something more on the order of being attacked by tongue worm. Have you ever seen how wheat rots? From within? . . . In any case we are dealing with a sickness, a disease imported from abroad and developed in an environment receptive to it. (Al-e Ahmad 1982: 3)

The medical aspect of the *gharbzadegi* discourse is not exceptional. Since the early twentieth century, the state of Westernization has been seen as a syndrome, and addressed with medical terminology, such as "cultural schizophrenia" (Shaygan 1992), "mental confusion" (*ashoftegi-*

e fekri) (Shadman 1326/1947), or "indigestion" (*sou-e hazemeh*).[10] Such arguments are not necessarily made only by Islamists. Many secular intellectuals—usually educated in the West—use the same approach. For instance, Daryoush Ashuri compares the Westernization of Iran with the historical invasions by Alexander the Great, the Arabs, and the Moguls. He claims that Westernization is the latest invasion of Iran. Unlike previous invasions, which were military, this one has "gradually penetrated our skin" (Ashuri 1376/1997: 145–47). Since the Revolution, the authorities have utilized such medical jargon to legitimate their occidentophobia. Conflating the language of health programs with cultural politics, the Islamic regime has depicted the way the nation's purity and health are demolished by "cultural microbes" (*mikrobha-ye farhangi*), which penetrate the nation's body and cause "cultural injuries" (*asibha-ye farhangi*). Accordingly, to immunize the nation, the regime emphasizes the necessity of a "cultural vaccination" (*vaksan-e farhangi*).

Since the youth are all seen as passion (*nafs*) and particularly vulnerable to "cultural threats," the focus of the Islamic regime has been on how to "protect" young people from moral hazards and prevent them from becoming the gateways of "cultural invasion." Uncontrollable mass communication from abroad, through radio, satellite TV channels, videos, and finally the Internet, have been identified as primary threats "broadcasting pollution." In December 1999, the *Valy-e faqih*, Ayatollah Khomeini, expressed his anxiety in this way:

Audio and visual waves that are worse than warships and warplanes are being used to disseminate a rogue culture aimed at reasserting the domination of the enemies of Islam. They have paved the way for the imposition of unethical values and Westernized ideas in order to captivate and humiliate Muslims.[11]

Mohammad Javad Larijani, then director of Islamic Republic of Iran Broadcasting (IRIB), believes that the influences of these foreign sounds and images will subvert the process of constructing the Muslim subject:

Can we believe that the highly motivated youth of the country will continue to be true patriots, correct in their way of thinking, and observant of religious duties while they are exposed to these destructive programs and watching them incessantly? Will they not dwindle into day-dreaming, humiliated, misled and self-deceived individuals?[12]

Conducting a war against nondomestic media has been the main task of the regime since the Revolution. Throughout the 1980s video recorders were illicit in Iran. Possessing, renting, selling, or buying them was punishable. In the early 1990s, the Majlis passed a law to legalize "owning and using a video cassette recorder." While the Iranian authorities were busy discussing whether or not to legalize videos, a more powerful threat arrived, namely satellite television, which has ever since presented the authorities with a problem. They are no longer able to control the flow, and a steady stream of TV programs is entering the country. While the Majlis were still confused about what to do, 500,000 satellite dishes were installed on roofs in Tehran.[13] The use of such dishes was the most controversial cultural issue in Iran throughout the 1990s. The conservatives began a rigorous propaganda campaign against satellite TV. The satellites were called an "enemy device for eliminating Islam,"[14] and seen as to signifying "hooliganism and social corruption."[15] The director of IRIB used a "purity and danger" discourse in his statements against the satellite:

It infatuates [people] by unhealthy information. . . . The contamination caused by satellites is far more dangerous than the pollution of the living environment. Now that sensitivity to pollution of the environment has reached such a state that smoking is forbidden in public places and even in apartments and large buildings, how can we remain indifferent to broadcasting pollution?[16]

The moral police conduct sporadic hunts for receiver dishes on roofs or in courtyards. People are encouraged to check if their neighbors have receivers. Helicopter hunts to identify houses with satellite dishes have also been conducted. A wave of attacks on satellite dishes was launched in late October 2001, on the order of the authorities. The police impounded more than 5,000 satellite dishes in Tehran and some 150,000 nationwide in less than two weeks.[17]

Engineering Goodness

Another modus operandi of the war against cultural crimes has been the reshaping of morals. The "salvation-oriented" mission of the Islamic government has been directed to helping the country achieve an "inner piety" (safa-ye baten). This requires cleansing the nation from "internal impurities" caused by "satanic temptations" and warding off the external threats of "cultural invasion" and "Weststruckness." This was conducted first through a Cultural Revolution (Enqelab-e Farhangi) and then by establishing the Ministry of Islamic Culture and Guidance in 1986 in order to orchestrate the national culture and control over cultural activities and productions.

The Islamic Republic then converted the media, the education system, art and film production into vessels for promoting Islamic and revolutionary values (see Benard and Khalilzad 1984: 117). The IRIB became an ideological apparatus for legitimating the clergy. The content gradually became dominated by religious seminars. Programs such as *Akhlaq dar khanevadeh* (*Ethics in the Family*) or Mr. Gherra'ti's lectures on Islamic ethics and rules supported and reinforced Islamic values and lifestyles. Through its numerous soap operas, TV serials, programs on martyrs and their families, documentaries or feature films on the war, and mythologizations of clerics and personalities of the Revolution, IRIB attempts to (re)produce images of the ideal Muslim revolutionary man and woman. Soap operas of historical personalities are usual, such as *Emam Ali* (biography of Imam Ali), *Maryam-e Moghadas* (life story of Saint Mary), *Amir Kabir* (biography of a reformist prime minister in the mid-nineteenth century), and *Bu-Ali Sina* (biography of the tenth-century philosopher called Avicenna in the West). Programs about the "cultural invasion" and its "domestic agents" also occupy a large part of IRIB's broadcasting. *Hoviat* (Identity) and *Sarab* (Mirage) were two controversial programs that attempted to defame Westernized Iranians.[18]

IRIB usually puts youths into two categories, either as zealous revolutionaries and faithful Muslims who, through heroic efforts, will save the country and build a decent future, or as deceived and *bidard* hedonists. It creates an image of an army of young people ready to execute their leaders' directives (*ummat-e hamishe dar sahneh*). They forge the ideal image of an "Iranian Muslim youth," a conscious (*agah*) warrior (*mobarez*), ready for self-sacrifice (*isargar*) and a "guardian of values." For instance, the soap opera *Khaneyi Misazim* (We Build Our House) is a melodrama that attempts to offer "proper models" for building a life based on "correct social and economic relationships." Work, endeavor, humanity, correct relationships, and economic discipline are central themes. The stereotype of *bidard* youth is also a recurrent theme in soap operas. For instance, *Khat-e Ghermez* (The Red Line) is about the "identity-lessness" (*bihoviyati*) of two young men. Free from "family ties and norms" (*gheyd va bandhay-e khanevadegi*), the two embark on an aimless journey.[19] Anti-*bidard* youth propaganda is also a central theme in state-run youth magazines, such as *Iran-e Javan, Omid-e Javan* (Hope of Youth), *Javanan-e Roosta* (Village Youth), *Javan-e Khanvadeh* (Family Youth), *Donya-ye Javanan* (World of Youth), *Roshd-e Javan* (Youth's Growth), *Javanan-e Emrooz* (Today's Youth), *Fazilat-e Javanan* (Youth's Virtue), and *Mo'oud-e Javan* (The Promise of the Young).

The "principle of mutual discipline" is a central component of the strategy of engineering goodness. In post-revolutionary Iran, the practice of mutual discipline, *amr-e be m'arouf va nahi az monkar* (the promotion of virtue and the rejection of vice) became a guiding principle of domestic politics. The expression stands for an obligation on the part of every Muslim to guide others toward goodness and save them from evil, a duty that operates both at the interpersonal level and in relation to hierarchical governance and subjection. In accordance with the Qur'anic verse (9: 71), the Iranian Constitution declares:

In the Islamic Republic of Iran, *amr-e be m'arouf va nahi az monkar* is a universal and reciprocal duty that must be fulfilled by the people with respect to one another, by the government with respect to the people, and by the people with respect to the government. The conditions, limits, and nature of this duty will be specified by law.[20]

However, in post-revolutionary Iran, "the principle of mutual discipline" has been used by Islamists to justify the violent oppression of young people.

Hierarchical relations in Iran, whether teacher/pupil, father/child, or master/disciple, are often based on a common paradigm, in which the role of the senior partner is to encourage, exercise, and inculcate appropriate practices in order to stimulate reason and to constrain the space for passion, the two contradictory forces. The youth have to be led toward *aql* by tutelage and discipline (Rosen 1989: 12). The mutual discipline of *amr-e be m'arouf va nahi az monkar* is a crucial feature in the process of learning:

The individual's acquisition of appropriate agency and its exercise are articulated by responsibility, a responsibility not merely of the agent but of the entire community of Muslims severally and collectively. In this tradition, the body-and-its-capacities is not owned solely by the individual but is subject to a variety of rights and duties held by others. (Asad 2000: 50)

To understand the context in which notions of "cultural crime" are mobilized, we have to look at the genealogy of the "principle of mutual discipline" and its roots in the history of political Islam. As a "collective duty," a Muslim who lives under an Islamic regime should struggle for the survival of the regime. One who lives under a regime hostile to Islam should struggle for its overthrow (Enayat 1982: 2). Thus the principle of mutual discipline is not only an ethical issue but a political one as well. Ali Shariati, one of the ideologues behind the Islamic Revolution, interpreted "prevention of vice" (*nahi az monkar*) as a revolutionary act directed against social injustice and against "cultural imperialism," "Weststruckness," and dictatorship (Rahnema 1998: 307). Morteza Motahari, another key figure in the formation of the Islamic revolutionary movement in Iran, delivered a series of lectures in 1969 in Tehran under the title "*Amr-e be ma'rouf va nahi az monkar* in Imam Hossein's movement." In these lectures he declared that "the prevention of vice" was the principal aim in Imam Hossein's battle against the despot Yazid and his injustice. Thereby he linked "the prevention of vice" to the contemporary social issues in Iran and made a political agenda of it (see Motahari 1379/2000).

The essence of the "principle of mutual discipline" is not to preach to individuals, but to apply moral order in society in order to achieve a state of equilibrium. Neglect of such order is seen as a vice that harms not just the individual sinner alone, but also the entire community (*ummat*), which is why the sinner is also a criminal in post-revolutionary Iran. To assert the significance of the principle and to promote it in society, a squad (Setad-e Ehya-ye Amr-e be m'arouf va nahi az monkar) has been established, devoted particularly to this purpose. Furthermore, the first week of the holy month of Ramadan is assigned as the "Week of the principle of mutual discipline."[21] The motto *amr-e be m'arouf va nahi az monkar* combines two different techniques of power: oppressive surveillance and Foucaudian salvation-oriented "pastoral power." The former is wielded by the moral police through the constant checking of bodies and spaces. Pastoral power, in its original sense, is a form of power whose ultimate aim is to assure individual salvation in the next life and which takes the shape of paternalistic care.

Father's Shadow

A child who does not grow up under the protective "shadow of parents" (*zir-e say-ye pedar va madar*) is supposedly heading for delinquency. Only the shadow of an elder (*say-ye yek bozorgtar*) can guarantee one's well-being. *Tarbiyat kardan* in Persian is used for both educating and punishing. Iranian schools are not very different from military bases imposing harsh discipline and punishment. Disobedient children are called *nakhalaf* (deviant). Young people are thus exposed to torment and discipline by teachers, masters, and fathers who "want the best for them" (*khobeshan ra khastan*). *Delsozi* (empathy) is a term frequently heard in political discourses. The severe ways teachers or officials treat youth are legitimated by claiming that they are *delsoz*, they care. In public debates the authorities defend their violent guidance by claiming they are expressing care and concern (*delsozi kardan*). The art of government is characterized by the continuity of the individual's self-government and its connection with morality, from the father's government of the family to the science of ruling the state. There is continuity and transmission running from the family to the state. The art of government is thus the extension of the "pastoral power" of the father over his household and wealth into the organizing technicalities of the state (Foucault 2000).

Iranian law legitimates the father's total authority over his child. In the process of tutoring punishment is justifiable even if it results in the death of the child (Bahnassi 1982: 183).[22] Backed up by *shariat*, Iranian Civil Law allows fathers' endorsement to punish their children physically. Article 1179 in the Civil Law says: "Parents are permitted to penalize their children but not outside the restriction of punishment." There is, however, no definition of restriction. Article 220 in the Penal Law goes even further: "Father or father's father who kills his child will not be punished afterward (*qessas*). He would be sentenced to pay *dieh* [blood money] to the murdered person's heirs" (quoted in Kar 1378/1999: 117). Within families a harsh system of control is applied to youths in order to protect them from "social and ethical delinquency" (*enherafat-e ejtemai va akhlaqi*) (Rejali 1994: 86–89).

Pastoral power is a supplement to discipline-oriented power. It is imposed not only by states or religious institutions but also by parents and teachers. It concerns the care of young people: the moralization of their bodies, welfare, and salvation. This is best expressed by a former member of the Supreme Judicial Council, Ayatollah Bojnourdi, who declared that "Penalty in Islam is correction rather than punishment."[23] While disciplining attempts to achieve normalization by drilling individuals, salvation-oriented tutelage does it by engaging in dialogue. In his study of torture in modern Iran, Rejali observes,

Individuals are treated not as objects that require training, but as subjects of questioning and guidance. Tutelage alters self-understanding and so behavior. In this respect, it assumes that individuals possess within themselves a deeper self that is realized through speech. In practicing tutelary techniques, individuals realize themselves as normal members of a moral speech community. (Rejali 1994: 84)

To understand the mechanisms of pastoral power in Iran, and in particular the ways power and hierarchy legitimate themselves, we need to study the institution of the *morad/morid* relationship and the way it is expressed in Sufism, family life, the bazaar, and the educational system. Originally coming from Sufism, the *morad/morid* relationship is a generational hierarchy that allocates power to the elders, a system that schools youngsters into total obedience to the patriarch. *Morad* is the master and *morid* the disciple. The master is also called *pir* (old) in Sufism. To find the right path in life, one needs a master, a *pir*. A person without a *pir* is "like a wild tree that bears no fruit."[24] The Sufi master not only is a teacher, but is himself the goal (*morad* literally means goal), a beloved role model for living. The disciple loves his master and devotes a large part of his life to serving him.[25] The master/disciple relationship is not very different from that between father and son. During education the master replaces the disciple's father. Total obedience to one's father is transformed into total obedience to one's master. While this pattern of obedience and loyalty (*morad/morid* relationship) originally had religious underpinnings, very similar forms can be found in secular political movements. Analogous patterns of interaction also mark the relationship between a master and his apprentice in the bazaar. Humiliation is perhaps the primary aim in the power system.

Contemporary pastoral power has been reshaped in new and mundane forms. Worldly salvation in terms of health, security, and welfare replace (Foucault 1983: 215) or supplement religious salvation (see also Ong 1999). The "caring power" in Iran emphasizes that sin is a violation not only of divine rule, but also of the sinner's well-being. The metaphors used in political discourse condemning the "cultural invasion" are often related to the body and health—"injection," "rape," "dissipating youth's energies," "poison," and "drugs."

The Cultural Foundation of Islamic Messages (Bounyad-e Farhangi Payam-e Islam) has published a series of handbooks on how to discover and clear out moral corruption in society. One of its publications, entitled *Javanan, Chera?* (Youth, Why?) is concerned with masturbation; how to prevent it and how to cure it. The book regards masturbation as a form of addiction that damages the eyesight, weakens the body, reduces the sexual drive, causes loss of memory or even madness, increases agitation, and finally damages the institution of the family (Zamani 1379/2000). In a similar way, gambling is seen as a sin and immoral because it damages the gambler's household economy (see Sanadjian 1996). It is by demanding "physical and spiritual hygiene" (*pakizegi-ye rouhi va jesmi*) that the forces of Islamic pastoral power authorize themselves to impose discipline and tutelage upon young people.

Ways of talking about morality and its relation to health are extended metaphorically to the level of the collective health of the Iranian nation or society by the notion of "Weststruckness." The Parent-Teacher Association (Anjoman-e Ulia va Murabian), a government organization with a "caring mission," publishes books for parents on how youth should be disciplined and how to counter "Weststruckness." These handbooks provide good illustrations of how pastoral power stimulates individuals to internalize discipline. In one of these handbooks, which is about the regulation of relations between boys and girls, we read:

We should note that we do not make our child faithful and restrained. She or he alone finds faith and control her/himself. We are just her/his guides. We do not direct our youth away from misdeeds: she/he does it herself/himself. We merely inform them, remind them of values, and explain the strength of willpower. (Ahmadi 1380/2001: 70)

Responsibility for proper self-government, alongside the collective duty of conducting *amr-e be m'arouf va nahi az monkar*, draws individuals into the power relations. As Rose and Miller put it, "Power is not so much a matter of imposing constraints on citizens as of "making up" citizens capable of bearing a kind of regulating freedom. . . . [M]ost individuals are not merely the subjects of power but play a part in its operation" (1992: 174, see also Foucault 1997).

The Eye of Power

As an effect of Islamic rule, social space has been partly transformed through attempts to strengthen moral control. Public places are turned into arenas for preventive demonstrations of punishment and are constantly scanned by the agents of the regime for transgressions and cultural crimes. This section deals with the various organizations mobilized for surveillance.

Revolutionary Committees (*komiteh*) were established in order to maintain Islamic order inside society. When in 1991 the *komiteh* were amalgamated with the police organization, the *basijis* became the major guardians of moral order on the streets.

The term *basij* (mobilization) refers to the militia of volunteers who provided the teenage "human wave" in the war against Iraq. In the early stages of that war Ayatollah Khomeini called upon young men to join the *basij*, which he called the "army of 20 million," referring to the 20 million young men in Iran; *basijis*, however, fought at the various fronts, joining the army and the Islamic Revolutionary Guard Corps (Abrahamian 1989: 70). Today, the *basijis* stand close to the hard-liners of the government. The *basiji* is the ideal young person (man). As Ayatollah Khamenei described the *basiji*, he is one

who cares for Islamic values, who is humble before God, who wants to be righteous and pure, who keeps away from moral evils, who struggles diligently for the development of his country and the emancipation of humankind from injustice.[26]

The last week of November each year (according to the Iranian calendar) is Basij Week, when special ceremonies and activities are organized in order to commemorate the establishment of the *basij*. Many *basijis* have military ranks conferred on them during these celebrations, and military manoeuvers are held. There are also sporting contests, a nationwide display of *basijis*. Among the programs scheduled for the week, *basij* Youth Clubs offer activities in various areas of interest such as Islamic teaching, as well as art, film, photography, theater, and competitions. The authorities claim that, during the 1990s, the *basij* has been expanding, and now controls 300,000 full-time men. During the same period its annual budget has increased by a factor of four (Zahedi 2001: 163).

In 1994, some 180,000 members of the *basij* forces went through ideological and religious courses in order to become better prepared to carry on their tasks of controlling corrupt practices and moral laxness. During Basij Week, *basiji* teams supervise public places and give guidance (*ershad*) and correction (*eslah*). An annual report delivered during the 1995 week claims that the *basijis* have "managed to give oral guidance to about 1,889,000 people whose families have expressed satisfaction with the constructive move by the *basij*."[27] In official speeches *basijis* are thanked on behalf of families whose "immoral youth" have been guided and corrected by them.

TABLE 2. SCHEDULE OF DEMONSTRATIONS AND MANEUVERS, AMR-E BE M'AROUF VA NAHI AZ MONKAR (1999)

Name of maneuver	Beginning	Destination	Aim (warning to)	Date and time
1 Ya Lesarat ul Hossein	Valiasr St. & Fatemi St.	Valiasr/ Jomhori St.	Vendors of western clothes (ties, etc.)	Thur. 9/6 5 p.m.
2 Solidarity with Martyrs of the 17th Shahrivar	Jam-e Jam St.	Mellat Park	Rap kids and immodest veiling	Thur. 16/6 5 p.m.
3 The Martyr Nasser Ebdam	Enghelab Square	Laleh Park	Corrupt music and unlawful relationships	Thur. 23/6 5 p.m.
4 The Sacred Defense	Darband Square	Shrine of Ebrahim	War against corruption	Fri, 31/6 6 a.m.
5 Ya Zahra	Daneshjo Park	Jihad Square	In defense of Velayat-e Faqih	Fri. 16/7 3 p.m.

The *basiji* play prominent parts in the maintenance of public Islamic order. Alongside these groups, the police devote a large part of their forces to dealing with "moral issues." I use the term "moral police" to refer to this part of the police. "Cultural crime" is not very precisely defined in Iranian law but is constituted by any act deemed to be against the cultural principles of the country. Due to this lack of precision, the application of the law regarding "cultural crimes" is left to the discretion of the moral police on the streets. Alongside the permanently patrolling moral police, the *basijis* sporadically take over the streets and public places to fight against "cultural corruption," as illustrated in Table 2, which I found on a notice-board in a mosque.

The Islamic Revolution has constructed its "art of government" by engineering a new social order based on Islamic family ethics and values. The social order in post-revolutionary Iran is indeed a juxtaposition of the patriarchal family structure, the *morad/morid* hierarchical ethos, and the police. Claiming to guard the "health and purity" of the nation as a "protecting" father guards his household, the Islamic governmentality arranged its "caring" politics by conducting its own "normalization" of the Muslim subject. This politics is based on modes of disciplining—e.g., the "panopticon" and punishment—and through the "pastoral modality of power," guidance (*ershad*) and correction (*eslah*). Despite the surface of its politics—referring to "early Islam" and striving after the ideal *ummat*—the Islamic Republic has had to adapt its social order to the logic of a nation-state: a juristic system with strong elements of centralization and codification, a centrally controlled mass media and education system. The next chapter deals with how this social order has been embodied in individuals in their everyday lives.

Chapter 2
The Aesthetics of Authority

A prisoner's meekness is a prison's pride.

—*Vladimir Nabokov*

Strange times, my dear!
And they chop smiles off lips
songs off the mouth.
We should hide joy in the larder.

—*Ahmad Shamloo*

In order to understand the criminalization of youth culture, we have to explore the aesthetics of authority, which have produced the notion of *bidard* youth. A crucial aspect of the post-revolutionary social order is the hegemonic discourse of self-abasement. An overwhelmingly religious Revolution has sought to sacrifice the self for a "higher value." Its mobilizing ideology (as I shall show in this chapter) is grounded in an "aesthetic of the modest self" and a "culture of sadness," both profoundly rooted in the Iranian/Shiite tradition. The order of things is designed to be sustained by the Iranian self through mechanisms of normative modesty and politics of emotion.

In Shiite Iranian culture the self is understood in terms of the dichotomies of *'oumq/sæth* (depth/surface) and *sanggin/sæbouk* (weighty/light). An *'amiq* (profound) and *sanggin* (weighty) person is quiet, gentle, serious, and thoughtful. A *sæthi* (shallow) and *sæbouk* (light) person is playful, unserious, childish, and joyful. The personal character most valued in Iran is quiet and gentle, demonstrating *nejabat* (modesty) by conspicuous self-abasement. The immense value of the "modest self" is also reflected in the Persian language.

In his study of language and power in Iran, William Beeman indicates how Persian pronouns and verbs correspond with basic orientations in social relations. He argues that Persian interpersonal discourse is based on relationships of inequality and a process of "other-raising" versus "self-lowering." Basically, in interpersonal interaction "one uses terms that serve to place oneself in an inferior status and the other person in a superior one. . . . Thus self-reference may use the expression *bandeh* (slave) in place of the neutral pronoun *man* (I)" (Beeman 1986: 16). Similarly, there are two versions of the verb "to say" (*goftan*): *farmoudan* (to command) is used for others and *'arz kardan* (the self-lowering version of the verb) for oneself. In Persian, it is "you *mifarmaeid*" and "I *'arz mikonam.*" This principle of "self-lowering" is the core of *ta'arof*, a major code of communication among Iranians.[1] The accomplished use of *ta'arof* is taken as a sign of social sophistication, while an inability to observe the rules of *ta'arof* in interaction is indicative of social ineptness. "*Ta'arof* is valued because it is viewed as an expression of selflessness and humility" (Beeman 2001: 47). This favored self-abasement is also expressed by many Iranians in their choice of modest names for children; for example, a not unusual name for men is *Gholam* (slave), which is often combined with the names of Imams, like *Gholam-Hossein* (Hossein's slave) or *Gholam-Ali* (Ali's slave).

The norm of modesty is well expressed in veiling as a form of highly valued self-effacement. The highly regarded personal quality of being *mahjoub* means to be both veiled and modest. Another feature of this social ethic is to value grief. A person's capacity to experience and express grief is an indication of his/her "deep" and "weighty" character. The verbs *gham khordan* or *ghosseh khordan* (to eat sorrow, to grieve) also mean "to care" and "to be concerned." The hegemonic ideal of noble suffering and normatively desired dysphoria is best expressed in Persian as *sokhtan va sakhtan* (burning and enduring).The ideal self is well acquainted with sorrow.

The experience of sadness, loss, melancholy, and depression is rooted in two primary meaning contexts in Iranian culture: one associated with an understanding of the person or self, the other with a deep Iranian vision of the tragic, expressed in religion, romance and passion, and in interpretation of history and social reality. (Good et al. 1985: 385)

An emulation of sorrow is based on pre-Islamic mythology, in classical Persian poetry, and Iranian interpretations of history. Primarily, however, it relates to the central Iranian religious traditions and the tragedy of Karbala (Good et al. 1985: 387).

What follows is a discussion of how the new regime in Iran has used these symbolic resources to implant the desired social order in its subjects. Articulated as resistance to the consumer culture (*farhang-e masrafi*) and "Weststruckness" that characterized the pre-Revolutionary, West-oriented Shah era, the contemporary Islamic order builds on an aestheticization of modesty manipulated through three mechanisms: a Revolutionary romanticization of poverty; veiling practices; and the emotionalization of politics.

Consumption and Purity

As will be shown below, both Islamist and secular intellectuals in Iran
have regarded consumption as a primary cause of corruption, self-
alienation, and dependence on neocolonial capitalism. They argue that
in a consumer society there is no place for native identity, authentic culture, or morality. Throughout his book *Gharbzadegi* (especially chapter
9), Al-e Ahmad attempts to persuade the reader that the most conspicuous syndrome of Weststruckness (*gharbzadegi*) is the consumption of
Western goods. The Weststruck man is described as an unauthentic (*bi-
essallat*) "prissy" (*qerti*), who superficially mimics the West.

> He is always primping; always making sure of his appearance. He has even been
> known to pluck his eyebrow. He places great importance on his shoes, his
> clothes, and his home. You would think he had just emerged from golden wrap-
> ping paper or just come from some European maison. . . . The [Weststruck]
> man is the most faithful consumer of Western manufactured products. (Al-e
> Ahmad 1982: 70–71)

Later on the author condemns the "Weststruck man" because "It is on
account of him that we have such unauthentic and unindigenous
[urban] architecture . . . under the ugly glare of the neon and fluores-
cent lights" (Al-e Ahmad 1982: 71).

Shariati too declares that "worldliness" has tainted Iranian culture.
He defines "worldliness" as the nihilism of Western culture, which promotes individual hedonism (Shariati 1979: 79), stripping nations of
their authenticity and transforming human beings into "consumer animals" (see Mirsepassi 2000: 122). In Shariati's view, the main consequences of consumerism are "self-alienation" (*az khod biganegi*) and
uprootedness from authentic Iranian/Islamic culture. Shariati's and Al-
e Ahmad's occidentophobia and attack on consumerism are presented
in a patriarchal way. Throughout his speeches and publications Shariati
expresses anguish that consumerism has converted Iranian women into
"European dolls" (*arousak-e farangi*) who can only consume and consume. Al-e Ahmad's "Weststruck" person is, in contrast, always a male,
whom he labels "effeminate" (*zan sefat*) to belittle him. Women cannot
themselves be Weststruck, but, on the other hand, they are used as
means to deceive men.[2] Ali Shariati, influenced by Frantz Fanon, also
uses postcolonial discourse to condemn consumerism. Shariati developed a populist version of Islam, combining Fanon's views, Marx's crit-
icisms of capitalism, and Shiite traditions. He believes that the "West,"
in order to enslave the "East," first turns it into a consumer of its products. Consequently the "East" becomes alienated from its own native
culture, turning into an eternal identity-less consumer and slave of the

West. Shariati believed that modernized meant modernized in consumption. "One who becomes modernized is one whose tastes now desire . . . European new forms of living and modern products." Non-Europeans are modernized for the sake of consumption. Therefore, the Europeans had to make non-Europeans equate "modernization" with civilization" to impose the new consumption pattern upon them, since everyone has a desire for civilization."[3] Such fears affect secular intellectuals, too. Obsessed by concerns with authenticity but also influenced by neo-Marxist intellectuals such as Marcuse, Iranian intellectuals have targeted consumerism as a crucial feature of the Shah's cultural policy.

A fear of consumerism has been the main theme in literature and films since the 1970s, most visibly in the book *Tars va Larz* and the film *Keshti-ye Yonani*. *Tars va Larz* (Fear and Tremble), written by the celebrated psychiatrist and novelist Gholam Hossein Sa'edi (1380/2001), tells stories about coastal people along the Persian Gulf. The arrival of a foreign (European) ship changes the life of the coastal people. The foreigners are beautiful and offer the local people a large amount of food and commodities. Overconsumption metamorphoses the people from human beings into a kind of parasites waiting for the arrival of other boats.

CINEMATIC VIGNETTE

Keshti-ye Yonani *(The Greek Ship, 1999, by Nasser Taghvai)*

This short film is one of six episodes making up the film *Tales of Kish* (*Qeseha-ye Kish*). Kish, a little free trade zone island in the Persian Gulf with its pleasing coasts, has become a popular tourist attraction in Iran. As in Dubai, life on the island is organized around shopping. One of the attractions of the island is an old ship stranded on the southwestern shore. It is said that, a long time ago, a Greek cargo vessel reached this part of the sea for unknown reasons, but was stranded for ever. The natives say that the owners of the ship set it on fire before leaving it: and indeed nothing is left of the ship but a steel structure. Taghvai's film tells the story of two workers who collect cardboard containers— marked by Kodak, Dauoo, Toshiba, Konica, and Aiwa brand marks— washed up on the beach from passing ships. The men dry out the boxes to build their huts. The wife of one of the men, who gathers some objects left by a passing Greek ship, is afflicted by a strange illness. The village medicine man claims it comes from the boxes. After a *zar* ritual, the woman is cured and the men throw the boxes in the sea. The film graphically shows how the local culture, health, and authenticity are endangered by consumerism and foreign culture. When a journalist asked Taghvai why he had chosen the Greek ship as a metaphor, the director answered: "Why not. Was Greece not the cradle of Western culture?"

* * *

Condemning the immorality of society prior to the Revolution, Ayatollah Khomeini often used commodities and consumption as examples. The Revolutionary agenda was to save the virtue and purity of the *ummat* from consumerism, by promoting self-restraint (*qena'at*) and idealizing poverty. Excessive consumption (*esraf*) and an ostentatious lifestyle (*tajamulgarai*) became synonymous with "bourgeois aesthetics" and were automatically defined as signs of adopting an anti-revolutionary position. People preferred to conceal their wealth, in order not to be stamped as anti-revolutionary. For instance, many hid their luxury cars in their garages for several years.[4]

The Noble Dispossessed

At the end of the 1970s, the slum dwellers in Tehran numbered as many as a million (Bayat 1997: 29). Ayatollah Khomeini, as the opposition leader, found potential power among them for revolting against the Shah. Claiming that Islam stands on the side of the disenfranchised (*mahroumin*) and the "dispossessed" (*mostaz'afin*), Khomeini characterized the Revolution as a movement against the "oppressors" (*mostakberin*). Its goal was to induce more social justice for the poor. The "dispossessed" were praised and deprivation was glorified. While the "oppressors" were depicted as venal, decadent, and corrupt, the "dispossessed" were "portrayed as the repository of innocence possessing genuine human values. If unbridled pursuit of material wealth had rendered the elite heartless lackeys of capital, the suffering of the dispossessed had humanized them" (Dorraj 1992: 221). Thus, pain (*dard*) and suffering (*ranj*) had become hallmarks of "high human values."

Ayatollah Khomeini frequently attested his commitment to the disenfranchised in his speeches: "I kiss the hands of the simple grocer" (Khomeini 1981: 184); or "Islam belongs to the dispossessed" (quoted in Abrahamian 1989: 22). The clerics and officials of the Islamic regime were zealous in presenting themselves as belonging to the lower classes, and the gradual romanticization of poverty became a salient feature of the theocrats' political populism (see Abrahamian 1993; Dorraj 1992). The ideological romanticization of poverty pursued by the Iranian authorities draws nourishment from Sufi traditions and literature. Poverty and a working-class lifestyle are celebrated in Iranian popular movies and soap operas. Following the famous phrase of Imam Ali, "The best wealth is self-restraint (*qena'at*)," the Iranian media glorify poverty and self-abasement by an endless restaging of the martyrs' testaments and life stories.

Even primary school textbooks are used to promote ideas of poverty and modesty. The most illustrative example of poor-is-beautiful-assessment may be in the textbook for the first grade. In the pre-Revolutionary first grade textbooks there is an illustration of a middle-class family sitting around the breakfast table.[5] The father wears a suit and tie and is shaved. The mother has short hair and is unveiled. The teenage girl is dressed in red and has her arm on the table. She is the image of self-confidence. Her brother, dressed in yellow, is talking. The parents are looking at him. On the table are coffee cups, a milk jug, a sugar bowl, plates, and knives. After the Revolution this picture was replaced with a more humble one, where the family is clearly less affluent. The family members are eating dinner sitting on a rug. On a damask cloth there is traditional Iranian food, rice, vegetables, and bread. The mother is veiled and wears a simple overall. The father is modestly dressed and wears a beard. The daughter, barely a teenager, is veiled in an overall and a scarf. Like her mother, she looks down shyly. The children are sitting on their heels (*du zanou*), a position showing respect to their parents. An interesting aspect of the illustrations is their body language, which indicates the modesty expected from the young people. Sitting on one's heels (*du zanou neshastan*) is a gesture whereby one lowers oneself and acknowledges a superior other. The common Iranian expression "kneeling out of politeness" (*zanou-ye adab zadan*) demonstrates a relationship between "sitting on one's heels," "good manners," and modesty. In front of Allah, this gesture is part of daily prayers.

Female modesty is confirmed by veiling, but normative modesty defines its own fashion for men as well; khaki pants, military overcoat, boots, a Palestinian shawl, and an unshaven two- to three-day beard, testify to one's neglect of the worldly life. This dress code gives one a "*hezbollahi* look" (*qiyafeh hezbollahi*). Paradoxically, however, the Revolutionary aesthetic has also favored American and German military overcoats.[6] The Revolutionary morale has forged a kind of cultural capital, based on a working-class lifestyle, a simple appearance, and unpretentiousness. To present oneself as simple and indigent is seen as a measure of one's commitment to the Revolution. Such an aestheticization of poverty can also be traced among secular leftist movements in Iran.[7] In encounters with representatives of the authorities, "*hezbollahi* style" and use of Arabic/Islamic phrases play a significant role. Many times I asked my informants why they did not shave, and they answered that they were going to visit certain authorities. Dara said that when he was going to visit an authority he wore the oldest and most ragged clothes he had, adding half-jokingly, "When I attend a meeting at university I wear the dirtiest socks I have. The more they stink, the more I look like a revolutionary." The "*hezbollahi* style" evokes the "proletarian style" promoted in the communist states.[8] The Islamic Republic, however, has fashioned its own distinct "judgment of taste."

Basiji

The government's ideal model for Iranian youth is the *basiji*, a modest, self-restrained (*qanne*), self-possessed (*mattin*) young man. He is "profound" (*'amiq*), "weighty" (*sangin*), serious, and ready to sacrifice himself for Islam and the Revolution. The archetype of the *basiji* is Hossein Fahmideh, a thirteen-year-old *basiji* who at an early stage of the war destroyed an Iraqi tank by a suicide attack. Books retell his life story, and his picture is paraded on posters and stamps. Ayatollah Khomeini called him "the real leader." After the end of the eight-year Iran-Iraq war in 1988 *basijis* somehow lost their significance. These men had left their school benches or jobs when they were still teenagers. They were seen as national heroes as long as the war lasted. They had sacrificed their careers, youth, friends, and frequently their health or parts of their body. Returning from the front, many *basijis* who came from poor backgrounds were disappointed to see that the original revolutionary ideas they had sacrificed themselves for were gone. An ideal *basiji* is modest in attitude and thereby spiritually rich but materially poor. "A rich *basiji*" is a contradiction in terms.

Nevertheless, sometimes the ideal necessitates a reforging of identity. Merhdad, a young *basiji*, comes close to pretending to be deprived. Merhdad is thirty years old and the only child of the family. He lives with his parents in the same alley where I resided during my fieldwork, in a wealthy neighborhood in North Tehran. His father is a well-off physician. Merhdad neither has nor needs an ordinary job. However, he has been active in the *basij* since the mid-1980s. While his father goes to his clinic in a suit and tie and his mother goes to meet her friends "not properly veiled," Merhdad is always dressed as a *hezbollahi*. He goes to the mosque he belongs to unshaven and dressed in a white shirt hanging over his military pants.

In his case, this is not a matter of any generational revolt. I can see clearly that he likes his parents and respects them. Yet he is ashamed of belonging to a wealthy family. He never invites his *basiji* friends home. He told me how he had tried to hide his bourgeois background from other *basijis*:

The first month I joined the *basij* we went for a military training in the mountains. When we opened our lunch boxes I was embarrassed. All had simple cheese sandwiches except me. My mother had put rice and chicken in my box. The group leader said "We have a rich kid here." It was embarrassing.

Merhdad told me that he sold the Peugeot his father had given him as a birthday present the previous year, to buy a second-hand Iranian-made Peykan. Merhdad wants to keep his family distant from his *basiji* comrades, because he knows that his family's ostentatious lifestyle is seen by other *basijis* as "superficial bourgeois aesthetics," which is in stark contrast to the ideology of the *basij*.

However, the majority of *basijis* come from the working class, and being *basiji* empowers them in the daily class conflicts on the Tehran streets. A former *basiji* from the working neighborhood Javadieh confessed:

It was just to have fun, to tease the rich *sousol* [effeminate] kids of north Tehran. With some other *basiji* friends we jumped in a car and drove to Shahrak-e Gharb or Miydan Mohseni. We put a "Stop, Check Point" sign up and annoyed "rich kids" in their *khareji* [foreign] cars. If one had a beautiful girl in his car we teased him even more. Sometimes if we did not like one, we cut his hair to belittle him before the girls.

For this young man as well for many others, *basij* has been a means to transgress the social hierarchy, albeit temporarily and symbolically. The state attempts to fit *basijis* into the educational system and the labor market by quotas and to retain their loyalty by granting them special privileges. They are given priority for subsidies for building houses or the *hajj* pilgrimage. Almost 40 percent of university places are reserved for *basijis*, their children, or the families of martyrs (Zahedi 2001: 119–20). This has widened the gap between *basijis* and other young persons who consider such favoritism to be discrimination.

A Veiled Society

Another side of the aesthetic of modesty has been the politics of veiling. The first stage was a project for the desexualization of society. Modesty and chastity are conflated in the Islamic notion of female virtue. Veiling is its instrument. Religions often regard sexuality as a menace and therefore repress it in order to keep people focused on salvation, and this view of what was necessary for the task of forming modest citizens has been shared by the Iranian clergy. Women are supposed to possess an uncontrollable sexual passion which is regarded as a threat to or calamity (*fetneh*) for the social order. Thus, sexuality is recognized only within the boundaries of permanent or temporary (*mut'a*) marriage.[9] In an ideal Islamic society the sphere of the family (the site of sexuality) should be separate from society. Such a separation purifies society from social corruption such as adultery and prostitution and takes the form of veiling, a responsibility that falls on women.

A woman's beauty and sexuality are to be reserved for her husband. A woman is expected to make up and wear attractive clothes only for her husband's gaze. It is women's responsibility to ensure that their faces and bodies are not being watched by unrelated (*namahram*) people. Even sexual relations between spouses are regulated by Islam. Married couples should not have sex during the *hajj* pilgrimage or fasting, as it is thought to cause impurity, and such activities require prior ritual washing. A married couple may not hug or kiss in public, not even at their own wedding. Any sexual expression in public is discouraged. The preservation of "public chastity" (*'effat-e 'omoumi*) demands the absence of anything that can be associated with (female) sexuality.[10]

Desexualizing society has its roots in how sexuality is conceived in Iranian society. In Iranian culture, a beautiful woman can be admiringly described as a "calamity maker" (*fetneh angiz*) or "one who causes confusion in town" (*shahrashob*) (cf. Mernissi 1975). Interestingly the "calamity making" of women is inherently linked closely to their pattern of consumption. A "chaos-making" woman is "a super-consumer of imperialist/dependent-capitalist/foreign goods; she [is] a propagator of the corrupt culture of the West. . . . She [wears] too much makeup, too short a skirt, too tight a pair of pants, too low-cut a shirt. [She is] too loose in her relations with men, she laughs too loudly and smokes in public" (Najmabadi 1991: 65). One way to control her is to constrain her sexuality by veiling.[11] A woman who has been denied both her sexuality and her individuality is assigned to the single recognized role of motherhood, a role celebrated in soap operas and textbooks.[12]

ETHNOGRAPHIC VIGNETTE

Actress Gohar Kheirandish (in her fifties) kissed the forehead of Ali Zamani (in his twenties) as he received the top director's prize at a ceremony in the central Iranian city of Yazd in October 2002. The clerical leaders organized protests after the kiss and the pair were accused of harming Islam. Kheirandish and Zamani were charged with immoral behavior and could face a jail sentence or up to 74 lashes for their actions but were more likely to be fined. The pair apologized for the kiss and said that it was a spontaneous, maternal gesture by Kheirandish.

The Science of Sexuality in Iran

In Iran, the suppression of sexuality has likewise extended it. In the Islamic Republic sexuality started to become repressed, that is, condemned to prohibition, nonexistence, and silence. Only one single and utilitarian locus of sexuality was acknowledged, the fertile heart of every household: the parents' bedroom (cf. Foucault 1990: 3). But turning sexuality into "sin" did not make it disappear. On the contrary, it was reinforced and became something to be observed everywhere. The repressive fascination with sex resulted in an explosion of discourses—in medicine, psychiatry, and education—about sexuality. It has resulted in a pervasive discourse on sex that is a form of power/knowledge. As Foucault points out, the repression of sex in nineteenth-century bourgeois society demanded a science of sexuality, *scientia sexualis* (Foucault 1990: 58), in order to understand, catalog and identify the very perversion that needed to be controlled or eradicated.

Its focus [was] not the intensification of pleasure, but the rigorous analysis of every thought and action that related to pleasure. This exhaustive articulation of desire has produced a knowledge which supposedly holds the key to individual mental and physical health and to social well-being. The end of this analytic knowledge is either utility, morality, or truth. (Dreyfus and Rabinow 1983: 176)

Since the Revolution a huge market for manuals, instruction booklets, and educational guidance on sexuality and sex life has emerged. A large part of these publications are published by the state, but individual clerics and religious institutes are also producing them. Publications by the "Parent-Teacher Association" (Anjoman-e Uleá va Murabian) and by the "Cultural Foundation of Islamic Message" (Bounyad-e Farhangi Payam-e Islam) aim to teach young people how to have "proper" (*monaseb*) and "healthy" (*salem*) sex. Numerous blogs and websites deal with sexual issues. One example is Weblog of Temporary Marriage,[13] which, based on religious sources, aims to "configure sexuality in society." The blog offers "information" on sex and sexual relations, such as "how to stop sickly [sexual] behavior"; "the harms of masturbation"; "ethics of sex"; " advantages of temporary marriage."

Furthermore, every ayatollah is supposed to have published his own *Towzihoule Masael* (Practical Treatise), a comprehensive guide to life in general and religious/juridical matters in particular. Sexual life is a major theme in these books. What follows is an excerpt from Ayatollah Mosavi Ardebili's *Towzihoule Masael* (1380/2001), which deals with rules of the senses.

Rules of Look, Touch, and Voice

Article 3032. It is *haraam* [unlawful] for man to look at the body of the *namahram* [unrelated] woman, regardless of whether it is with the intention of pleasure or not. It is also *haraam* to look at the faces and the arms, up to the wrists, of such women with the intention of pleasure. Similarly, it is *haraam* for a woman to look at the body of *namahram* man, without the intention of deriving any pleasure.

Article 3032. It is *haraam* to look at the private parts of another person, even if it they are seen through glass or reflected in a mirror, or clean water, etc. As an obligatory precaution, it is also *haraam* to look at the genitals of a child. However, a wife and her husband can look at the entire body of each other.

Article 3039. If a man and woman, who are *mahram* of each other, do not have the intention of sexual pleasure, they can see the entire body of each other excepting the private parts.

Article 3040. A man should not look at the body of another man with the intention of sexual excitement, and also, it is *haraam* for a woman to look at the body of another woman with the intention of sexual excitement.

Article 3043. If a man has to look at or touch the body of a *namahram* woman for the sake of treatment, there is no harm. But, if he can treat her with looking and without touching, he must not touch her, and if he can treat her with touching, he must not look at her.

Article 3044. If one is obliged to look at another person's private parts for treatment, he must look in a mirror, but if there is no way but looking, then there is no harm.

Article 3045. A woman is allowed to speak loudly before *namahram* men unless her voice makes the men sexually excited.

Article 3046. Women and men are allowed to hear each other's voices if they do not have the intention of sexual pleasure.

In 2005 a "Marriage Calendar" (*Taqvim-e zanashoui*) was published by a religious publisher in Qom. Printed in 100,000 copies, the Calendar contains sex instructions and quotes from religious leaders about sexual issues. Each day is marked as an "appropriate" or "inappropriate" day for sexual intercourse. For instance, according to the Calendar, sexual intercourse in a standing position is improper because it resembles animals' sexual intercourse. Based on quotes from religious texts, men are recommended to do foreplay before penetration.[14] Another example of expansion of "the science of sexuality" is shown in the aims and plans of the government National Youth Organization.[15]

National Youth Policy

Article 36: Hygiene of adolescence
• Being aware of physical and mental health, physical changes and mental developments during the period of maturation and directing sexual instincts toward preserving physical health and reproduction.

•Providing suitable grounds to obtain the youth's trust in expressing their problems arising from adolescence with parents and teachers.
•Planning for physical and mental activities to moderate the adolescents' sex instinct up to their marriage time.

Article 37: Rites of maturity
•Learning the rites of maturity and responsibilities of becoming an adult on the basis of religious laws & understanding the reasons of impermissible premarital affairs between boys and girls.
•Guidance of the youth to acquire restricted useful & necessary sex knowledge and prevention from acquiring unnecessary and perturbing information.
•Immunization of the social environment and removal of probable backgrounds of the adolescents' sexual abuse in their mutual relations.
•Expansion of the sex hygiene and individual cleanliness among girls and boys.

Article 38: Chastity
•Improvement of the spiritual disposition and moral training of the youth to preserve their health and restrain their sex instinct.
•Preservation of the sanctity and protection of chastity, honour, and family dignity.

* * *

Since sin and crime are seen as equivalent by the authorities, confessing one's crime (*'eteraf*) and repentance (*toubeh*) are also usually the same. Unlike Catholicism, there is no explicit verbalized confession in Islam, but Muslims are expected to repent (*toubeh*) alone and in their hearts.[16] Summons to make *toubeh* became pervasive in various forms, such as in official speeches, religious lectures, graffiti, and in textbooks. In the religious handbook, *Javanan Chera?* (Youth, Why?), we read "One should see him/herself before the Divine Justice [*'adl-e elahi*] and make *toubeh* for his/her bad deeds" (Zamani 1379/2000: 155). Another instance: "We watch her/him from afar and let her/him take his/her own steps. If we choose these methods, our children will easily tell us their secrets and control themselves. This is what faith means" (Ahmadi 1380/2001: 70).

Confession is a central component in the expanding of "techniques of discipline" and control of bodies and society, especially "telling the truth" about sexuality (Foucault 1990: 59): "in confession after confession to oneself and to others, this *mise en discours* has placed the individual in a network of relations of power with those who claim to be able to extract the truth of these confessions through their possession of the keys to interpretation" (Dreyfus and Rabinow 1983: 174). In the Iranian context the border between confessing (*'eteraf*) one's crimes and one's sins (almost always sexual ones) has collapsed.

It has been very common for accused journalists, intellectuals, and political activists to "confess" their sexual sins/crimes alongside what they are actually accused of. Political offenses are linked to sexual misdemeanors. Confessions of the individual's sexual life have become part of politics in Iran. Every day on the streets people are forced by the moral police to confess to their sexual "sins." Two unrelated persons of opposite sex found in the company of each other are forced by the moral police to "confess" to what kind of (read sexual) relationship they have. The young couples are interrogated separately and then the girl's story is compared with the boy's to check if they are lying or not. Prepared for this, young couples adopt tactics to deceive the system. The boy borrows his sister's identity and even ID-card for his girlfriend, or they prearrange a story to mislead the police.

Elli's trouble with the moral police is an illustrative example. She told me she was once stopped by "moral policewomen." They first ordered her to correct her veil and then began to insult her, saying that she looked like a whore. Elli wore an overall on which there were several lines that made an arrow pointing downward. The policewomen claimed that the pattern "pointed at Elli's cunt" in order to attract the attention of boys.

Veiling and Modesty

Imposing veiling and unveiling has been seen metaphorically by Iranians as a hallmark of the "tradition/modernity" (*sonat/tajadoud*) dichotomy. While "modernity" took the concrete form of unveiling, one of the first concerns of the Islamist movements is veiling.[17] Although veiling and modesty in Iran go back in time well beyond the Islamic Republic, it was only after the Revolution that veiling and sex segregation for all were enforced and given a political and juridical dimension. Sex segregation of public spaces was ordered at the very beginning of the Islamic Republic. Rules prescribing the *hejab* as a proper and modest attire for women were written into the law. One form of "cultural crime" is *bad-hejabi* (improper veiling). Women had to cover their hair and skin in public, except for the face and hands. In 1983, Parliament made "observance of the veil" compulsory in the Penal Law, on pain of 74 lashes (Kar 1380/2001: 126–27). In 1996, the Penal Law was reformed and the punishment of *bad-hejabi* was reduced to prison and a fine. *Bad-hejabi* is only vaguely defined by the law. "Uncovered head, showing of hair, make-up, uncovered arms and legs, thin and see-through clothes and tights, tight clothes such as trousers without an overall over them, and clothes bearing foreign words, signs, or pictures" (Paidar 1995: 344) can be understood as *bad-hejabi*. But the term can also refer to the use of nail varnish, brightly colored overalls, or even modes of body movement or talking (Kar 1380/2001: 127). Mehrangiz Kar, a lawyer and activist for women's rights, states that the fines paid by women accused of

bad-hejabi represent a considerable revenue for the judiciary. According
to the Article 638 of the Islamic Penal Law, "Unveiled women who appear in public places and in the public's sight will be sentenced to
prison from ten days to two months or to pay a fine of 50,000 to 500,000
Rials."

Patterns of dress are often a form of communication. Veiling expresses modesty, as in the expression, "My sister, your veil is a sign of
your chastity" (*Khaharam, hejab-e tou neshane-ye effat-e toust*). In political
discourse the veil is presented both as a symbol of inner purity and
modesty (*nejjabat*) and as an ideological device in the war against "cultural invasion." That women are improperly veiled is seen as caused by
plotting by the internal and external enemies of the Revolution. This
view is best formulated in the famous slogan, "My sister, your veil is
more vital than the blood of the martyrs." An improperly veiled woman
"dishonors the blood of the martyrs of Islam" (see Paidar 1995: 339).
Violence against so-called *bad-hejab* women has been a daily scene since
the Revolution.[18] To find a solution for the *bad hejabi* "problem," the
Majlis (parliament) started a debate and research for creating a "national dress code" for Iranians in October 2005.

Veiling is a gender question involving men also. Historically, men in
Middle Eastern societies were also supposed to be "veiled" (see El
Guindi 1999: 117–28). Men are concerned, even if to a different degree, with veiling in a more abstract sense, and in the concrete sense of
covering bodily parts seen as immodest. Like women, men are not allowed to exhibit their bodies or to adorn them by wearing ties or bow
ties, sunglasses, necklaces, or earrings. Having long hair is taken as a violation of the Islamic order. Wearing short-sleeved shirts or shorts is
against normative modesty. Men's averted gaze is also a consequence of
veiling. As Abu-Lughod has noted, modesty means more than veiling
according to strict Muslim reading. It means hiding your natural needs
and passions, for instance, by not smoking, laughing loudly, or talking
too much. Modesty is about "masking one's nature, about not exposing
oneself to the other" (1986: 115). Covering "sexual shame," the veil
makes sense of the dichotomy between related and unrelated people. A
woman should cover her sexual shame for men she is not related to,
that is, men who might be potential sexual partners.

Both men and women must be protected from being seen by unrelated persons of the opposite sex by following a set of rules of modesty
that apply to architecture, dress, behavior, eye contact, and forms of interaction (Milani 1992), but they must also veil themselves in more in-
direct ways. Women must to some extent veil their voice. "Veiling of the
voice includes using formal language with unrelated males and females,
a decorous tone of voice, and avoidance of singing, boisterous laugher,

and generally any emotional outburst in public other than the expression of grief or anger" (Naficy 2000: 562).

The salient side of normative modesty is effacement. In the Iranian culture, face (*rou*) is a common metaphor for self-assertion and is used as a symbol in measuring the social ethic. *Kam-roui* (little-face, shyness) or *rou nadashtan* (not having a face) is a sign of humbleness, while *rou dashtan* (to have face) or *pour-roui* (full-face) stands for self-exposure, brashness, and free expression, in what is perceived as an aggressive and arrogant manner. The expression *roum nemishe* means "my face does not allow me to say or do it." A person's honor and reputation are his/her *aberou* (water of face). Similarly, the expression *sharm-e hozour* (shame of presence) refers to the same high-valued self-effacement. One who has *sharm-e hozour* (one who is ashamed of his/her presence) is a meek and respectful person. The *mahjob* (veiled one) is a courteous person. Thus self-abasement (symbolic self-sacrificing) and self-effacement (veiling) are main features of the social ethic that the Islamic state has constructed.

Moral Space

The norm imposed on Iranian youth is that they have to be "veiled" in the abstract meaning of the word, to be modest. In their social practice they should maintain the distinctions and segregation between related and unrelated (*mahram* and *namahram*) people. This protects the moral values of society from corruption, by evil lusts or "cultural invasion" by the earthly Great Satan, the United States. Another feature of the politics of veiling is strict gender segregation, which is enforced in public places such as beaches, swimming pools, schools, hairdressers, or sports halls. According to the law, there should be separate sections for the sexes at political meetings, conferences, weddings, funerals, demonstrations, and even different queues in front of a bakery. Buses are divided into two parts separated with a metal grille. Men should get on and off through the front door; the rear section and rear door are for women. Women are excluded from sports halls, where "unveiled" men play football or wrestle in shorts. Mixing the sexes was seen by Ayatollah Khomeini as a plot "designed by foreigners to propagate promiscuity, and to weaken the Muslim youth's determination."[19] All places where segregation cannot be imposed, for example, in the street, shopping centers, or parks, are under the supervision of the moral police.

Another noticeable feature of Iranian normative modesty is the division of space into public and private spheres. Private space (*andaruni*) is associated with women and family relations (*mahram*). Public space (*biruni*) is associated with men and unrelatedness (*namahram*). Traditional urban house designs use high walls and inner rooms to protect the family from the public. In southern Tehran, the quarter (*mahalleh*) still functions in its traditional role, as an interstitial space between private and public, under the control of neighbors. If this moral geography is violated, it might cause stigmatization. One way of understanding the *chador*—the black veil that covers the body from head to foot—is to see it as a "mobile *andaruni*." Just as the walls of a house protect the inhabitants, the *chador* protects women moving through public space from being looked at by unrelated men.

Imposition of the Islamic order has transformed traditional definitions of space. The urban sociologist Amir-Ebrahimi (1380/2001) argues that after the Revolution even public spaces in the cities have to some extent been transformed into *andaruni*. The patriarchal father's attention to the female virtue (*namous*) of his family is now part of the way the state manages space (Foucault 2000: 207). Although traditional principles of marking off public space from morally controlled "private" space are not followed in modern architecture and urban planning in Tehran, the attitude maintaining them is still powerful in some places. For instance, in all public places such as cinemas or restaurants there is a section "specifically for families" (*makhsous-e khanevadeh*), which is separated or "protected" from the single male's (*afrad-e mojarad*) erotic power.

I experienced this "spatial morality" personally several times when I was asked to leave restaurants in Iran because I did not respect the "family space." Once I was refused entrance to a well-known traditional teahouse. "It is only for families. We do not want to have *mojarads* [single people] here," the doorman told me. *Mojarad* generally means single, but usually refers only to a single male. The discrimination against *mojarads* does not include women. While single men are not allowed to enter "family spaces," single women can do so. A single man is called *azab*, an Arabic word which means unmarried but also "to be distant." So, the dangerous single men are supposed to be distant, unattached, and isolated. At the entrance to the traditional teahouse, upset by being discriminated against, I insisted on entering, and the porter repeated: "Here is only for family-possessed [*khanevadeh-dar*] persons." Being "family-possessed" brings connotations of morality, civility, or virtue. To call somebody "without-family" (*bi-khanevadeh*) is an insult, meaning that the person is vulgar and undignified. The moral geography in Iran is thus organized in a way that segregates the family (read women) from unrelated, particularly single, men, who are supposed to be potential challengers of the order of sexual purity that is upheld and protected by the omnipresence of the patriarch. The most blatant discriminations against young bachelor men are done by the *basij*.

Once I asked Bahman, a *basiji* in the Shahrak-e Gharb (I shall return to him in the next chapter), "Why do you stop only cars in which there are young people, while cars in which there are families can go through?"

Bahman: "Families usually are not a problem. But be honest and tell me don't you become suspicious, if you see three well-dressed young men in a car at midnight?"

To summarize, the personal modesty that is designed and imposed from above implies a social control of the body that acts not only by covering hair and skin but also by desexualizing the body in public and by imposing a normative poverty. Modesty in appearance and behavior thus operates both as a symbol of Islamic order and as a mechanism for maintaining it, in a combination of self-regulation and external control. The modest body demonstrates the normative values of the social body (see Douglas 1982), defining its social boundaries and confirming a person's loyalty to the social order. Operating by humiliating the self, the body and its desires, the social order is turned into a project of self-abasement. If one side of this is to create an aestheticization of modesty, the other side engenders the celebration of sadness.

Iranian Blues: The Politics of Grief

When you are among Iranians, don't smile too much; they don't. (Lewis 2000: 333)

Iranians frequently complain that the Iranian culture is "a culture of sadness" (*farhang-e gham*), "a culture of mourning" (*farhang-e azadari*). Contrary to Western conceptualizations of it, in the Iranian culture sadness in its various shapes of grief and despair is not an indication of anomaly or a destructive feeling, but rather is normal and even valued.[20] The medical anthropologist asserts that dysphoria is central to the Iranian ethos (Good et al. 1985: 384). Such feelings are usually seen as symbols of inner purity (*safa-ye baten*). Once, while attending a concert, Dara and I saw Davod sitting close to us. Davod is a young man from Shahrak-e Gharb. An activist in the Local Association (*anjoman-e mahali*), he is accused by many other youths of being a political opportunist and having a "businessman style" (*bazari maslak*). Dara and his friends in Shahrak-e Gharb rarely missed a chance to criticize and belittle him. During the concert, Dara told me to look at Davod who, impressed by an old sorrowful melody, was shedding tears. Apparently surprised by Davod's tears, Dara said after the concert: "Did you see? He cried. He is sincere. Despite his deceitfulness, his heart is clean." Sadness and grief (*qam o qosseh*) are marks of social sophistication and personal "depth" ('*oumgh*) and decency. Cheerful persons who express their joy frankly, laugh loudly, and joke with others risk being stamped as "happy-go-lucky" (*alaki khosh*), "unconcerned" (*bi-khiyal*), or *bidard*. In rural Iran it is still usual for people after long laughs to say "forgive me, God" (*astaqforella*), as if laughing is in itself a sin.

The centrality of tragedy to collective consciousness in Iran is reflected in popular culture and mythology. The Iranian national epic *Shahnameh* (Book of Kings) consists of tragedies. The best known of them are the tragedy of *Rostam and Sohrab* and the story of *Siavash* (I will return to these myths later). From the pre-Islamic mythologies in *Shahnameh* to the drama of Karbala, tragedy is related to the most conspicuous form of self-abasement and martyrdom. However, the Iranians' vision of tragedy is first and foremost rooted in Shiite history and principally in the drama of Karbala.

The Tragedy of Karbala

The Karbala massacre took place in the month of Moharram 61 A.H. (ca. October 680 A.D.), on the plain of Karbala, located in today's Iraq. Imam Hossein, son of Imam Ali and grandson of the Prophet, was martyred on the tenth day of Moharram, known as Ashura.[21] The detailed history of Ashura is a story of loneliness, thirst, loss, torture, and bereavement. The anguish and regret of the Shiites are expressed and performed in a commemorative ritual of Ashura.[22]

The annual ritual of Ashura has since then been celebrated everywhere in Iran for ten days (1st to 10th Moharram). The ritual is a complex arrangement of collective, ritualized mourning through public recitation and the chanting of elegies (*rowzeh-khani*); *ta'ziyeh* (a theatrical representation of the tragedy); and the Moharram procession (*dasteh*).

It is no exaggeration to say that the whole Iranian population, more than 90 percent of them Shiite Muslims, go through the ritual every year. Even the lives of nonbelievers and religious minorities are affected by the ritual. Moharram is the first month of the Arabic/Islamic lunar year. It is often called *mah-e azadari*, the month of mourning or "the time of sin." Public morale forbids weddings and marriage preparations during the month of Moharram. No joyful ceremonies take place; TV and radio programs are cheerless, "weighty" (*sangin*), and "serious" (*jeddi*). During the ten days of Moharram, the whole society is driven into a state of depression. TV and radio broadcast programs about the Karbala tragedy and the rituals. Thus, even non-Muslims are involved, albeit indirectly.[23]

The Karbala tragedy has also affected Iranian art and literature.

Ta'ziyeh has been praised and developed as a particularly Iranian style of drama. There is a painting style related to the Karbala tragedy, known as *pardeh* or "coffeehouse painting," that visually narrates the battle. A new generation of artists have developed "coffeehouse painting" into a modern art genre known as the "Saqakhaneh School" (see Chelkowski and Dabashi 1999). The main purpose of the Ashura rituals is to maximize lamentation. Shiite tradition encourages and promotes weeping as a way to salvation. Weeping for Hossein, called the "Lord of Martyrs" (Sayyed-ul Shohada), not only brings divine forgiveness, but also contributes to the triumph of the Shiite (see Enayat 1982: 182). A recurrent expression in official speeches is that "Islam needs tears." Tears would even help Imam Hossein: "A learned man saw in a dream that the Imam [Hossein] had recovered from all the wounds [inflicted on him at Karbala]. He asked the Imam how his wounds had healed so miraculously. 'With the tears of my mourners,' replied the Imam."[24]

As Motahari formulates it, the Karbala tragedy is a "school" (*maktab*) and a "culture" (*farhang*) (see Motahari 1379/2000). Another Islamist, Emalduldin Baghi, in his book *Jamm'e Shenashi Qiyam-e Emam Hossein* (Sociology of Imam Hossein's Movement), agrees that the rituals of Ashura fulfill various social functions. They protect the society from cultural impurity and alienation and revive ethical values, such as "faith," "martyrdom," "sacrifice," "dignity." The cult of Ashura guarantees social cohesion and represents an "ideal lifestyle." It imposes a norm and is a means for social control and guidance of the young people (1379/2000: 76–82). Thus, the Karbala tragedy is more than a historical event. As Michael Fischer puts it, it provides a paradigm, because it is

(a) a story expandable to be all-inclusive of history, cosmology, and life's problems; (b) a background contrast against which the story is given heightened perceptual value: in this case, primarily Sunni conception, but other religions at times serve the same function; and (c) ritual or physical drama to embody the story and maintain high levels of emotional investment. (Fischer 1980: 27)

Good et al. (1985) and Good and Good (1988) also believe that the Moharram ritual organizes a "prototypical" view of the social order and the self in Iran. The central concept of the Karbala paradigm is "self-abasement." Mourning and self-flagellation represent the feelings of guilt of all Shiite Muslims who were not there to help Imam Hossein. They represent the Kufan people repenting their abandonment of Hossein. How a "sense of guilt" and "valued dysphoria" has been manipulated and utilized in the political mobilization before and after the Revolution will be examined below. A recurring slogan since the Revolution has been "We are not like Kufans to abandon the Imam alone" (*Ma ahl-e Kufe nistim Emam tanha bemanad*).

Before discussing the role of the Karbala tragedy in the emergence of the current social order in Iran, I want to comment that, despite the fact that the shadows of the overwhelming ritual of Moharram reach out into all parts of the nation, there are subtle variations in the interpretation of the Karbala tragedy. For instance, in rural areas the Moharram ritual is only an excuse for teenage boys to have fun. Being together in long nights spent at the *hosseinye*, they make jokes or play cards (Fischer and Abedi 1990: chap. 1).

One way to avoid a fatalistic and static representation of Iran—as entirely subject to the ubiquitous sadness (e.g., in Good et al. 1985; Good and Good 1988)—is by "historicizing" the process whereby the Karbala tragedy has been transformed from a central symbol of folk religion into the focus of a state ideology.

The Politicization of Karbala

For Ayatollah Khomeini, the Karbala events had transformed not only the history of Islam, but the whole of human history. Imam Hossein's heroic movement was depicted as an archetype representing the eternal struggle of Goodness against Evil, injustice, and tyranny. This new interpretation of the Karbala tragedy became popular among young people, despite the disapproval then shown by orthodox clerics.

Shariati's revolutionary model is a combination of gnosticism and political engagement. Gnosticism liberates individuals from worldly ties. It indoctrinates them to value pain and martyrdom. Revolutionary gnosticism has been the ideal model not only for Islamists but also for secular political activists.[25] Revolutionary Iranian discourse has been based on the dichotomy between "Hosseini" and "Yazidi" people, using it both as a pattern for action and a central symbolic frame for the organization of the early Revolution and later on to mobilize people in the war against Iraq. Both the Shah and Saddam Hossein have been called the "Yazid of the time" (*Yazid-e zaman*). The Islamic state was established by manipulating Karbala-related symbols, rituals, and emotions (see Good et al. 1985; Good and Good 1988; Fischer 1980; Enayat 1982; Mottahedeh 1985; Hegland 1983; Gieling 1999; Dorraj 1999; Khosrokhavar 1995; Aghaie 2004; Varzi 2006).

A widely used slogan in official speeches, mass media and wall graffiti is "Kullo yawm'in 'Ashura, Kullo arz'in Karbala" (every day is Ashura and every land is Karbala).[26] The message has been, "if you were not at Karbala at that time to aid Imam Hossein, you can perform your duty today." Utilizing the tragedy of Karbala, the Islamic regime has sought to induce a "sense of guilt" that would thrust people toward such self-reproach. By transforming hegemonic cultural discourse and everyday life into a melancholic ambiance, the Islamic authorities have attempted to canalize young people's emotions in order to make them attached and devoted to the system.

Half a million young Iranian men are estimated to have lost their lives in the war (Amani 1992).[27] The state used all available means to promote a "martyrdom-seeking attitude" (*rouhi-ye shahadat talabi*) among the young people of the nation.[28] Martyrdom is regarded as analogous to "sweet syrup," drunk by those who are ready for self-sacrifice. The official news of the martyrdom of a son killed on the battlefield, when delivered to his family, was regularly initiated with "Congratulations and Condolences" (*tabrik va tasliat*). Media propaganda incessantly showed warriors who expressed their wishes to become martyrs, awaiting their martyrdom with joy and triumph. Returnees from the fronts complained that they were "disqualified" from being martyrs (*liyaqat-e shahadat nadashtan*).

The symbolism of martyrdom is all-prevalent in Iranian society. In the spring of 2000, in addition to the traditional rituals, a Karbala exhibition and workshop was arranged for the first time in Tehran. A model of Karbala was built which showed the events of Ashura. Other activities were arranged such as theater playing, a puppet theater for children, and narration of the history of Karbala. Several workshops were organized for young people: one for "Painting the Karbala," others for collective mourning (*rowzeh-khani*) and breast-beating (*sin-e zani*), or for learning how to organize Karbala rituals. The exhibition and workshop lasted three days. Schools all over Tehran sent their students to visit, and similar activities were arranged in other cities as well. Since the end of the war, a huge organization has been constructed for cultural activities, such as large wall paintings of martyrs around the city, publishing "war literature" and collecting slang expressions, and memoirs of the war, to be published in the series "Culture of the Front" (Farhang-e Jebhe). In Tehran alone, 1,400 streets had their names changed to the names of martyrs (Chelkowski and Dabashi 1999: 121). Furthermore, the state supported a new cinema genre called "Cinema of the Holy Defense."[29] Up to 10 percent of the themes in the textbooks from second through fifth grade are about death and martyrdom (Nafisi 1992: 168). Interviews with the families of martyrs make part of media programs every day. The six TV channels, all state-owned, play a crucial role in reproducing the hegemonic grief-stricken ethos.

Since its establishment, the Islamic Republic has placed lamentation on its social agenda. Weeping is often part of the official speeches made by political leaders. Expressions of grief have become a sign of religious and political commitment (Good and Good 1988). Common expressions such as "crying refreshes the heart"; "weeping makes hearts pleased"; or "better than weeping is weeping itself" are frequently heard in officials' speeches. More grief indicates more faith. "Whom God loves more, gains much grief." Politicians frequently mention Imam Hossein in the middle of their speeches and weep. Ayatollah Khomeini formulated the significance of grief for the Islamic state as follows: "It is the lament which keeps us alive" (quoted in Gheissari 1998: 114). The mass media have recurrently campaigned for a promotion of the "culture of weeping." A look at the Iranian almanac also shows that holidays in Iran are mainly "mourning days"—dates of the martyrdom or the death of the Prophet, Imams, or Revolutionary personalities.

The hegemonization of the Karbala discourse and the reproduction of a "martyrdom-seeking attitude" (*rouhi-ye shahadat talabi*) construct an atmosphere in which one is induced into a sense of guilt, shame, and gradual self-abasement. The official culture of the theocracy is characterized by a tone of petrified seriousness, based on religious awe, lamentation, and humility. This religious seriousness is supposedly the only tone fit to express the true, the good, and all that is essential and meaningful. Accordingly, hilarity is seen as indicative of the reverse, of triviality, falseness, and meaninglessness.

The Politics of Colors

If I had to choose a colour to characterise Iran, I would choose black. (Briongos 2000)

To Iranians, the symbolic range of colors is divided between, on the one hand, "weighty" (*sangin*), "respectable" (*bavaqar*) dark colors and, on the other hand, "light" (*sabouk*) disgraceful (*zannandeh*), bright ones. Color is an important symbol of the revolutionary culture. According to the authorities, the most appreciated color for clothing, particularly for veiling, is black. The black *chador* is regarded by the clergy as the "superior veil." It is obligatory for a large number of women, such as government employees. According to an order from the Ministry of Education, students too are obliged to wear somber colors close to black, such as dark blue, gray, and brown. The *basijis* and semi-official militia Ansar-e Hezbollah symbolize their standing by wearing black shirts. "Wearing black" (*siah poushi*) has become a criterion for dividing people into "good" and "bad" categories. The feminist journal *Zanan* criticized the political use of color by the state:

Darkly dressed persons were classified as "one of us" [*khodi*] and ones dressed
in light colors as "not one of us" [*ghayr-e khodi*]. Darkness [*tiregi*] has become a
symbol for a willingness to protect Islamic rules and revolutionary values, while
lightness [*roushani*] is a metaphor for mimicry of the corrupt Western culture
and lack of respect for the blood of martyrs.[30]

In Iranian culture, black has connotations of both grief and shame.
The very common expression *roum sia* (let my face be blackened)
means "How ashamed I am." Another well-known expression is "siyahy-
e zemeston be zoqal mimone" (the blackness of winter is left on coal).
It is used to express "Time passes. She/he will be ashamed of her/his
misdeed." This relationship between shame and black is noted by,
among others, Abu-Lughod (1986), who concludes that the veil "black-
ens the face" and symbolizes shame, particularly sexual shame (Abu-
Lughod 1986: 138). In many parts of Iran, after her husband's death a
widow is expected to wear black for the rest of her life. There is thus an
apparent relationship between dark colors and modesty and sexual
shame.

Shariati also uses color to denote the division between the passive
pious Shiite (black Shiite) and the heroic revolutionary Shiite (red Shiite). Shiites have a complex relation to the color red. While it symbolizes blood, sacrifice, struggle, and martyrdom, it is also used to denote
the personality most hated by Shiites, namely Shemr, the one who killed
Imam Hossein. In *ta'ziyeh* the one who plays the role of Shemr is
dressed in red from head to toe. In the national referendum after the
Revolution people could choose to vote "Yes"—a green card—for an Islamic republic or "No"—a red card. Bearing in mind that green is
Imam Hossein's color and red is associated with Shemr, voting "Yes" was
tantamount to fighting alongside Imam Hossein and voting "No" was
the same as fighting on the side of Shemr (Chelkowski and Dabashi
1999: 75). Along with other "cheerful colors" such as pink, orange, or
yellow, the color red signifies one's sense of self-esteem, joyfulness, and
worldliness—hence an anti-Revolutionary attitude.[31]

After two decades of all-black clothing, several surveys by psychiatrists
have warned that Iranians, particularly women, have become depressed.[32] Alarming prognoses of growing depression and suicide
among schoolgirls have forced the authorities to allow some relief. The
expansion of depression among young people has been described as a
"national malady" by the experts. According to a survey, four million
people under age of twenty are depressed due to the low level of social
enjoyment.[33] More than 20,000 persons attempt suicide annually in
Tehran alone.[34] In summer 2000, the Ministry of Education announced
that, in order to create a happy atmosphere, raise hopes, and preserve
the mental health of students, girls in elementary schools would be en-

couraged to wear brightly colored clothes. Since the late 1990s, the government, worried by the social consequences of the ubiquitous sadness in society, has started to "command" people to be joyful. In the 1990s, the reform-minded mayor of Tehran, Gholam Hossein Karbaschi, painted the city in bright colors and put up large placards saying "Smile citizen" (*hamshari labkhand bezan*). In March 2002, even the conservatives admitted the nation's need of joy for the first time. Haeri Shirazi, representative of Vali-ye faqih (Ayatollah Khamenei) in a Friday sermon in Shiraz emphasized teaching people jubilation.

It is not good that Muslims are incapable of expressing joy [*shadi kardan*] in times of joy [*ayam-e shadi*]. There are persons who even condemn applauding [*dast zadan*]. Applauding and cheering have never been against Islam. Unfortunately, many do not know how to rejoice. They should be taught and trained how to rejoice.[35]

In several cities, such as Shiraz and Mashhad, "Festivals of Laughter and Joy" (*jashn-e khande va shadi*) were organized by the authorities in the Summer of 2002. Daily papers and magazines publish interviews with "moderate" religious scholars who, with reference to *hadiths*, announce that hilarity is not un-Islamic.[36] By arranging folk festivals and using folk music and customs (clothes, food, and rituals), the authorities are attempting to shape an officially recognized form of happiness.[37]

The vague presence of happiness and cheerfulness in Iranian public life still faces strong opposition from conservative forces. Concerts and ceremonies that play live music, even if these have been given official permission, are occasionally attacked by conservative forces. The authorities seek to launch a "definition" of happiness. President Ahmadinejad and the Majlis (parliament) show a more conservative approach toward what "happiness" is. Mehrdad Bazrpash, Ahmadinejad's adviser on youth, says that "with the right tools, we can define what is happiness for the youth."[38] Similarly, Mousa Alreza, a Majlis deputy, states that "in our society, unfortunately no definition has been presented to the public about happiness." He adds that people's behavior gets out of hand for the smallest expression of happiness. He asked the ministry of Islamic guidance to come up with standards for one specific form of expression of happiness, and punishment for those who violate it.[39]

For more than two decades, the Islamic government has tried to redesign Iran's social order. It has been able to realize its ambitions through the political reconstruction of myths, or rather, the mythologizing of its politics, and through the reconfiguration of collective significances. A complex "semiotic politics" of personal emotions is involved in the state ideology. The Islamic Republic has attempted to create its own particular subject: an oppressed (*mazlom*), modest (*najib*), poor, sad (*qamgin*), and veiled (*mahjob*) individual. In the cultural ideal ruling Iran, suffering pain is a token of dignity and purity, while being *bidard* signifies one's immorality and an anti-revolutionary standing. The Islamic Republic has also created its own aesthetics, in terms of appearance, style, and jargon—a form of "cultural capital" in some situations. By creating and using the emotions of people and creating a community of sentiment, the authorities have tried to canalize individual desires (such as the desire for martyrdom) in ways that endorse and sustain power.

Through manipulation and control of the body, clothing, color, emotion, and sexuality, the theocracy has created its own rituals. According to Bloch's functionalistic perception, rituals are strategies of power in the reproducing of structures. By "hiding reality" (Bloch 1989: 33) rituals constitute an imaginary, static, transcendental order using formal, repetitive, non-arguable means that legitimate authority (see Kelly and Kaplan 1990: 125). Kelly and Kaplan argue that rituals can be "acts of power in the fashioning of structure: acts that make gods, kings, presidents. and property rights by declaring that the authority of the priest, judge, or police officer resides in a higher source" (140). Furthermore, rituals limit agency. In Bloch's view, roles and acts in rituals are authorized by a superior authority and not by those who participate in the ritual. "Ritual is a kind of tunnel into which one plunges, and where, since there is no possibility of turning either right or left, the only thing to do is to follow" (Bloch 1989: 42). In the ideal social order the theocracy is attempting to establish in Iran, public life is like participating in a ritual—or theater—with predetermined roles and little space for agency.

Chapter 3
A Dissident Neighborhood

Shahrak-e Gharb, Dalghak-e Gharb
(Shahrak-e Gharb mimes the West).

Faith, No more!
—*Wall graffiti in Shahrak-e Gharb*

In 1994, Shahrak-e Gharb was a hot news topic among Iranians. A story, about which the official media and the state were entirely silent, spread through the country and even to outside Iran, where foreign broadcasts (of which BBC, Radio Israel, and the Voice of America were the most popular in Iran) sent the news back to Iran.[1] The story was about the mysterious death of a teenage boy (we shall call him Babak) at his birthday party in Shahrak-e Gharb. In the absence of his parents, he had arranged a party in their apartment in a high building in Zone 1 in Shahrak-e Gharb. Young boys and girls mingled, drank homemade vodka, and danced to illicit music. *Basijis* stationed in Shahrak-e Gharb were informed and sent a patrol to investigate. When they rushed into the apartment, Babak fled to the balcony. Frightened of the punishment awaiting him, he tried to jump to the neighbor's balcony. He did not make it and fell to his death. This was the officials' version. However, no one was recognized as responsible for the incident.

The tragedy of Babak underlined the reputation of Shahrak-e Gharb as a neighborhood distinct from other parts of Tehran—a neighborhood with a more liberal attitude toward sex and youth culture, a neighborhood constantly in conflict with *basijis* and the moral police. As it is formulated in Tehran, Shahrak-e Gharb is "a different world." My interest in this neighborhood was sparked by all the rumors I heard and read about Sharak-e Gharb long before I started my fieldwork. In this chapter, I examine how young people of Shahrak-e Gharb construct their neighborhood identity as a space of defiance against the dominant social order. Shahraki identity is forged by dissociating from poor, "traditional,"

"local" (all favorable attributes according to the Islamic regime) South
Tehran. With the help of ethnographic glimpses, I shall try to show how
supposedly "modern" (*motajaded*) and globalized young people in
Shahrak-e Gharb distance themselves from the identity imposed upon
them by emphasizing their individuality or by linking themselves to the
transnational youth culture. But first I shall present a picture of the wider
urban milieu in Tehran, and the geography of the city as a whole.

Tehran

Until 1796, when Agha Mohammad Khan, founder of the Qajar dy-
nasty, chose Tehran as his capital, Tehran was an unimportant little
town. Unlike other large Iranian cities like Isfahan and Shiraz, Tehran
lacks Oriental features, that is, Islamic urban planning, with elegant
mosques or palaces. Tehran is a giant Third World "city without memory" (Pakravan 1971: 9).

Tehran is situated on the southern slopes of the Alborz mountains,
almost 100 km south of the Caspian Sea, at an elevation of 1100 meters
above sea level. Although it has been the capital for more than two centuries, its urban development did not begin until the 1930s. The inflow
of migrants from rural areas and little towns to Tehran has been increasing dramatically since the 1960s (Bayat 1997: 29). After the Revolution, refugees from the Iran-Iraq war, as well as from Afghanistan,
have further contributed to the enlargement of the population. Usually
poor and unskilled workers from various ethnic backgrounds, they have
settled in the slums of southern Tehran. The city has gradually encompassed the surrounding satellite towns and villages. For the past three
decades, the population has grown from barely 4 million in 1966 to
over 6 million in 1986. In a similar way, according to the mayor of
Tehran, the land area of Tehran has expanded from 200 square kilometers in the first year of the Revolution (1980) to 600 square kilometers
in 1992 (Bayat 1997: 79). Until the 1960s, the urban structure in Tehran
was concentrated around the bazaar. In today's Tehran, this area is situated in the southern part of the city. Northern Tehran, with its green
spaces and beautiful calm gardens at the foot of the mountains was the
summer resort of the city dwellers.

Because of its location, Tehran grew along a sloping north-south axis.
The resulting difference in altitude reflects the socioeconomic hierarchy, making the north-south duality a salient feature of the urban structure. The north, with its green spaces, more moderate climate, and
beautiful vistas, is the home of the affluent Tehranis; the south belongs
to the lower middle class and poor. Urban morphology in the north is
well planned and characterized by wide, tree-lined streets, large houses,

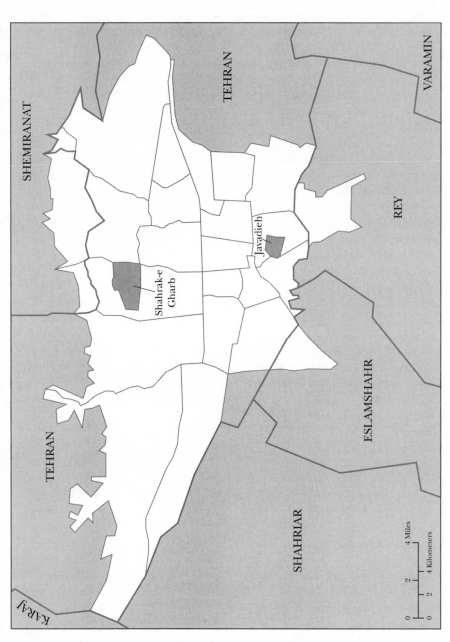

Map 1. Tehran. Courtesy, Tehran Geographic Information Center (TGIC).

and a lower density of population. There are parks and modern shops. North Tehranis enjoy high rates of literacy, income, and land values, and lower unemployment than southern Tehranis.[2]

The class division between north and south has in turn produced a "status division." The rural origins and ethnic backgrounds of the migrant poor in the southern suburbs have set them off culturally and socially from the Westernized urban rich, who stigmatize the poor as *dehaati* (rural/backward), and *hamal* or *amaleh* (literally unskilled construction laborers; see Bayat 1997: 30–32). Stereotypes also represent south Tehranis as traditional and religious. Naziabad and Javadieh are perhaps the neighborhoods most clearly stigmatized as *jonob shahri* (south Tehrani). Social inequality continuously reproduces itself in a dichotomy between a modern, affluent, "global," urbane north and the traditional, "local," rural poor south, traditionally delimited by Enqelab Street, which crosses Tehran from east to west (see Madanipour 1998).

Tehran, crammed with more than 12 million inhabitants in 2004, is a large city, faced with serious urban problems, such as traffic congestion, air pollution, and a shortage of water. The city is divided into 22 districts (see Map 1). Recent surveys of the social geography of Tehran indicate that it is divided not just by a north-south duality, but also along a center-periphery axis. Three districts—2, 3, and 6—make up the "center" of Tehran. They show higher rates of literacy, education, employment, income, and presence of women in the labor market (Amir-Ebrahimi 1992, 1999). These districts are surrounded by middle-class districts. Poor neighborhoods (districts 15, 16, 17, 20) lie below the bazaar area and around the railway station, Goumrok, and Shoush Square. Districts 18 and 19 are the poorest areas in Tehran.

Shahrak-e Gharb: "A Different World"

During the 1970s, thanks to oil dollars and increasing transnational flows of commodities, signs, and lifestyles, Tehran was spatially transformed. The construction of Shahrak-e Gharb was a central step in the spatial modernization of the city. It is a modern neighborhood in northwest Tehran (in District 2). It was planned to be an American-style neighborhood for wealthy Tehranis. The name of the neighborhood, "Shahrak-e Gharb," means the Little City of the West, referring to its geographical location but also to the Westernized character of this neighborhood. The very name has been controversial in the eyes of the Islamic state. After the Revolution, the neighborhood was semi-officially renamed Shahrak-e Quds (Little City of Jerusalem). However, it has continued to be called Shahrak-e Gharb, and the local association fought for a long time to regain the original name.[3]

Designed by French architects, Shahrak-e Gharb was, according to the original plan, to cater to the elite. A population of between 30,000 and 40,000 was estimated in the first plan. They would reside in 2,000 houses and more than 7,000 modern apartments. Today, the population of Shahrak-e Gharb is estimated to exceed 70,000. Large villas and luxury flats built with imported materials and equipped with swimming pools, playgrounds, green spaces, and shopping centers were features providing a modern lifestyle. The point was to segregate Shahrak-e Gharb. Equipped with its own school, sports clubs, cinemas, shops, and so forth, it was to be self-sufficient and cut off from the dirty, chaotic, noisy, confused, backward Third World Tehran. Shahrak-e Gharb is divided into zones, or *fazs*, numbered one to seven. The construction of Zone 1 was already almost finished at the dawn of the Revolution. The rest of Shahrak-e Gharb was built afterward, by the Housing Ministry.

In 1989 the Foundation for the Dispossessed took over Shahrak-e Gharb. Land confiscated from rich people north of the original boundary of Shahrak-e Gharb was allocated to poor people from south Tehran and appended to Shahrak-e Gharb as the seventh zone. The urban design of this zone differs from the rest of Shahrak-e Gharb. In a similar way, more than 100 different housing cooperatives built apartments for government employees in Zone 6. Five- or six-story buildings, with three to four apartments on each floor, are inhabited by lower-middle-class Tehranis who have been able to move to Shahrak-e Gharb with government subsidies. These buildings were aesthetically poor with a crude interior design. Zones 2, 3, and 4 are more or less identical and do not differ from the original pattern of Shahrak-e Gharb. Zone 1 is obviously the most attractive section. With its higher land prices and rents than the rest of the area, its green parks, its luxury houses and apartments, its "community school," and its modern shopping centers, Zone 1 has become what the "Shahrak-e Gharb concept" was planned to be, an isolated resort for the elite. It is a "car-neighborhood" with wide symmetric streets. Streets and alleys are usually cul-de-sacs, unlike the network of alleys in the central and southern parts of Tehran.

Shahrak-e Gharb is separated from the rest of Tehran geographically by two highways on the eastern and southern sides, and by a riverbed and another highway on the west. In the north it borders Saadat Abad neighborhood, which itself ends at the mountains. This neighborhood is accessed directly by highways. The main entrance to Shahrak-e Gharb is from the south at San'at Square, where all public transport from different parts of Tehran arrives and leaves Shahrak-e Gharb.

The sociological profile of district 2, where Shahrak-e Gharb is located, shows that this neighborhood occupies a high position in the socioeconomic hierarchy of the city. Shahrak-e Gharb is usually put in contrast to Javadieh and Nazi Abad, two working-class neighborhoods (both in district 16), where many of the young people strolling around in Shahrak-e Gharb and the daily visitors at the Golestan shopping center come from.

TABLE 3. OCCUPATIONS OF INHABITANTS, DISTRICTS 2, 16, AND TEHRAN (%)

District	2	16	Tehran
Manager and administrator	11.1	1.6	4.8
Professional	27.5	7.3	13.8
Technician	9.5	4.9	6.2
Clerical personnel	10	9.2	8.7
Commercial personnel	15	19	17
Agricultural laborer	0.6	0.5	0.7
Laborer	20.1	49.8	38
Occupation not described	6.2	7.6	10.8

Source: Statistical Center of Iran, Tehran 1996 Census. Unemployment in district 16 is double that in Shahrak-e Gharb (*Atlas of Tehran Metropolis*, 134).

The literacy rate in district 2 is 97 percent, compared with less than 85 percent in district 16 and barely 90 percent in the whole of Tehran. Similarly, while in Shahrak-e Gharb 40 percent of the nonstudent population have a university degree, this is the case for less than 5 percent in district 16. In Shahrak-e Gharb 55 percent of the young people between ages fifteen and twenty-nine are university students, whereas the rate in district 16 is only 10 percent.[4] District 2 accordingly has a much higher status in the labor market (see Table 3). Unemployment in district 16 is double that in Shahrak-e Gharb (Tehran Geographic Information Centre (2005). The price of a square meter of land in Shahrak-e Gharb is four times that in Javadieh.[5] The average size of a household in district 2 is 3.8 persons, compared to more than 4.2 persons in district 16 and 4 in Tehran as a whole.

Another measure I was curious to look at was types of women's activities. Table 4 shows that women in district 2 are more active outside the home than women in the rest of Tehran, thereby indicating a more liberal attitude toward women's participation in public life.[6]

TABLE 4. OCCUPATIONS OF FEMALE INHABITANTS, DISTRICTS 2, 16, AND TEHRAN (%)

District	2	16	Tehran
Housewife	49.8	62	56.6
Employed	13	5	8
Student	31	27	29.5

Source: Statistical Center of Iran, Tehran 1996 Census.

We Are Modern—They Are Traditional

Shahrak-e Gharb is segregated from the rest of Tehran not only by geographic borders, but also by a "symbolic boundary." It is seen not only as a neighborhood but also as a "state of mind," a lifestyle. Although its inhabitants (hereafter Shahraki) do not make up any homogeneous modern, Westernized elite category, they nevertheless share an idea that their identity and culture differentiate Shahrak-e Gharb from other parts of Tehran. The borders affirm a distinction between the concept of "us" and the construction of "others" (Cohen 1985). Throughout my fieldwork different expressions of this Shahraki identification struck me, and I attempted to understand how it was formed through my conversations with Shahraki and non-Shahraki Tehranis. The notion that it is a "modern" district built for the elite is obviously very central. Dr. Amiri, director of the local association, stated that it was the most progressive part of Tehran, the one with the highest potential. He did not miss the opportunity to name a list of "prominent" historians and musicians who happened to be Shahraki. "The best of each group and category live in Shahrak-e Gharb. Before the Revolution Shahrak-e Gharb was thought to be a residence for *taftey-e jodda bafteh* [privileged category]. But the Revolution made it different." Dara is an active member of the local association and works for the local newsletter, *Bavar*. He once presented me with a long list of famous poets and writers resident in Shahrak-e Gharb.

The average education is higher in Shahrak-e Gharb than in the rest of Tehran. They [the state] want to destroy our reputation, because there are so many Shahraki intellectuals. They say that they do not like Shahrak-e Gharb because of its westernized culture and life style. But in fact they are scared of our intellectual young people.

According to my informants, Shahrak-e Gharb possesses a modern, urban culture. Its symmetrical "imported" style of urban planning is dis-

tinct from the rest of Tehran. In southern neighborhoods there is a grocery store, a butcher, and a bakery in each alleyway. Residents and shopkeepers know each other and a large part of the trade between them is
based on trust and credit. In Shahrak-e Gharb, transactions take place
in the anonymity of the shopping centers, and this very anonymity is
perhaps the main feature of its urban milieu. Dara frequently reminded
me of the "huge difference" between Shahrak-e Gharb and southern
Tehran:

Southern Tehran neighborhoods have a rural pattern [or social structure].
There is still a *mahallegari* [neighborhood patriotism] over there. Here it is
more like Europe. There is more individualism compared with other neighborhoods. If you pass an alley in Javadieh, they will stop you and ask why you are
there. Everybody knows everybody. Here nobody cares who you are or what you
are doing here. You have more freedom and meet more tolerance. They [south
Tehranis] have no culture of urbanism. Shahrak-e Gharb is the only district in
Tehran which has its own non-governmental local association and newsletter.
That is what I call urban culture.

Another man similarly emphasized the role of the culture: "Difference is not in the soil and the air. There is the same soil and air here as
there is in Javadieh. It is a matter of culture."[7] The "we" feeling that
Shahrakis have constructed is not based on any conventional "community warmth" or on face-to-face contacts, but on a shared idea of being
"modern." This neighborhood self-esteem is based on a belief in being
well-educated, Westernized, egalitarian, free-thinking, and transnationally connected. The claim of a distinct "being modern" neighborhood
identity can also be found in other parts of Tehran, for instance among
the "kids of Gisha," a middle-class quarter in central Tehran (see Shirali
2001: 46).

Shahrakis use any argument available to emphasize distinction from
other city dwellers. It could be an environmental point: "Shahrak-e
Gharb's air is less polluted than other areas in Tehran because the wind
blows from west to east." It could be a historical one, as they identify
Khorvardin park—in the north of Shahrak-e Gharb—as an ancient
Zoroastrian temple. It could be demographic. At the local association,
I frequently heard that Shahrak-e Gharb could exist independently of
Tehran. Local newsletters, such as *Bavar* and *Akhbar*, frequently pub-
lished the names of famous writers, artists, and sportsmen who lived in
Shahrak-e Gharb. In addition, each year a person has been chosen by
the *Bavar* newsletter as the Man of the Year of Shahrak-e Gharb.

This feeling of distinction and emphasis on being unique, either in
terms of being the victim of the state's policy or of being the best, sustain people's sense of identity and community, and to some extent characterize Shahrak-e Gharb. *Qasedak*, a weekly advertising paper, has a

map of Shahrak-e Gharb in each issue, contributing to the "image" of
Shahrak-e Gharb as a community (see Anderson 1983). The local association (*anjoman-e mahali*) was founded in 1981 by the people of
Shahrak-e Gharb themselves, when the Pahlavi Foundation was discontinued. Dr. Amiri, as he is called by Shahrakis, has been the director of
the association since its initiation. Dr. Amiri is a respectable man in his
late fifties. He has a Ph.D. in economics from the University of London,
but is retired and is engaged in Shahrak-e Gharb's affairs full-time. He
called himself Shahrak-e Gharb's *kadkhoda* (village headman). On
many occasions when I was with him, people came to him for advice or
help. One man asked for help to register his son at a school. On another occasion a man requested help because he had a problem with
the secret police. Dr. Amiri told me that the Shahraki local association
was the first urban local association in all Iran. It was thus a pioneer and
should be a model for other parts of Tehran.[8] The association has six
committees, Green, Economic, Urban Affairs, Security, Publication,
and Youth, which work with different affairs.

   The Youth committee was the most active. Dr. Amiri said that they
were attempting to register the Youth and Green committees as non-
governmental organizations and link them with UNESCO. The association is nonpolitical, nongovernmental, and financed by Shahrak-e
Gharb's inhabitants. They occasionally publish newsletters and the
youth committee has its own newspaper, *Bavar*. The daily newspaper
Akhbar has also published a special supplement on Shahrak-e Gharb.
Most members of the management council have a university degree,
mainly from Western countries. They still retain connections with the
West through family links. Dr. Amiri and his wife, for instance, usually
visit their children in Canada in the summer. Another member of the
council occasionally visits her children in London. Mrs. Azizi, chair of
the Green Committee, was educated in the U.S., where her brothers
still live. They have helped her to establish contacts with international
environmental organizations. Another is married to a German woman.
At the weekly meetings, English terms and expressions are frequently
used. Some write notes in English. The majority of the men come in
suits and ties. Such "cosmopolitan traits of taste" distinguish this association from other associations in Tehran, which are usually government-
organized and managed by *basijis* and *hezbollahi* persons. Another
significant feature of the association is the powerful presence of
women.

   I participated in most of the activities of the local association, such as
the seminars the youth committee arranged twice a week. On Sundays, it
was "cognition of self" (*khodshenasi*), on Thursdays a "political analysis"
seminar followed by a "literature" one. Usually about fifteen young people

aged between eighteen and twenty-four gathered. The seminars started at
4 p.m. and lasted three hours. The participants often invited non-Shahraki
friends or cousins to attend, and these latter admitted that the seminars
were unique in the city. The "cognition of self" seminars were the most
popular ones. Topics ranged from women's rights, "generation clash,"
"love," and "boy-girl relations" to "psychoanalyzing" each other.

A Deterritorialized Neighborhood

Traces of globalization are more apparent in Shahrak-e Gharb than in
any other part of Tehran. Transnational connections through the diaspora, the globalizing media, and patterns of consumption have given
Shahrak-e Gharb a distinct character. This does not mean that local
identity is lost. Globalization produces the local rather than demolish-
ing it. One important consequence of globalization is the recovery of
the concept of place (Beck 2002: 23). In the following pages I examine
how transnational connections have formed Shahraki identity and even
its *Javad* Other (see below). A significant connection with the global
culture is through the Iranian diaspora.

Madres-ye Tatbiqi are "adaptation schools," catering to children of returnees from the diaspora. There are only two such schools in Iran, one
for girls and one for boys, both located in Shahrak-e Gharb. After an intensive two-year program, the children are expected to have readapted
not only to the Iranian educational system but also to Iranian customs
and tradition. Due to the sex-segregation rule, I was not allowed to visit
the girls' school, but I regularly visited the boys' school, where I got to
know some of the young students. I spent hours in the school courtyard
chatting with students, parents, and teachers. Returning from different
countries, predominantly the U.S., the students have formed a transnational atmosphere. The school authorities show a much higher level
of tolerance toward "improper behavior and clothes" than in ordinary
schools. Apart from serving returnees, the school also offers intensive
Persian courses to diaspora children, who are sent to Tehran for "language travel." Moreover, the school offers a limited range of foreign
language courses to "ordinary" Tehrani youngsters. The transnational
atmosphere is fascinating for many Tehranis:

I like the milieu. People have a higher culture here [*farhang-eshon balatare*]. I
enjoy hearing children talk English to each other. It's like being abroad
[*kharej*]. I bring my children here to learn English and become familiar with the
environment abroad [*faza-ye kharej*].

Other traces of diaspora connections are ubiquitous throughout
Shahrak-e Gharb. Mr. Modir, principal of the high school in Zone 1, a

block behind the Golestan shopping center (hereafter Golestan), told me that many of his students' parents spend several months in Europe or the U.S. every year visiting family members or relatives.

BIOGRAPHICAL VIGNETTE: ARVIN, AN IRANIAN SATAN WORSHIPPER

When Hamid mentioned Arvin I thought he was joking: A Satan worshipper in Tehran! Hamid arranged a meeting some days later. Arvin was born in 1978, one year before the Revolution. He lived in his parents' luxury house just a few blocks beyond Golestan. Arvin opened the door himself. He did not have the attributes of a Satan worshipper, a black robe, long hair, or chains. When he started his education at Tehran University he had been forced to change his appearance, he said. However, on the door of his room I did read "Welcome to Hell." All over the walls in his room, verses of Heavy Metal music were written. Words such as "Death, Suicide, Hell" were written in black and decorated with drops of blood.

I was fifteen years old, when I became interested in the worship of Satan. At first it was about music. At that time, everyone listened to Madonna and Michael Jackson. Very few were familiar with Heavy Metal music. In the whole school there were five or six kids who listened to such music. Now it is the fashion and everybody says that they listen to it. I don't believe them. Nowadays I listen to rock from the 1970s, which is difficult to find. The mother of a friend of mine is an air-hostess. She brings new music each time she comes from Europe. Our numbers grew and we formed a group. Later on, one of our members, whose father was very rich, invested a huge sum of money in this. He smuggles metallic music from Turkey, makes copies and distributes them in Tehran. Gradually, I became interested in the philosophy of Satanic worship. You know, I like its sorrow, loneliness, and hatred. The world is full of misery, war, and hostility. It means that it is Satan who dominates our life and not God. The Master is indeed Satan. Look at our own society, which is called "divine" [*elahi*]. I seek refuge from this divinity in Satan.

Thanks to his economic and social resources, Arvin has a vast network through which he builds up his subcultural capital. His leaning toward Satanism was to me a way of dissociating himself from others and from the current situation in Iran. He was seeking individuality.

I buy my clothes from a shop with clothes that cannot be found anywhere else in Tehran. The owner travels a lot to Germany, Malaysia, and Dubai and imports fine things. We receive information through the Internet. There are a huge number of sites, from which I can download music and even print pictures. I was beaten up several of times by the *basijis* because of my appearance. I was lucky they did not take me seriously.

*   *   *

Alongside transnational personal ties, an imagined "cultural continuum" (Hannerz 1987) between the local and the global is also omnipresent. Graffiti all over Shahrak-e Gharb refer to the names of exiled Irangelesi pop artists, such as Ebi, Dariush, and Siyavash, or to non-Iranian pop and rock music bands such as Metallica, Iron Maiden, or Pink Floyd. Comparing and associating the local with the West contributes to this imagined "continuum." Once a Sharaki man expressed it this way: "Shahrak is Iran's Paris." I found similar assumptions of participating in a global cultural sphere when Dara asked me for help to find a way to study sociology in Paris, "the center of sociology," as he called it. Another young man in the association, Farhad, dreamed of studying philosophy in Germany, where he "could read Nietzsche in the original language." The "transnational" aspect of the Shahraki lifestyle was illustrated in many ways, for example, in home decoration. English books, a piano, abstract paintings on the wall, art magazines in French and English on the table were tokens of the cosmopolitanism and modern lifestyle I saw in many informants' houses. Such demonstrations of "transnational cultural capital" are, however, not only a matter of taste but also of capital and information, hence of class.

The transnational features of Shahrak-e Gharb have made it a newsworthy topic that international journalists have "discovered" in recent years. Since the Revolution, news on Iranian issues wired by Western agencies has for a long time been dominated by accounts of anti-Western fundamentalists and Revolutionary Islamists. In contrast to this stereotype, foreign journalists have sought to demonstrate the complexity of Iran and its people during the more open mid-1990s. Shahrak-e Gharb offered the most suitable alternative narratives. Almost all the reports I have read about Tehrani youth came from Shahrak-e Gharb or were associated with Golestan. These places would represent the "global" (read American) side of Tehran's daily life. Sometimes such representations become romanticized, presenting the place as a site of resistance against the Islamic state.[9] During my fieldwork, I witnessed foreign correspondents, one after the other, coming to Shahrak-e Gharb to contribute to the "global" image of this neighborhood. One French journalist asked several young Shahrakis I knew for interviews. They consulted me and I warned them not to let the journalist make political points that would endanger them. In spite of the youths' initial demand that the interview be "nonpolitical," they were depicted as political opponents of the state. The article was translated into Persian and a summary was published in several of the dailies.

Shahrak-e-Gharb is not just a neighborhood, it is a state of mind and a symbol. This affluent neighborhood in northwest Tehran, though less extravagant than some of the northeastern Tehran suburbs, has developed a certain reputation in town that is bolstered by the looks and behavior of its own youth. Maybe because demographically it has the highest percentage of teenagers and young men and women in their early twenties, it also has a certain public face. One Shahraki young man told me at a party that he only hangs out with other Shahraki youths, because they are a "certain type." Whether his veiled meaning is that he discriminates by class, I do not know. But everyone insists that there is a Shahraki type of young man and woman. This type—if there is such a thing—is the young man with slightly longer than politically approved hair, slicked back, clean-shaven, dressed impeccably in tight jeans and a nice shirt, perhaps with a Western logo, and the girls, made-up, with colorful scarves pulled back to reveal as much (dyed) blonde or red hair as possible, with painted toenails in open-toed shoes even in the winter or with stylish chunky shoes. (www.iranian.com, an online magazine, accessed March 17, 1999)

* * *

Significantly, the "deterritorialization" of identity represented by Shahraki transnationality has forged a nostalgic sense for the "territorialized" lifestyle. On the east side of Golestan, after one block of luxury houses, there is an attractive small park. On the eastern edge of the park stands a *chaikhane sonnati*, a traditional teahouse, called the Silk Road. It is a cottage made of clay, in a rural style. The interior is decorated with old rural paraphernalia, such as fire irons, coal-fired samovars, wooden cases, Bakhtiari kelims, and brightly colored cushions made by Qashqai nomads. Instead of chairs and tables there are wooden couches on which guests sit with their legs crossed. The waiters wear old-fashioned village dress—*shoular* (wide black trousers), white shirt, black vest, hat, and *giveh* (white village shoes). The teahouse was built and run by Shahin, a young architect returned from a long period of residence in Austria. He traveled throughout rural central Iran to collect the decorations. The ambition of his teahouse is to represent a romantic and authentic rural milieu, close to the modern high buildings. Since the mid-1990s, many "traditional teahouses" have appeared in Tehran, mostly in the northern part of the city. The Silk Road teahouse is a site where an invented and chic "tradition" is performed for "modern" Tehranis.

Paradoxically, the teahouse objectifies a lifestyle that "modern" Shahrakis want to distance themselves from. By displaying rural lifestyle as a museum object, "modern" Shahrakis trace a clear boundary between what they regard as "tradition" and "modernity." It is in contrast to traditional rural lifestyle that "being modern" makes sense. However, this "nostalgia for the present" (see Appadurai 1996: 30) is a consequence of modernity. The Silk Road teahouse presents tradition as if it belonged to the past, whereas it is in fact still alive and practiced as ordinary daily life in rural Iran. However, while Shahrakis are nostalgic for an imagined *sonat*, they disassociate themselves from its real life counterpart. Below I explore this theme as it is embodied in *javad*.

The *Javad* Other

Like any kind of social identity, Shahraki identity is built on contrasts with others. Such categorization is the other side of group identification (see Barth 1969). To construct a pure Us, Shahrakis need an "impure" Other. Who, then are the "others" against which the Shahrakis construct their selves? They are the "traditional, backward, poor, village-minded, southern Tehranis" whose character is summed up in the epithet *javad*. *Javad* is an Arabic boy's name, but in Shahrak-e Gharb it is used as a metonym for the residents of Javadieh. As I already mentioned, this is a lower-class neighborhood in south Tehran, generally inhabited by second- or third-generation migrants from rural Azerbaijan. Among Shahraki youths, *javad* is a reference to the working-class and "backward" attributes of the young men living there. Young people frequently use the term when they talk about south Tehranis. There is also a less well-known epithet for women, Manizheh, an old-fashioned girl's name.

Arvin, the Satan worshipper, has never been in Javadieh but is convinced that it is a dangerous place: "If you go there and do not know any local person, you will be beaten up. They are uncultivated [*bifarhang*] and savage [*vahshi*]. It is not easy for us to go to Javadieh. People in Javadieh have other norms. If I go there in the clothes I usually wear here, I shall have problems." To be *Javad* is seen to be tough and masculine. "*Javad*-ness" is a source of both proud male identity and low status. As will be discussed in the next chapter, "*javad*-ness" is primarily defined by the pattern of consumption. Nevertheless, it is more than clothes that makes a person *javad*. Bodily comportment, ways of walking, gestures, and attitude are also indicators of "*javad*-ness." To be *javad* means to be "nonmodern," "rural" (*dehati*), and "traditional." The consumption of the *javad* is defined as tasteless and therefore has come to stand for the embodiment of vulgarity and "traditional" lifestyle in

the eyes of those who strive for a "modern" identity. In non-Western societies the integration of young people into the stream of "global consumerism" has given rise to urban stereotypes who portray a particular
style of "lumpen" and "uncultured" masculinity (e.g., *maganda* in Istanbul; see Öncü 2002).

The "social dominance" of Shahrakis became more evident when I
witnessed how the idea of "*javad*-ness" was internalized by the people of
Javadieh and other parts of poor southern Tehran.[10] Many young men
from southern Tehran, even from Javadieh, used *javad* as an epithet to
tease one another. One group of south Tehranis were at Golestan every
day. They appeared around six or seven P.M. and stayed until ten. The
group usually consisted of five or six young men in their early twenties.
The youngest called himself "Simon." I never got to know his real
name. When I asked him "why Simon?" he said he just liked the name.
He was a handsome young man with hair down to his shoulders. He
told me:, "I have been arrested several times for my hair. They say that
it is non-Islamic." He had not finished high school but had been on the
run from home for a month. Robert, another guy in the group, had
chosen the pseudonym because he was enchanted by Robert De Niro
when he saw *The Deer Hunter*. Both worked in the bazaar in Tehran but
were faithful daily visitors to Golestan.

One evening I was chatting with them as they were hanging around
outside Golestan.

Robert: "My parents . . ."

Simon butted in: "Who live in Javadieh"

Everyone laughed. Robert smiled and said: "Shut up, you bastards.
Javadieh is Paris compared with where you come from, Naziabad and
Darvaz-e Ghar."

Mr. Aber, a middle-aged man and one of the six security guards at
Golestan, lives in Javadieh but believes *javads* are "uncivilized." He con-
siders that the roots of the problems in Golestan lie in south Tehran: "I
like it here, even if young people often get into fights with each other.
Last month a colleague of mine was badly beaten up. Shahraki kids are
okay. They listen and do what we say. I do not know where these wild
ones come from. Perhaps from Naziabad or Javadieh."

The hierarchical ranking of social categories is manifested in having
an "attitude." "Attitude" is expressed in speech, way of walking, and
style of dressing, rather than in economic resources. Newly rich people
(as will be discussed later) without the "right attitude" can also be classified as *javad*. *Taze be deoran resideh* is the common term Iranians use to
name the rising nouveau riche. The hierarchy is based on social status
rather than social class, that is, it is defined by practices that emphasize
cultural distinctions to maintain social stratification. Status is not only

about political entitlement and legal location within civil society, but also involves style. Style is undoubtedly a matter of the individual's taste and preferences. Yet it is obvious that in Iran some groups have more power than others to ascertain what is stylish and what is uncouth.

When representatives of "otherness" appear inside Shahrak-e Gharb, concern arises over the threat they pose to the values Shahraki identity is based on: modern-ness, elitism, "gender morality." Examples of such threats are daily *javad* visitors, *basijis*, "bad girls," prostitutes, new rich people, and gypsies.

Hamid, a Shahraki man in his early twenties, strolled around with me in Golestan one evening. We sat down on a stone bench in the western yard to watch people. In Tehrani slang he said:

All the girls you see here are *bezar* [sluts]. They come here from other parts of Tehran and after a while become "a known face" [*tablow*, lit. tableau]. Then they leave Golestan. They can not stay. Every body knows that they are *kharab* [lit. ragged, prostitutes]. Shahraki girls are not like them. You do not see Shahraki girls around here. They do not come here just to stroll. If they want shopping they come with their mothers, but never alone. Shahraki girls are *najib* [modest and virtuous]. People see these non-Shahraki girls and think that Shahraki girls are easy-going.

Haddi is a man in his early twenties who works as a sales assistant in a boutique in Golestan. He is from a lower-middle-class family and lives in Zone 6. He has not finished high school and dreams of a new life abroad. Once on his lunch break we went to a café next to his boutique. I pointed out a group of *bad hejab* (improperly veiled), cheerful, noisy young girls at a table in the opposite corner of the café. They were engaged in secret communication with a group of boys at a nearby table. I asked Haddi if they were Shahraki. His answer was firm and clear:

No. Shahraki kids are pure [*pak*]. Our girls do not even smoke cigarettes. Girls from south Tehran come here to pick up rich Shahraki boys. Even girls from the provinces run away from their home to come to Shahrak-e Gharb. They dream of picking up a rich Shahraki boy. Instead, they become "homeless." We call them *kartonkhab* [those who sleep in cartons] because they have no place to live. They sleep one night in my place and the next in your place. People give them a place to sleep in return for a fuck.

Mina, a seventeen-year-old Shahraki young woman from a well-to-do family, could not hide her anger when I asked her about non-Shahraki girl visitors. She said:

I get mad when I see that Shahrak-e Gharb has become a meeting place for drug sellers and whores. During the daytime the parks are full of drug sellers and their customers. At night our streets are occupied by greasy painted girls looking for their customers. They all come from southern Tehran. Shahrak-e Gharb is a lucrative niche for them. They give Shahrak-e Gharb a bad reputation. Shahraki kids are modern, chic, and rich. They go to parties and mingle with the opposite sex. All these drugs and whore-affairs come from outside.

Although prostitution is forbidden in Iran and both parties are severely punished, the rumor throughout Tehran is that Golestan and Iranzamin Street are red light districts. Dr. Amiri said furiously, "Nobody cares that these women who stand on Iranzamin street come from Darvazeh Doulab [a neighborhood in south Tehran]. They blame it on us and say Shahrak-e Gharb is a nest of corruption." The purity of Shahraki girls was frequently emphasized in conversations with Shahrakis. They were concerned to prove both to me and to the state that moral corruption originates from outside Shahrak-e Gharb.

This other-making also had ideological aspects. Time after time Shahrakis proudly emphasize that there are no Shahraki *basiji*. Those who are posted in Shahrak-e Gharb come from outside. Dr. Amiri stated with a grin:

Shahrakis do not attend Friday prayers [*namaz jom'e*]. They do not even go to the mosque. There is no *daste-ye Ashura* [Moharram procession of young men dressed in black beating their breasts] here. Shahrakis vote differently from people in Meydan-e Khorasan [in south Tehran]. Shahrakis take no part in the "theater" called election. Most votes go to Googoosh and Dariush [two exiled pop artists from the pre-Revolutionary period].

The ideological differences between Shahrakis and other Tehranis, particularly southern Tehranis, were stressed: the former were not involved in the state's political activities, were not *hezbollahi*, were not religious, did not engage in the Karbala ritual. Once after a seminar at the local association, one of the participants told me with pride in his voice: "Outside Shahrak-e Gharb young people believe what society tells to them. They just accept their situation and never protest. But here youths are sharp and freethinking." All these ways of distinguishing themselves from others heightened the "ideological purity" of the Shahrakis.

However, the "other" does not always come from outside. One day, in the local association, Dara and Farhad said they wanted to show me something interesting. We walked through several alleyways in Zone 1 until we reached a large house that apparently had never been completed. Clearly, it was a luxury house that had been abandoned for a long time. A large number of people called by Shahrakis *kouli* (gypsies) live in the house, whose owner had fled the country after the Revolution. Dara said "They are strange."

I asked, "How are they strange?"

Dara said, "They live like people in Javadieh. They are different. For example, the door of their house is always open. Their children are all the time outside and play on the street. Their children are dirty. Several families live in the same house."

The "other" of the Shahrakis also includes the class category living in Zone 6, farthest to the west in Shahrak-e Gharb, with its less aesthetic residences allocated to low-grade government employees. Farhad recognizes a clear distinction between Zone 6 and the rest of Shahrak-e Gharb:

Zone 6 is totally inhabited by government employees. They come from different parts of Tehran and from different backgrounds. They have changed the pattern of Shahrak-e Gharb. There are a lot of problems there, because of the mixture of different cultures. There are many people from southern Tehran who are not familiar with the apartment lifestyle. For example, they keep hens and chickens on their balconies.

Hanging clothes on the balcony or going out in pajamas is also identified with southern Tehran. Arvin the Satan worshipper thinks that

People from southern Tehran have invaded Shahrak-e Gharb and just imitate the culture of the *bala shahr* [northern Tehran]. These people don't understand our culture. They just mime it without knowing why. For example, all family members sit and watch pornographic films together just as they watch an ordinary film. They think that is how to be modern. Almost all of the bad girls on Tehran's streets come from religious families. They got a culture shock when they moved to North Tehran.[11]

In one of the Sunday seminars, I got to know Said. He is twenty years old, from a lower-middle-class family and lives with his parents in Zone 6. He is a bright young man with moderate religious beliefs. After the seminar, I accompanied him to his home for a cup of tea. Unlike other houses in Shahrak-e Gharb, the little family apartment was simple, decorated with Iranian miniature paintings and handicrafts. In his room I saw a *setar* (a traditional musical instrument) and books by Shariati, Al-e Ahmad, and several other Islamist thinkers. While he served tea, he said:

They laugh at us, just because I am religious and pray. Here in Shahrak-e Gharb we are in a minority. I do not agree with the kind of Islam the state imposes on people. I search for the authentic Islam. My friends in Zone 1 tell me that I am already like an adult and have no youthful life. Their parents are wealthy and have no problems. What they care about is partying and girls. That is it. They are *bidard*. I hate to go to Golestan. The only time I visited Golestan was when my cousin came from the provinces to visit us. He insisted on seeing Golestan. In one shop I saw how a young man, my age I guess, paid 25,000 toman [ca.

U.S.$30] for a shirt. It is as much money as I have to buy clothes for a year. I hate the capitalist atmosphere in Shahrak-e Gharb. I would prefer to live in another part of Tehran.

Shahrakis in the Other's Eyes

"Othering" is usually a mutual process. The prejudiced image the rest of Tehran has of the Shahrakis is gendered. Shahraki girls are seen by them as less pure than their sisters in other parts of Tehran, particularly in the south. Since the girls are not considered "pure," the boys are not credited with honor (*gheyrat*). Consequently, they are not as masculine, as "real men," as southern Tehrani boys are supposed to be. Naser, a thirty-eight-year-old cabdriver from Javadieh, liked to be identified as a *luti sefat* (a man with *luti* qualities, namely courage, honor, modesty, humanity, and rectitude). A *luti* is always a roughneck. Naser is a wrestler and his teenage son has a black belt in karate. Naser told me:

My son must be able to defend himself and his family. I sent him to the karate club when he started school. Last year he beat a boy who had said *mattalak* [an erotic verbal taunt] to one of the girls in our neighborhood. The boy was some years older than him. My son beat the boy thoroughly. My nephew is as old as my son, but he has lost his direction. I tried and tried to guide him but he is lost. He gels his hair and dresses like Shahraki kids. Wealthy Shahrakis do not care what their children do. Shahrak-e Gharb is a bad place. You cannot find any virgin girl there. They fuck with their boyfriends and when they get married they have their hymen restored surgically. Poor bridegrooms, who think that their wives are pure virgins!

One evening while I was talking with Simon and his friends in the yard of Golestan, all the young people suddenly streamed toward Iranzamin Street. Simon ran out to see what was going on. After a while he came back. Grinning, he described enthusiastically how Shahin Dragon's gang had beaten the Shahraki "mamma's boys." A young man from Ekbatan (a neighborhood in West Tehran), Shahin Dragon, who got his nickname for proficiency in Kung Fu, occasionally came with his gang to Golestan to fight with Shahrakis. Simon said:

Shahraki kids are not real men and are effeminate [*sosoul*]. You can never trust them. They are friends as long as you have got money. Unlike Shahraki kids, they [Shahin Dragon and his gang] are good friends. Shahrakis know nothing about the quality of manliness [*mardonegi*].

South Tehrani young people draw a distinction between the coldness, distrustfulness and femininity of Shahrakis and the warmth, masculinity, and trustfulness of south Tehranis.

The stereotypical presentation of the neighborhoods corresponds to stereotypical comments about the bodies of Shahrakis and *javads*. The construction of Shahrak-e Gharb as a "modern space" requires "modern bodies" as well. While the Shahraki's body is seen as "soft," "feminine," "polished," and lazy, the *javad's* body is seen as "rugged," "masculine," and "uncouth." There is an explicit linkage between sexuality and morality within these representations. The identification of Shahraki men as effeminate *na-mard* (non-men) and *sosoul* by *javads* is accompanied by a representation of Shahrakis as "lazy," and "snobbish," whereas the representation of *javad* as "masculine" and "vulgar" by Shahrakis suggests that they are "wild" and "uncivilized" in word and deed.

Table 5 illustrates some of the Shahrak-e Gharb/Javadieh dichotomies—made by Shahrakis and non-Shahrakis—formed through images of lifestyle, economic and social landscapes, and political orientation.

TABLE 5. IMAGES OF SHAHRAK-E GHARB AND JAVADIEH

Shahrak-e Gharb	Javadieh
Wealthy	Poor
Socioeconomic elites	Working class
Modern	Traditional
Transnational	Local
Individual orientation	Community orientation
Liberal attitude	Morality
Center	Periphery
Bidard and Weststruck	Suffering and faithful

The *Basij* in Shahrak-e Gharb

To complete the complex image of Shahrak-e Gharb we also need to look at things from the opposite side, the *basijis*.

I met Bahman one hot afternoon, a *basiji* who was a distant acquaintance of Said's (from Zone 6). I had seen him many times patrolling around with his colleagues in Golestan. Bahman, in his early thirties, was stationed and served in Shahrak-e Gharb. Contrary to the stereotype of a *basiji*, he was friendly, humble, and extremely polite. During my teenage period, Bahman, as a representative of the *basij*, and I as a rebel youth, would have had an antagonistic relationship. He believed in keeping society pure from the "cultural invasion" embodied in youths like me. As vessels for the "invasion," we were guilty. On the other side, many of us regarded the *basijis* and their violent ideology as inhuman encroachments on our integrity and individuality. But now, when we were both in our thirties, I had a complex and ambivalent feeling toward him. While I refused to go to the front during the Iran-Iraq war and left the country to find a safe life in the West, Bahman fought against Saddam's army, lost friends, and risked injury and death. A decade after the end of the war, I returned from my safe life in Sweden, educated, with credit cards in my pocket, an anthropologist who wanted to "study" him.

Bahman grew up in a village near Shiraz, a city 850 km south of Tehran. At age nine he lost his father, and his mother worked hard until her death ten years later. They moved to Shiraz in the hope of a better future. Bahman and his three sisters, all older than he, witnessed how exhausted she was from her hard work as a domestic servant. The social injustice Bahman experienced in childhood made him and his family zealous disciples of Ayatollah Khomeini, whom they saw as arriving to help the dispossessed. At age of ten or eleven Bahman followed his mother and sisters in demonstrations against the Shah. Several years later, not yet fifteen, he joined the *basij* and went to the war. Until the ceasefire in 1989, he spent a large part of his life at the front. After the war, he moved to Tehran. He refused all benefits earmarked for war veterans. He had "fought for God not for money and rank." As he himself put it: "It was a deal with God not with His creatures." He could not or did not want to change his *basiji* lifestyle. In Tehran, he continued his *basiji* mission at the Squad for Revival of Amr-e be m'arouf va nahi az monkar. He commands a team consisting of ten or so *basijis*, all about twenty.

Shahram: "Why did you stay in the *basij* after the war?"

Bahman: "To watch over martyrs' blood and to fight against cultural invasion."

Shahram: "Don't you think there is a conspiracy theory behind the youth problem?"

Bahman: "No. I have no enmity against Shahraki youth. It is more anguish I feel. They are victims of the cultural invasion, which imperialism is organizing against us and other Muslims."

Shahram: "Whose hand do you think is behind the problem?"

Bahman: "Iranian anti-Revolutionary groups, supported by the CIA, are trying to demoralize us. They do it by satellite TV channels, Irangelesi music, and sexy [pornographic] films. They send money to their agents inside Iran, who arrange parties. At these parties girls and boys meet each other and consume alcoholic drinks and God knows what else they do. All this is to destroy our revolutionary values. Young people make mistakes and we should guide them. God knows that it is only for their own good."

Shahram: "So, why do you focus on Shahrak-e Gharb and its young people?"

Bahamn: "Shahraki youths are *bidard*. They did not participate in the war and do not suffer from economic pressure. They do not care what is going on in the country. Their life is pleasure [*khoshi*] and frivolity [*bikhiyali*]. You cannot imagine the cases we see everyday in Shahrak-e Gharb. To have free sex is the only thing that matters for them."

From Fokoli to Bidard

Bidard is a term I frequently heard in public debates by the authorities and *basijis* to refer to Shahraki youths. It refers to the wealthy and comfortable life Shahraki young people are supposed to lead. These *bidard* youths are regarded as deviants, not "authentic" Iranian youth. The virtue of youth is seen to be endangered by the "Weststruckness" that today is embodied in the *bidard* youths. Although the term *bidard* was coined after the Revolution, as a concept its roots go back far beyond the Islamic Republic. The concept for which it stands has been expressed by different terms during different periods of the twentieth century, such as *gharbzadeh* since the 1960s, *fokoli* after World War II, and *farangima'ab* (with European style) in the early twentieth century. In the genealogy of the concept *bidard*, the most pervasive and fascinating term is *fokoli*.

Fokol is the Persian variant of *faux col* (French for detachable collar). *Fokoli* (faux col wearer) is used to refer to the Iranian dandies who adopted European dress and style, using foreign words in their speech. *Fokoli* recalls Naipaul's "mimic man." The *fokoli* is a liminal person, neither authentic Iranian nor pure European. Since the late nineteenth century the term *fokoli* has been used in the "authenticity discourse" to condemn Westernization. *Fokoli*s have been attacked both by religious conservatives and by intellectuals who criticized them for being modern in appearance without any substantial cognition of European modernity. The Iranian thinker Shadman (1326/1947) characterized *fokoli*s as "pseudomodern" and as the "dirty enemy from within." In his view the *fokoli* was "a shameless Iranian who knows little of some European language and even less Persian, yet claims that he can describe to us the European civilization of which he has no knowledge and through a language he does not know" (Shadman 1326/1947, quoted in Gheissari 1998: 85). The *fokoli* endangers the Persian tradition. According to Shadman, "The *fokoli* is the biggest enemy of Persian [culture and language] and therefore the obstacle in the way of true progress. He will never [be able to] lead us to European civilization, because the wretched man is himself lost in perplexity and darkness" (86–87).

The term *fokoli* was also used by Islamists and "religious intellectuals" in political rhetoric against the Shah's modernization policies. *Fokoli* embodied *gharbzadegi* (Weststruckness) in the 1960s and 1970s. Al-e Ahmad, for example, wrote about Westernized intellectuals:

The intellectual first was *fokoli*, and "modern." . . . Nowadays intellectual is *farangima'ab* [with European style]: one who wears European clothes, hat, and shoes. He drinks liquor and sits on a chair. He shaves his beard and wears a tie. He eats with a spoon and fork. He uses European terms. He has been in Europe or will be. He takes examples from Europe or America. He has heard about microbes . . . and talks all the time about "vitamins" and "calories." He goes to movies and dances. (Al-e Ahmad 1357/1978: 44)

In his two-volume critical book *Dar Khedmat va Khyanat-e Rowshan-fekran* (On the Service and Treason of the Intellectuals), Al-e Ahmad continued to condemn the *fokoli* intellectual for being areligious and alien to Iranian culture and tradition, pursuing a "scientific world view," taking care of his body through exercise, and going on a diet (Al-e Ahmad 1357/1978: 43–46). There are several interesting angles to this portrayal. First, like the Weststruck person in Al-e Ahmad's *Gharbzadegi*, the *fokoli* is always a man. Second, the definition of a *fokoli* is mainly based on the consumption of Western commodities. Third, the *fokoli* is concerned about his body and physical needs; he is condemned principally for his self-assertion. Fourth, the *fokoli* has abandoned "tradition" (*sonat*) and is "modern" (*motajaded*).

The *fokoli* has gradually become a comic figure in Iranian popular culture. Peter Chelkowski, in his study of Iranian improvisatory comic theater known as *Rou Hozi* in the late nineteenth and early twentieth centuries, writes that the *fokoli* was one of the main characters of the performance. The *fokoli* was represented as "a dandy and a person educated in the West. He is a pitiful man who either pretends to be superior to his peers or is confused about his place in society. Sometimes this man represents a European with absurd and laughter-provoking manners" (Chelkowski 1991: 779–80). The satirical play *Jafarkhan az Farang Amadeh* (Jafar Khan Is Back from Europe) by Hasan Moghadam is perhaps the best-known drama about *fokoli*s. Staged in the second decade of the twentieth century, the play is about an Iranian who, after a visit to Europe, apes Western speech patterns, attire, body motions, and manners (786). The *fokoli* remained a popular satiric type in the world of Iranian entertainment for a long time.

The image of the *fokoli* as Westernized and "self-alienated" was brought into people's consciousness through melodramatic films, known as *filmfarsi*.[12] Iranian popular cinema recurrently used *fokoli* in the movies during the 1960s and 1970s, for example in *Joje Fokoli* (Fokoli, the Chicken), a well-known movie made by Reza Safai in 1974. When in 1964 *Agha-ye Gharn-e Bistoum* (Twentieth-Century Man, by Siamak Yasami) was screened, an anti-*fokoli* cinematic type was created, a poor young man from a "traditional" background who defended Iranian cultural identity. The economic success and good reception of this film led to this theme being repeated in a large number of movies produced throughout the 1960s and 1970s. A few years later a new genre known as *film jaheli* was established, its main character being a lumpen-proletarian man who embodied the most sordid traits of patriarchy. The *jahel* (lit. ignorant) represented forms of male chauvinism in which masculine "honor" was vested in the chastity of the man's female relatives (Dabashi 2001: 26). The *jahel* was often illiterate, athletic, and folksy, and made fun of *fokoli*s and their lifestyles. He was also represented as sexually "immoral" and "corrupted." Unlike the *fokoli*, who is a faithful consumer of foreign commodities, the *jahel* shows self-restraint. This difference is explicitly illustrated in the consumption of food. The *jahel* loves to eat *abghost* (traditional Iranian cuisine) with his hands, sitting on a carpet. The *fokoli* eats *farangi* foods with a knife and fork, sitting at a table (see Heidari 1379/2001).[13] The *jahel* identity is built on performance. In a simple black suit and a white shirt with the top buttons undone, his body movements will demonstrate his strength, self-assurance, and supremacy.

However, the most interesting dichotomy between *jahel* and *fokoli* is their degree of "manliness." While the *jahel* has a large mustache and hair on his chest, fights well, and has several mistresses at once, the *fokoli* is feminine. He has a weak body and is not virile. Since the *fokoli* is not bothered by seeing his sisters or daughters having relationships with strange men, he is "honor-less" (*bighayrat*). In the phallocratic world of the *jahel* (who penetrates), possessing an active penis is a way of maintaining sexual rights over the *fokoli* (who might be penetrated). The contemporary novelist Amir Hassan Cheheltan (1380/2001) has based his novel *Tehran Shahr-e Biaseman* (Tehran, the City Without Sky) on this dichotomy, between the masculine *jahel* and the feminine *fokoli*, to illustrate parts of the social roots of the Revolution.

The main character in Cheheltan's *Tehran Shahr-e Biaseman* is a Keramat who left his village in his early teens to find work in Tehran. He came of age under harsh circumstances around World War II. Gradually he turns into a *jahel*. His "genuine manliness" and physical virility make him a sexually attractive to women. He is an allegory of the Iranian phallus both in his sexual power and in his patriarchal attitude. On the eve of the Revolution, he becomes a zealous *hezbollahi* and a respected Revolutionary figure. The following passage is from a scene where he comes into contact with the "modern and *fokoli*" Tehrani upper class. An affluent woman, whose sexual lust cannot be satisfied by "*fokolis*," takes him to a party.

He was not like these men. Men who cleaned themselves with perfumed hand-kerchiefs. They were poets, writers, doctors, engineers, actors, pilots, singers, journalists. . . . They could talk to *farangis*. They wore white womanly stockings and played tennis. They wore sunglasses and slept on air mattresses in the pool. . . . They ate caviar and crayfish and after shower used to cream their body. . . . They went to cocktail parties. They drank cappuccino and espresso. They smoked *farangi* tobacco. Like women, they put their palm to their mouth when they yawn. . . . They disgusted him. The phallus of the nation was femi-nized by men's feminine manners, costly perfumes and face powder, *farangi* cuisines and jewelry, foreign languages . . . , short skirt and tight trousers. (91–92, my translation)

*   *   *

Thus the feminine, consuming, "modern" (or detraditionalized) *fokoli* embodies the peril which threatens Iranian cultural purity. It is basically this idea that the Islamic regime has adopted to shape the category of *bidard* youths. There seems also to be a continuity between the associa-tion of the *jahel* with cultural nativism and the *hezbollahis*' struggle for au-thenticity (although they are quite different on other questions). The best-selling movie *MAXX* (by Saman Moghadam 2005) is another exam-ple how a *fokoli* (here a feminine Westernized returnee pop-singer from Los Angeles) is put in contrast to the masculine interrogator whose aim is to protect the cultural values of the nation. Table 6 summarizes the bi-nary opposition model on which the national ideology of manliness and cultural purity is based. Not surprisingly, after the Revolution, *fokol*, the tie, became a charged symbol of *bidard*-ness. Subsequently, wearing a tie has for many men been a way of demonstrating their defiance.

TABLE 6. IMAGES OF *BIDARD* AND *HEZBOLLAHI*

Bidard/fokoli	Hezbollahi/basiji
Feminine	Masculine
Consumerist	Self-restraint
Westernized	Nativist
Weak	Strong
Mimic	Authentic
Honor-less (*bigheirat*)	With honor (*bagheirat*)
Modern (*motajaded*)	Traditionalist (*sonati*)

The stereotypes of *bidard* and *fokoli* youths are "discursive weapons" of power. Michael Herzfeld emphasizes the significance of the act of stereotyping in the mechanisms of power. The power that the state exercises through its agents depends on the selective manipulation of stereotypes already in popular circulation (Herzfeld 1997: 30), and actively deprives the "other" of certain properties. Stereotypes do serve the interests of power, but carry the potential of subversion and are sometimes used to achieve it (157–58). The categorization of youth as either *hezbollahi* or *bidard*, like the categorization of women into either "virtuous mother" or "whore" (cf. Stephen 1995), enables the *basijis* to identify a majority of young people as subversive.

Pain and Purity

The relation between suffering or having pain (*dard*) and inner purity (*safa-ye baten*) is a significant feature of the Karbala paradigm. Imam Hossein, his family, and his followers went through enormous physical pain. The memory of the tragedy of Karbala is a source of emotional pain demonstrated in mourning and self-flagellation. In Shiism pain is regarded as a "necessary" experience in the way to becoming "fully human" (cf. Asad 2000). One needs to go through pain to understand the significance of the Karbala tragedy. Acknowledgment of pain is a part of the sense of guilt Shiites are supposed to feel.

The Iranian nation is represented by the Islamic regime as a people who have suffered from the Shah's despotism, an "inflicted war" (*jang-e tahmili*), and the U.S. embargo. This common suffering is used in the construction of the moral order. Those who have not "suffered" are seen as "outsiders" (*ghayr-e khodi*, lit. not one of us), such as Iranians in exile or wealthy Weststruck Shahrakis. *Delsokhteh* (lit. one with a burned heart) is a term used to refer to people engaged in social and political issues. Ali Shariati was perhaps the first one who explicitly associated "pain" with virtue and "being socially committed." Shariati's life was a story of pain (Rahnema 1998: x).

Shariati associated suffering and pain with consciousness and responsibility and a *bidard* deportment with ignorance and irresponsibility. In a similar way, joyfulness, the display of happiness and enjoyment were seen by Shariati as "a wave of despicable and contemptible stupidity" (Rahnema 1998: 43). For Shariati, pain was also a force which cements a nation. According to his definition a nation was "the sum of all human beings who feel a common pain" (Rahnema 1998: 120). In the Iranian culture pain generates purity.

> Sacrifice in the pursuit of honour incurs pain. The pleasure of pain and longing becomes the motor of life. In this society worthy men are those who have a pain, who live with it and never directly divulge it. It is the inward and outward scars that make a man. The hedonistic happy-go-luckys are boys who need to mature. In this tradition, romantic youth fall in love not to consummate their love, but to cherish the longing and the pain. (Rahnema 1998: x)

Pain takes a central place in Iranian literature and arts. The most celebrated contemporary poet, Ahmad Shamloo, also sees pain a necessary experience of being: "A mountain begins with its first rocks and a man with the first pain" (Shamloo 1343/1964). Ebrahim Hatami Kia, a well-known director of war-genre films, who identifies himself as a *basiji*, uses pain to show the virtue and innocence of *basijis*. His famous films deal with the fate of *basijis* in postwar Iran. In his most celebrated movies, *Azhans-e Shishe-ie* (Glass Agency, 1997) and *Az Karkhe ta Rein* (From Karkhe to Rein, 1993), we see *basijis* suffering from chronic physical pain caused by injuries from the war. The heroes have difficulty fitting into the postwar atmosphere of the 1990s. Their pain and suffering are the only souvenir remaining from the "old-good" time of the war, a time of self-sacrifice, selflessness, and purity. Sayyed Morteza Avini, a *hezbollahi* filmmaker and celebrated *basiji*, believes that "pain is a necessity with which humanity can be realized" (Avini 1379/2000: 161). Since "pain" is assumed as a necessary sign of human dignity, *bidard* Shahrakis are stripped of their social identity and characterized as "inauthentic" and "false."

Hajj Agha Kiani, director of the bureau for research on youth issues at the Education Ministry, belongs to what is called the "moderate group" (*gorouh-e mianerou*) and stands behind President Khatami's reform-oriented policies. He told me that

There are three youth groups in Iran. Two minorities at the ends and the majority in the middle. At one end there are *basijis* and at the other end *bidard* Weststruck persons [*qeshr-e bidard va gharbzadeha*]. These two groups are lost [*az dast rafte*]. What we should do is to keep the middle group, which comprises the majority of our young people, away from the peril of the extremist *basijis* and the inauthentic [*na-assil*] *bidard* youths.

Hajj Agha Kiani directed research on issues related to young people and offered collaboration and assistance if I changed my research field from Shahrak-e Gharb to a neighborhood in south Tehran, which in his view would be more "valuable" research.

The idea that *bidard* Shahrakis are "licentious" and "abandoned" is often met not only among the authorities, but also among "ordinary" people. Once at a dinner party in my cousin's apartment in central Tehran, I was asked about my fieldwork. Omid and his wife are a young middle-class couple with university education, and not at all *hezbollahi*. I was surprised by their reaction when I talked about my project on Shahraki youth. "Why Shahrak-e Gharb? You can find nothing interesting there," my cousin said while his wife nodded. "Go to Javadieh instead. There you meet people of every sort. War veterans, drug handlers, bullies, and a poverty you cannot see elsewhere in Tehran. Shahrak-e Gharb's kids are just mimics." He continued that Shahraki youth had no culture and their lifestyle lacked essence and was somehow ephemeral. When I complained and told them how awkward it could be listening to the problems and suffering of young people, Omid "assured" me: "Shahraki kids have no problem. These Rap-kids [*bach-e rapha*] are a stratum of *bidard* people. What they tell you are their imaginations. Their problem is why they do not have a better car, or how to find pretty girlfriends."

The article quoted next, which is one of many, illustrates how Shahraki kids and the milieu of the neighborhood are represented as non-Islamic, the young man's appearance in the company of a dog, for instance. Shahraki kids are stamped as "dog fanciers" (*sag baz*). In Islam the dog is seen as impure (*najes*). A Muslim should not even touch a dog. The interest Shahraki young people show for dogs is seen not only as a Westernized trait, but also as an anti-Islamic attitude. In the summer of 1999, the legislature declared that bringing pet dogs into public places was an affront to Muslims and would be punishable. In October 2002, a conservative Iranian official leader denounced the "moral depravity" of dog ownership and called on the judiciary to arrest all dogs and their owners.[14]

JOURNALISTIC VIGNETTE

"Here Is Another World."

He is a tall, thin young man with a wet-look hairstyle. He strolls around in
Shahrak-e Gharb in baggy trousers. His little sister holds the leash of a little
puppy, which she calls "Tou Tou, don't go away. . . ." On the other side of the
street is a shopping center. Its colorful boutiques attract passersby. Here is
Shahrak-e Gharb. . . . Friendship here is not based on emotion and feeling but
on money and goods. Shahraki kids do not make friends with poor people.
Here money matters and nothing else. Golestan is empty of emotion—an emotional vacuum. Human relationships are at a minimum here. Since most
Shahraki parents are employed and have little time for their children, they give
large amounts of money to their kids to make them happy. Some people believe
that the people of Shahrak-e Gharb have more freedom and possess a higher
culture than others. Others say there is more materialism in Shahrak-e Gharb
than there is spirituality. However, as a neighborhood in Greater Tehran
Shahrak-e Gharb has its own specific traits. (*Neshat*, 21 Tir 1378/12 July 1999)

* * *

Shahrak-e Gharb has been a politically loaded neighborhood and has
been used as a battlefield between two political fractions within the
state. During the presidential election of May 1997, the conservative
faction, frightened by the popularity of Mr. Khatami, orchestrated a
plot to discredit him. The plot aimed to "reveal" that Mr. Khatami's sup-
porters were Weststruck, corrupted, and anti-Islamic youths. Needless
to say, Shahrak-e Gharb was chosen as the most appropriate location for
the scenario. A week before the election, Shahrak-e Gharb witnessed an
incredible event on the Ashura evening (see Chapter 2): a joyful march
around Golestan. What was later called *Karneval-e Shadi-ye Ashura*
seemed first to be a spontaneous march of pro-Khatami youngsters of
Shahrak-e Gharb on Iranzamin and Mahestan Streets. Young girls and
boys, "improperly veiled," danced and waved pictures of Khatami. Luxury cars with their lights on sounded their horns. From the cars loud
Western pop music was heard. Pictures of Khatami were put up on the
windscreens and young people yelled, "Only Khatami, Only Khatami."
Police stopped the "carnival" and detained more than 200 in the police
station of Shahrak-e Gharb. Dr. Amiri, who was head of Khatami's campaign in Shahrak-e Gharb, protested against the "carnival." He declared that it was a plot against Khatami. He also stated that none of
those arrested were Shahraki. Instead, they came from other parts of
Tehran.[15] *Ressallat*, a conservative daily newspaper, recounted the event
to conclude that pro-Khatami people were immoral and corrupt as well
as Westernized and anti-Revolutionary. Considering the Iranians' love
for Imam Hossein and the respect they show to the Ashura ritual, this

event could have seriously damaged Khatami's campaign. Furthermore, the whole event was covered in film and photography by several people. Only a few days after the event a 20–minute film was copied onto 40,000 video cassettes and distributed over the whole country; the film was shown in every mosque and *hosseinieh* (religious centers dedicated to Imam Hossein, usually used for Ashura ceremonies). The "Karneval" became a political weapon for the conservative forces, who were prepared to do anything to stop Khatami's victory in the election.

Khatami's campaign, in turn, blamed the conservatives as organizers of the "carnival" for dishonoring Khatami and destroying his popularity among the people.[16] The editor of the local newspaper *Bavar* made a strong defense of Shahrak-e Gharb:

Shahrak-e Gharb is sacrificed. Why has only Shahrak-e Gharb been the concern of a specific group inside and outside the government? Why are the reports about Shahrak-e Gharb so biased, one-sided, and prejudiced? Why did the directors behind the Ashura Karneval choose Shahrak-e Gharb for their scenario? . . . Unlike those who think this hostility is based on the "type" and "appearance" [of Shahraki youth], I think it has another reason. Shahrak-e Gharb is different from other districts, not in appearance [*zaher*] but in inner state [*baten*]. What makes Shahrak-e Gharb different is the presence of intellectual Shahrakis. The massive attack on Shahrak-e Gharb in the name of "appearance" is no more than a slogan. The attack is against the Shahraki intellectuals, or rather their thought.[17]

Explicit anti-Shahraki rhetoric first appeared in public debates when the conservatives wanted to challenge the reformists. *Shalamche*, a radical journal of the *basijis*, advocated an aggressive Revolutionary attitude. Its name was taken from a well-known front during the war, where a huge number of young *basijis* were killed by the Iraqi army. The reformists succeeded in closing the journal down in 1998. The editor's note on the first page of the last issue said: "We congratulate Shahrak-e Gharb's *fokolia* on our disappearance."

Misrepresentation of Shahrak-e Gharb has had social consequences for the inhabitants, who have suffered from how they and their neighborhood are represented in the official media. Media reports have caused a hostile attitude on the part of the Islamic state toward Shahrak-e Gharb which has affected the Shahrakis' daily life as well. Dr. Amiri was upset when he told me:

As the director of the local association I have fought for two years to bring a gas pipeline into Shahrakis' houses. Our request was rejected by the authorities time after time. They said Shahrakis were *taghouti* [idolaters, rich Westernized people associated with the Shah's regime] and did not deserve the gas. We are *badnam* [have received a bad reputation]. The authorities are very cynical toward us. Shahrak-e Gharb is under the authority of the Foundation of the Dispossessed, which systematically ignores us. We are struggling to get under municipal authority. We have many social problems because Shahrak-e Gharb is seen as *taghouti*, We have no cinema, no theater, no sports clubs. There are only five bakeries for all Shahrakis. No organization cares about the traffic matters and other urban complications we face every day here.

The Center and the Periphery

Due to the imposed social order which oppresses poor and rich youth more or less equally, there seems to be a shared demand for "social freedom" (*azadi-ye ejtemma'i*) that transcends class boundaries. The consequence has been a homogenization of the needs and claims of young people throughout Tehran. More of the cultural influence, however, flows from north to south than vice versa. The wealthy Shahrak-e Gharb has more extended connections with the outside world. Through links to the Iranian diaspora and access to satellite channels and the Internet, the neighborhood has turned into a principal center for diffusing Westernized youth culture.

As mentioned above, there is a spatial social hierarchy between the "traditional" and peripheral south and the "modern" and central north Tehran. There is also an asymmetric relationship between Shahraki youth and *javad*s or provincial youth, based on access to the global culture. I asked Simon and Robert what was the attraction of Golestan. Simon answered:

We come here every day to see friends and look at girls. We come here because in Shahrak-e Gharb there is a relative freedom [*azadiye nesbi*]. Golestan is a meeting place [*patouq*] for youth.

Thanks to the relative freedom in Golestan, Robert and Simon could behave in ways banned in their own neighborhood. According to them, the harsher ambiance in southern Tehran not only was caused by the police but also reflected the generally severe attitude of the older generation. Simon quarreled frequently with his father over his hair and his daily visits to Golestan. He was upset when he told me about his arguments with his father.

I am not stupid. I know myself that I am an *allaf* [loiterer] here. But if they take even this from us what. . . . It is better to be *allaf* here than to be *mavvadi* [addicted to drugs].

Simon and Robert were forced to dress and behave properly and to use their real names when they were at the bazaar and in their neighborhood. Simon hid his long hair underneath a cap at work. They were *Javad* in the south and "modern" in north Tehran.

Simon and Robert's trip from Javadieh to Golestan usually took at least an hour. Since they did not possess any vehicle of their own, they had to take buses and taxis, a costly and tiresome daily trip. Nevertheless, they came all the way from south Tehran to the north to enjoy a couple of hours in Golestan. They said "we rarely go to other places. Outside Shahrak-e Gharb there is no freedom."

Robert said once in his Tehrani slang: "Here we have no police register [*âmâr*, statistic]. I mean we are not a known face [*tablow*, tableau] here." He means that in Shahrak-e Gharb he enjoys an anonymity he does not have in his own neighborhood. This "relative freedom" is what attracts young people from all parts of Tehran. As Farhad said, there was a higher tolerance of young people in Shahrak-e Gharb. In this scene they could do what they could not do in Javadieh or other neighborhoods in south Tehran. For the hairstyle, dress, or behavior they opted for in Shahrak-e Gharb, they would risk being pestered, teased, and derided in their own neighborhood. To perform this style might provoke what my informants called "traditional" thoughts, which were seen to be stronger in south Tehran. Golestan functions as a center of information, vision, and imagination for youths of the periphery, south Tehran neighborhoods, and the provinces. Simon and Robert had succeeded in shedding their *Javad* stigma and had learned the rules for being "modern." I asked Robert where he had learned "not to be a *Javad*." He answered, "Sit here an hour and you will see the latest fashion, that they [Shahraki young people] have seen during their trips to *kharej* [abroad] or on video films or satellite TVs."

Aptin and his sister Marjan, my cousins, live in Isfahan. At the time of my fieldwork, he was eighteen years old and she was seventeen. They came to Tehran for a short vacation. During the week they were there we used to meet at the home of a common cousin. Through our conversations the unequal center/periphery relationship became clearer.

Aptin: "Irangelesi music is still popular among Isfahani youth. Compared with Tehran, few households have satellite-receivers. Video is still the main medium. My sisters had a satellite receiver but did not dare use it. They were scared. Isfahan is a religious city, not like Tehran."

Marjan: "Tehran is different. People are more classy here."

Aptin: "Golestan is much better than the centers in Isfahan. Everybody who comes to Tehran, visits Golestan. It's like a holy shrine [*emamzadeh*]. In Isfahan there are much harsher restrictions. Now and then the *basijis* attack the *passage-e charbagh bala* and force young people to pray in the courtyard."

Aptin: "Tehrani girls are open. In Golestan they teased me. Believe me, one even pinched me."

Marjan interrupted him: "Tehrani girls are not fine! They think they are better than us. You know, we are *shahrestani* [from the provinces]."

Shahram: "But how can they know you are not from Tehran?"

Aptin: "It's easy. They can see it clearly. How we dress, how we move around, how we look at them, just like as we came from villages. Golestan is well known for its girls. They are not restrained and shy like girls from the provinces. Here girls are cool [*bahal*], they are cute and happy."

Marjan: "They use more make-up than we can in Isfahan. Both girls and boys spend more money on clothes and entertainment."

In order to "democratize" culturally prestigious activities which are otherwise unattainable for unprivileged south Tehranis, Tehran's city council has opened several "Houses of Culture" in different parts of the city since the early 1990s. The first and largest, Bahman House of Culture, was founded in 1991 on the edge of Javadieh. These Houses offer courses in languages, music, computing, and sports. Concerts of Iranian and Western classical music as well as art exhibitions are also arranged. The Bahman House of Culture, for instance, intensified the links between the wealthy inhabitants of the north, who come to visit the center, and the poor citizens of south, who are attracted by the center's sports and artistic activities. However, a survey of the visitors to the Bahman House of Culture between 1993 and 1994 indicates that there is still a difference in "cultural taste" between southern and northern Tehranis. Only 20 percent of the audiences at concerts of Western classical music came from the south. In contrast, the concerts of Iranian traditional music were only 27 percent attended by participants from north Tehran (see Amir-Ebrahimi 1374/1995). In 1996 Victor Hugo's famous drama *Les Misérables* was on stage in the Bahman House of Culture. A survey of the audience indicates that 75 percent of the spectators came from North Tehran and only 12 percent from the southern neighborhood (Amir-Ebrahimi 1999: 355–58). Furthermore, the Bahman House of Culture offers an arena where the participation of women can be as high as that of men. This is significant because the public spaces in Tehran and particularly south Tehran have hitherto been mainly male-dominated. The culture house project has faced strong opposition. Conservative forces see them as arenas where Westernization is promoted.

Shahraki identity, like "*Javad*-ness," is a source of pride, but it is also a stigma. Shahrak-e Gharb is usually imagined as synonymous with West-struckness, immorality, sexual freedom, and consumerism. It is also an emblem for "anti-Islamic values," the source and medium of the "cultural invasion," and a manifestation of young disobedience. Tehrani youth enact their rejection of the "imposed order" by consuming and performing modernity. In the next chapter I explore how they do this at Golestan, the heart of Shahrak-e Gharb.

Shahrak-e Gharb and Javadieh exist as much as imagined as real places. Undoubtedly, the Shahrak-e Gharb/Javadieh dichotomy is based on uneven distribution of wealth. Nevertheless, an idea of cultural distinction has also developed. Shahrakis tend to dissociate themselves from the Other, embodied in *Javad*, through culturalized lifestyle choices, such as individual autonomy, secularism, and globalism. The exclusion of *Javad*s by Shahrakis can be seen as a rupture from the wider society through the creation of an alternative "mentality," social organization, and neighborhood identity. On the one hand, this has happened through the ways in which Shahrakis, thanks to their transnational connections can determine trendy styles and represent Javadieh as "traditional," "poor," "backward," and "local." On the other hand, the state-dominated media have represented Shahrak-e Gharb as "corrupt," "Weststruck," and anti-revolutionary, with social and economic consequences for the inhabitants of the neighborhood. As I shall describe in the next chapter, there is a "cultural dispute" not only over the wealth of Shahrakis and deprivation of *Javad*s but also over the "tasteless consumption" of the new rich immigrants to Shahrak-e Gharb. The next chapter takes us to the Golestan shopping center (located in Zone 1), where youths from south and north Tehran negotiate their identity, through consumption and communication.

Chapter 4
A Passage to Modernity: Golestan

We have to wake up from the existence of our parents.
—Walter Benjamin

The mall is a theater.
—William Kowinski

As a teenager, in the early 1980s, I spent several hours a week in Passazh-e Sepahan or Passazh-e Chahrbagh Bala, in my home town of Isfahan. On Thursday evening these shopping malls were full of well-dressed young people with the "right" hairstyle. We strolled around to see and to be seen. While always in fear of the *basijis* patrolling around, we exchanged glances and a few words with girls. Sometimes phone numbers were passed between us. I obtained recent illicit pop music and met my friends in cafeterias. On the basement floor of the Passazh-e Chahrbagh Bala, there was and still is a gallery known as Bazar-e kuwaitiya (Kuwaitis' bazaar). The trendiest clothes could be found there. The name originates from the bazaar of Abadan, a border city close to Iraq and Kuwait, which in the 1960s and 1970s was the most cosmopolitan city in Iran. Bazar-e kuwaitiya was crammed with modern commodities, imported from Kuwait. Later on, Iranian labor migrants found an extra income in importing luxury commodities when they came back to Iran on visits. Nowadays the goods in the shops come from other countries, yet the name Bazar-e kuwaitiya points to trendy and modern commodities. Although we were constantly pursued and insulted by the *basijis*, who tried to drive us out of the mall, we knew that we were the winners. The state had successfully achieved its sex-segregation policy everywhere in society, except in the malls. By being constantly on the move through corridors, floors, shops, stairs, we could not be stopped and separated from the opposite sex.

* * *

Having experienced this side of "shopping" and social life in the shopping malls, I have always had difficulty with the hegemonic ideological theories that present consumer culture only in terms of the exploitative "global dictatorship of capitalism." For academics the idea of the mall usually evokes illusion and false consciousness.[1] It is an urban phantasmagoria, an entry into a dream world. Tehrani young people, among whom I carried out my fieldwork, have a different view on the topic. For them the shopping mall is not about illusion, it is rather about imagination, subjectivity, and defiance. This complexity is perhaps what Walter Benjamin meant by the "ambiguity of the arcades" (1999: 903). Benjamin, in his work on Parisian arcades known as *Passagen-Werk* (*The Arcades Project*), is ambivalent toward the arcades, which for him are at once utopian and dystopian (see Wilson 1992). On the one hand, influenced by Marx, Benjamin saw the arcades as a "primordial landscape of consumption" (Benjamin 1999: 827) which represented a vital essence of capitalism and the unconsciousness of the dreaming collective. In his own words: "Arcades: houses, passages, having no outside. Like a dream" (839).

Simultaneously, however, the arcades also reflected for him the utopias projected by the nineteenth-century visionary Charles Fourier representing the "anticipation and imaginative expression of a new world" (Benjamin 1999: 637). As Susan Buck-Morss, in an impressive and insightful study of *Passagen-Werk*, puts it, "this fetishized phantasmagoria is also the form in which the human, socialist potential of the industrial nature lies frozen, awaiting the collective political action that could awaken it" (Buck-Morss 1991: 211). In the Paris arcades, Benjamin saw not only revolutionary power in the mass culture, but also the rupture of tradition; "a rupture of those social conditions of domination that consistently have been the source of tradition" (1999: 279). The mass culture materialized a collective energy by which the "antiquarian effect of the father on his son" could be overcome. Such "rupture of tradition" is an aspect of what I have experienced in Golestan, where I carried out the major part of my fieldwork. Golestan represents a disjunction in continuity and coherence of the "local." In this chapter I show, through ethnographical illustrations, how Golestan is used by young people as a scene for performing, consuming, and learning "modern being." I shall also argue that Golestan is, above all, a "carnivalesque" space for demonstrating the "rupture of tradition." But first a quick history of modern shopping centers in Tehran.

The Emergence of the Passazh

The modernization policy of the Shah constructed a new urban-based, middle-class lifestyle. Urban development, population growth, and the emergence of a new Western-oriented category have led to the expansion of a new pattern of retailing in Iranian cities. Twentieth-century Tehran, capital of the first Iranian nation-state, was planned to be different from the old urban pattern. Modern urban planning would "rationalize" urban space. The new urban structure was thought to promote mobility and accessibility. Broad, straight avenues and wide squares, adapted for motorized vehicles, replaced, cut, and crossed the narrow, partly roofed alleyways, parts of the bazaar, and the labyrinth of culs-de sac shaped for pedestrian movement.

However, while in the late nineteenth century the bazaar was still the center of the city, in today's Tehran the bazaar is physically marginalized and encompasses a minority of all the shops in Tehran. The petroldollar middle-class Tehranis needed a different shopping experience. Western-style walk-in shops emerged on avenues throughout Tehran. Lalehzar Street and Berlin Alley (Kuche Berlan) were the first walk-in shopping streets in the 1940s and 1950s. Later on, in the late 1960s and early 1970s, a new form of shopping center emerged in Tehran and other large cities. These shopping centers have been called *passazh* (after the French term *passage*, used for shopping arcades in the early twentieth century). A *passazh* in present-day Tehran is a modern multistory building, usually housing a car park and served by elevators and escalators. It is designed with a good composition of light and color, and of course includes large spaces for interior gardens. The typical features of the traditional bazaar, such as the mosque, old-style coffeehouse, public bath, are absent here. Instead there are cafeterias and fast-food shops. Shops are crammed with imported goods. Recent chic modes from Europe can be found in these boutiques. The shops have fancy names and signs shaped in colorful neon. Unlike the traditional bazaar, all the shops have shop-windows. The *passazhs* are built outside the bazaar's physical boundaries and are usually located in the more modern parts of the city.

Not unusually for modern architecture, these *passazhs* rapidly become outdated and lose their attraction as spaces for economic and leisure activities. Passazh-e Safaviyeh, on Naderi Street, was regarded as a modern milieu for Tehrani flâneures in the early 1960s. Today it is an old-fashioned insignificant *passazh* in central Tehran. Although the emergence of the *passazh* and other shopping arenas has reduced the importance of the bazaar, they have never replaced the bazaar entirely. The *passazh* has rather been a supplement to the bazaar. Emphasis on the difference between the *passazh* and the bazaar should not obscure the continuity of the bazaar into the *passazhs*; the latter are in some sense extensions of the bazaar into the modern avenues. These institutions are economically affiliated. Many *passazhs* are built by capital generated by the *bazaris*. Some of the commodities marketed at the *passazhs* are supplied by the bazaar, which is still the main import/export organization in the country. Nevertheless, the two arenas offer different kinds of "sociability" (Shields 1992: 107), ways of relating the local community to the wider society and locating it in time and space. There are innumerable small and large *passazhs* throughout Tehran. I chose Golestan for my fieldwork because of its multiple dimensions in the realms of politics, commerce, youth culture, and transnational connections.

Golestan

The Golestan shopping center in Shahrak-e Gharb is the most famous *passazh* in Tehran, perhaps even in all Iran. It is a four-story building on the corner of Iranzamin and Mahestan Streets. There are more than 180 shops and offices in Golestan, and a large car parking area underground. Two main arcades, one north-south and the other east-west, join each other to make an L. The arcades are at least 6 meters wide with boutiques on both sides. Shops are dominated by clothes shops. The ground and second floors contain boutiques. On the ground floor one finds, besides clothes boutiques, three elegant handicraft shops, a jewelry shop, a bookstore, a Hi Fi shop, a photo shop, a travel agency, an Adidas sports shop, and a bank. On the second floor are a body-building equipment store, two cafeterias, two carpet shops, a handicraft shop, and several real estate brokers. The rest sell clothes and shoes. The third floor is allocated to offices, such as doctors' clinics, institutions for teaching languages and music, or trading firms. During my fieldwork two Internet cafés were also opened on this floor. Off the back yard on the west side there are three fast-food restaurants, a bank, and several groceries. The eastern back yard has a florist, two toy shops, a grocery, a pizzeria, and a taxi service office. In a narrow passageway that links the western to the eastern one there are several food shops. There is a Nan-e Fantazi (Fantasy Bread) bakery, with many Western kinds of bread but no traditional Iranian ones. The grocery stores are crammed with goods normally rare in Iran, cornflakes, Nescafe, and Swiss chocolate, to name but a few.

Since the emergence of the Islamic regime it has been officially forbidden to use Western names in shop signs. The names of some well-known boutiques in Tehran such as Maxim, Rose Lady, or Nostalgia were replaced with Iranian names. To circumvent the law, businesswo/men in Golestan have started to use ancient pre-Islamic Persian names, unusual names taken from ethnic cultures, or just modified foreign names. Armenian, Kurdish, or An Azari names are the most usual.

Azari names like Denis, Kurdish Hiva, or Bakhtiari Tiam, and other ethnic terms like Shemiz, or Poushni, are Iranian but not Islamic. Moreover, they still have connotations with "abroad" (*kharej*). One shop was
named Anoushé (an old Persian girl's name). The owner told me the
name was "pure Iranian, but sounds like a French name." Another
name was Si Mo, Si Tou (in the Luri ethnic language "For Me, For
You"), which was taken to sound Japanese.

ETHNOGRAPHIC SKETCHES

I

Rang Café, in the corner of the first floor in Golestan, is one of the
most popular coffee shops in Tehran. It is small but with a very chic interior. The walls are dark brown, the decoration is wood, and there is a
fireplace in the corner. Black and white pictures of old Tehran abound.
The pictures show Tehran between the two world wars, the first cars, the
first "modern" streets and squares, and so on. In the middle of the café
is a semicircular bar, behind which staff prepare orders. Although no alcoholic beverages are served, wine and beer glasses hang over the bar.
Two coffee machines are on the counter. While in most coffee shops in
Tehran you receive Nescafe when you order coffee, here you can enjoy
a "real" coffee. The most popular coffees are Qahveh Faranse (French
Coffee), a regular coffee, and Qahveh Turk (Turkish Coffee), a spicy
concentrated coffee. On the menu, which is written in both Persian and
English, European nationalities are used as prefixes for items, such as
Danish cake and Cookies, Italian ice cream, or French jelly.

The café is always crammed with young people. The owner, a woman
in her early fifties, sits behind the cash desk. Sometimes she leaves her
place and approaches "improperly veiled" young girls to gently ask
them to correct their veils. She told me later that she did it with anguish: "But what can I do? They closed my café for a month last summer. They said that 'Islamic values' were broken in my café. I cannot
afford them to close my café once more." I went to the Rang Café regularly to write down my notes over a cup of French coffee. The waiters,
all young males, knew me. Alan migrated from a Kurdish village to
Tehran in hope of a better life. As well as his work at the café he studies hard to get his *diplom* (high school degree). He dreams of emigrat-
ing to Canada. In pauses, he would come with a "Teach Yourself
English" book and a booklet and asks me to teach him English. I taught
him a little English and talked about how people emigrate legally and
illegally to Canada.

Our dialogue was amazing and somehow bizarre. While I was bombarded by his questions about living abroad, about how he could get himself to Canada, if Sweden gave asylum to Iranians, and so on, I asked him about Golestan, his life in Kurdistan and Tehran, if whether had friends in Shahrak-e Gharb or among the customers. He shared a rented room with two other co-village boys in a poor neighborhood in southern Tehran. He said that he had no Shahraki friends:

They are *bimarefat* [not true friends]. But I enjoy being here. It was not easy to get a job here. I tried very hard. Here I come in contact with people who come from abroad [*kharej*], like you. I ask them for advice and guidance. Until I can arrange my emigration to Canada, here is like *kharej* for me.

The day before my departure from Iran, I went to say good-bye to Alan. He tried unsuccessfully to hide his anguish over my departure, which meant that part of his dream world had vanished. He knew very well how little chance he had of realizing his dream. Yet perhaps he found another person coming from *kharej* to talk to about life in Canada.

II

In June 1999, a fast-food restaurant called Boof was opened in the courtyard of Golestan. Boof was a new fast-food chain in Tehran, and this was its third restaurant. Boof was a copy of the American McDonald's. After the Revolution the Islamic state closed all McDonald's restaurants in Iran. McDonald's was seen as a crucial medium of "cultural invasion." In the mid-1990s, an Iranian returnee from Spain opened a fast-food restaurant in Tehran. Its name began with "Mac." The authorities closed it after few weeks, arguing that it resembled the American chain restaurant "too much." However, in the political atmosphere of 1999 there was room for more tolerance toward Boof. The way the premises were decorated in red with metal trimmings and the staff dressed in red and white uniforms and caps, as well as the way the customers order, pay for, and receive their food, all mimic the traits of a McDonald's restaurant. The food offered is different kinds of hamburgers made with *halal* meat, and served with French fries. Beverages are Iran-made, such as Parsi Cola or non-alcoholic "Islamic beer," as it is called. At a long counter five cashiers take orders and receive payment. Above them is a neon board on which customers can see the names, pictures, and prices of the items. Cashiers pass the orders to the kitchen through an internal electronic system. It takes a minimal time from ordering and paying to receiving the food.

Three large fanciful color pictures hang on the walls; they are on glass and strong lamps light them from behind. The pictures, as I discovered in other Boof restaurants, are made especially for this company. The theme is the clash between modern technology (in most cases modern vehicles) and ancient buildings. One, on the left of the entrance, shows two columns of Persepolis. A picture of a man driving a jet ski on the sea is set on the first one. "This shows the clash between tradition and modernity," Dara said. The manager of the restaurant told me, the motto of Boof is "cleanness and again cleanness." The manager said: "You go to the restaurants in town and you feel sick at how dirty your table is. Imagine what it's like in the kitchen! Here I have two boys just for keeping the restaurant clean." He was right. The restaurant was always clinically clean. In his terminology "modern" and "clean" were synonymous. In the Western "civilizing process" hygiene was a crucial symbol of the "modern" lifestyle (Elias 1978 [1939]).

The restaurant has a little indoor balcony for around twenty persons. It is "only for families" (*makhsous-e khanevadeh*). One day I went to Boof to have lunch. To do an "ethnographic test," I went upstairs to the balcony. A waiter approached me and told me that the balcony was only for "families." The balcony was vacant; I said: "There are no families here now," and ignored his protests. He went downstairs. After awhile the manager came up and "respectfully" kicked me out. Boof illustrates the contradiction of the modern predicament Golestan represents. On the one hand, it attempts to emphasize modern values such as the rationalization of time and extreme cleanness. On the other hand, it is not able to liberate itself completely from traditional expectations, such as protecting the sacred institution of the "family" from sexualized young people.

III

The Mazi Internet café on the third floor is one of two in Golestan, but there are innumerable others in Tehran as a whole. It was opened by twenty-eight-year-old Shahab in the summer of 2000. Entering the Internet café, we come first to a little waiting hall. There is a table just beside the entrance. A young girl usually sits behind it and takes care of customers. The café has three rooms and a tiny pantry. The rooms are allocated according to the three different services the café offers. Beside providing Internet access, tutoring, and training, the café also offers cheap long-distance telephoning. These services attract customers of different age categories. The Internet room had six computers. In January 2001, the hourly rate was 2,400 *toman* (U.S.$4). According to Shahab, the users are mainly NRI (nonresident Iranians) who are checking their email. Another group of Internet users are young students searching for information about Western universities, probably to find a way to continue their studies abroad. While there was never a queue for using the Internet, there was always a handful of middle-aged people, primarily women, waiting their turn to make long-distance telephone calls. The owner told me that they are usually parents who are calling their children in the U.S. or Europe. Making a call through the Internet costs only an eighth of the price through the state telephone company. Coffee, tea, and soft drinks are also served. The owner, Shahab, had returned to Iran after 22 years in France: "I like to live here. I like my work, even if it is not yet profitable. I can hardly earn the capital it costs, let alone a salary. But I am sure it will be a good business soon, if the authorities do not disturb us of course. They can close the café any day they want."

He was right. The Internet has been regarded as a means of "cultural invasion." However, the reformists and President Khatami have advocated young people's right to have access to information. Shahab said there were restrictions on surfing on the Internet. According to him, pornographic sites and sites of Iranian political opposition groups were filtered. He told me that in the beginning the authorities had ordered that girls and boys should be separated in the Internet café. He had allocated one room for girls and one room for boys. Now, however, the situation was much calmer and they could sit in the same room. One day the table beside me was occupied by three teenage boys. They were so noisy that I could not concentrate on writing an email to Stockholm. They were chatting with some girls sitting together behind a computer elsewhere in Tehran. The result was a date.

Golestan Is Modern and the Bazaar Traditional

The identification of *passazh* in general and Golestan in particular as "modern" contributes to the construction of its opposite, the bazaar, as "traditional." Similar to the way Shahrakis disassociate themselves from *javads* to represent themselves as "modern," the representation of Golestan and other *passazhs* is based on a dissociation from the bazaar. The parallel is not arbitrary. Geographically the bazaar is located where the majority of *javads* live. *Javads* are supposed to consume *bazari* commodities and to have "*bazari* taste" (*saligh-ye bazari*). Through the economic conjunction, the bazaar and the *passazhs* play different, sometimes opposed, roles in the Iranian social world. The bazaar is represented as a forum for "continuity," the *passazh* for "disjunction." To understand the place of *passazh* in Iranian society, we need to know the bazaar. I therefore begin with a historical and ethnographic description of the bazaar.

In Iran, the bazaar has been the third foundation on which society is grounded, ranking only after the royal court and Islam.[2] The bazaar is a business district of the city characterized by a specific morphology and architectural design.[3] It contains premises for crafts and manufacturing, and some of the commodities offered are produced within the bazaar itself. Yet the Iranian bazaar has a broader meaning than just a marketplace. It is an "institutionalized organization"[4] with religious, commercial, political, and social elements. It is the center of personal transactions and communication in urban life (Floor 1984). The bazaar has its own moral codes of Islamic discourse (Fischer 1995). It is also the socioeconomic and political power base of the Shiite religious establishment and a bastion of political movements (Ashraf 1990).

In medieval Islamic urban society the mosque and the bazaar provided two principal recognized loci for male sociability (Udovitch 1987: 163). As institutions, they are still tightly intertwined. Exchange in the Islamic bazaar is not simply an economic transaction. It is also a matter of social value and religious morality.[5] The bazaar economy is religiously formulated (see Fischer 1995; Geertz 1979; Thaiss 1971). Islam and business are so integrated that the bazaar usually carries an "Islamic" adjective in academic discourse. As anthropologist Gustav Thaiss states, Islamic discourse is the cement that binds the structure of the bazaar together, providing a basic common denominator for different categories of *bazaris* (1971: 194).[6]

The relations between the bazaar and the mosque are marked by interdependence and reciprocity (Ashraf 1990; see also Keshavarzian 2007). One side of this relation is financial. The *bazaris* support the mosque and the religious schools and pay an amount (one-fifth of their net profits) as *khoms* to the clergy. The other side is the clergy's protection of the *bazaris* against the oppressive state. The clergy often interpret Islam in line with the *bazaris*' interests (Mozaffari 1991). Intermarriage between the two social categories is quite common. For the *bazari*, to have a good relationship with the clergy is a sign of piety and a way to maintain respect and honor in the bazaar community, a necessity for success in the bazaar. This interdependence, as well as the physical setting, has brought about similarities in the lifestyle and worldview of the *bazaris* and clergy. The bazaar is undoubtedly one of the most organized social categories in Iranian society. As a close-knit organization with vast networks among different social groups, enjoying financial power, and supported by the legitimacy of Islam, the bazaar had and still has the capability to challenge the regime in power. The bazaar/clergy alliance has been a significant factor in social movements in Iran since the late nineteenth century, for example, during the Tobacco rebellion (1891–1892), the Constitutional Revolution (1906–1911), and finally the Islamic Revolution in 1979.

The emergence of the modern state and the socioeconomic changes since the 1920s had dramatic effects on the bazaar. The Pahlavi period (1925–1979) was marked by modernization policies that went against the bazaar's interests. The well-organized state bureaucracy intervened in commercial activities and oppressed the merchants. Furthermore, urban developments threatened the integrity of the bazaar, and the secular state generally restricted the role of the clergy in society. Mohammad Reza Shah saw the *bazaris* not only as "a bunch of bearded idiots" (quoted in Mozaffari 1991: 383), but also as a barrier to his reform endeavors. In his book, *Answer to History*, he asserts that his fight against the bazaar was a mission for modernity: "The *bazaris* are a fanatic lot, highly resistant to change. . . . Moving against the bazaar was typical of the political and social risks I had to take in my drive for modernization" (Pahlavi 1980: 156).[7] A serious challenge to the bazaar was the government-sponsored cooperative societies. Department stores called *kuroush* were established in Tehran and other large cities, in an attempt to modernize the retailing and distribution system. Moreover, the cultural policy of the Shah challenged the *bazaris'* adherence to the traditional lifestyle. The increasing Westernization of urban life and the official un/anti-Islamic policies that governed the media and structured school curricula were incompatible with Islamic values. Not unexpectedly, the bazaar played a crucial role in the Revolution of 1979 against the Shah and the establishment of the Islamic Republic.[8]

The bazaar and *passazhs* play different roles in what is seen in Iran as the "traditional/modernity" (*sonat/tajadud*) dichotomy. While the bazaar is supposed to be an arena where "tradition" is reproduced and performed, the *passazh* offers a site where it is interrupted. The dichotomization is based on several contrasting features of these marketplaces, such as politics, gender roles, generational aspects, patterns of consumption, "taste," or attachment to locality and globality.

The origin of the *passazh* in the very process of modernization is reflected in a different political stance from that of the bazaar. For instance, Golestan supported Khatami against the conservative forces in his presidential campaign in 1997, whereas *bazari* people supported the conservative candidate. Two years later, in June 1999, Golestan had a big sale to celebrate the anniversary of the second Khordad (the day Khatami won the election). The profound alliance between the *bazaris* and the clergy determines their political inclinations. In spite of its demands for a more liberal economic atmosphere, the bazaar stands forcefully as a culturally conservative institution. The bazaar has been a faithful defender of traditional lifestyle and Islamic values against the immorality and disorder caused by the social disease of Weststruckness thought to be displayed in the *passazhs*.

Compared to the bazaar, there is more tolerance for women in the *passazhs*, where they have a strong presence, both as salesclerks or entrepreneurs and as customers or flâneurs. The authoritarian masculinity of the bazaar fades in the *passazh*. For instance, Mrs. Arki, owner of a children's clothing boutique in Golestan, was on the board of the shopping center. There were also two other women in the council of managers of Golestan. Many businesses are run by all family members jointly. Although the loudspeaker frequently orders women in Golestan to be properly veiled, young female flâneurs frankly violate the order. Genderwise, the bazaar is a homogeneous space, a "men's world." There are no businesswomen. Women might work as artisans for a *bazari*, but they are seen neither by the visitors nor by other *bazaris*. As visitors and customers, women are expected not to stay a long time in the bazaar. Unlike the *passazhs*, women do not hang around in the bazaar. An improperly veiled woman is not welcome and may even elicit aggressive reactions from male *bazaris*.[9]

In a similar way, while the traditional bazaar is dominated by middle-aged Muslim men, Golestan has a more democratic ambiance and openness to religious minorities as well as young people. Youth-oriented *passazhs* also require young entrepreneurs who can cater to the needs and tastes of the younger generation. These young businesswo/men are usually from other social categories than those of *bazaris*. They often have higher education and do not identify themselves as *bazari* (I shall return to this below).

Locality and Globality

Commitment to the preservation of "authentic" Iranian culture is much more evident in the bazaar than in the *passazh*. Through its religious rituals and ethical discourse and its support for the conservative forces within the Islamic state, the bazaar attempts to maintain loyalty and identification with the "local." Golestan is far from the long history, complex culture, and immense networks the bazaar possesses. In *passazh* settings there seems to be less anxiety about the hazards of commodification and threats to tradition. Golestan lacks the organic relationship the bazaar has with the mosque, religious rituals, or other social activities. The lack of loyalty to the "local" allows for more playfulness about identity, and the possibility of adding a transnational context to it (see Augé 1995). In Golestan the interior decoration and the strived-for ambiance evoke a transnational aesthetics. With its modern architecture, its luxury commodities, trendy cafés, fast-food restaurants, grocery stores crammed with foods of European cuisine, bookshops with foreign journals and books, Internet cafés, this space transposes imagination across spatial boundaries. At Christmas time most shops were decorated with a Christmas tree, Santa Claus dolls, and a "Happy New Year" written in white on the shop-window. To many visitors, being in Golestan gives an experience of being "modern" and being a part of what is called the global "aestheticization of everyday life." Golestan is linked to the local culture as well as to transnational modernity, through the references of its signs, sources of its commodities, and ambitions of its customers. For Tehrani youth, Golestan is where they construct their own social space beyond local boundaries and identity. The shopping mall, like the cinema, "offers a safe transit into other spaces, other times, other imaginaries" (Friedberg 1994: 121).

Khareji Contra Irani Quality

A central concept for understanding shopping at Golestan is "foreign quality" (*jens-e khareji*). *Jens* means both commodity and quality. *Kharej* literally means outside or abroad, but is mainly used to refer to the West. *Kharej* and its adjective form (*khareji*) carry an implication of high quality and standards. Iran-made goods (*jens-e Irani*) are synonymous with low quality and deficiency; foreign goods (*jens-e khareji*) are believed to be of high quality. The significance of *khareji* quality is shown best in the advertisement: "According to the latest method in Europe"; "Adapted to foreign [*khareji*] standards"; "Best service under monitoring by Ms. X with several years experience from Paris"; "Finally we have discovered the secret of European slimness."

Since the establishment of the Islamic state, importing *khareji* commodities, particularly those seen by the authorities as nonutilitarian "luxury consumption," has been forbidden. The concept of "luxury consumption" refers to a broad range of items (*ajnas-e lux-e masrafi*) from chocolate and chewing gum to BMW cars. Shops in Golestan and other *passazhs* are nevertheless crammed with the latest fashions in clothing, shoes, and cosmetics. There are two trade routes through which illicit commodities reach the boutiques in Tehran: the "suitcase trade" across the Persian Gulf and smuggling from Dubai and Turkey. The truck drivers traveling between Turkey and Iran are a main source of commodities for young consumers in Iran.[10]

For young Tehrani consumers, brands come first. It is important to possess the original (*asl*) brands. It is worth noting that the word *eslalat*, literally meaning authenticity, comes from *asl.* Bazar-e Ghaem, Bazar-e Ferdowsi, and Sorkhe Bazar in central Tehran are full of pirated copies of brands (*mark-e taqaloubi*). All kinds can be found, for instance, buttons with Levi and Wrangler logos, or the yellow trademark of Dr. Martin to be sewn onto shoes. On the border with Turkey there is a market solely for pirated copies of brands. The logos and buttons of famous brands are produced in Turkey and traded to Tehran and other cities. Iranian products, mostly clothes but also perfume, shoes, and so on are marked with them and sold at boutiques as *khareji* products.

It is difficult to distinguish between original and false brands. One afternoon I was visiting one of my informants in his boutique. He sells exclusive men's attire. Most of his customers are young men buying their wedding costume. That afternoon a young couple came in to find a suit for the husband-to-be. They brought with them the latest *American Bridegroom* catalog and pointed out the models they were looking for. Such a catalogue had not yet reached Tehran. The girl said her brother in Los Angeles had sent it to her. The couple did not find a suit identical to what they wanted, but were convinced by the seller that he could talk to a tailor who would make one, following the catalog picture. He asked if he could borrow it to make a copy. After the couple left the shop I asked him how he would use the catalogue. He answered, "I copy suits, mark them with an Armani brand, and sell them as original [*asl*]." He raised his head, looked at me, and grinned: "I'm kidding." I did not believe he was. I had already heard from two other boutique owners that he sells Turkish suits as Italian ones.

The best way to get Western goods is to ask someone who is traveling abroad to bring things back. Otherwise, you never know what you are paying for. If you import them yourself from "abroad," you feel assured that you are getting *jens-e asl* (original goods) or *jens-e fabrik* (unused, untouched goods). Once when Elli and I were strolling through Golestan I stopped in front of a cosmetics boutique and pointed at the diverse perfumes in the shop window: "Here you can find more brands than in Stockholm. Look, there are Chanel, Christian Dior, Eden, Safari, and all the other trademarks I do not see in shops in Stockholm."

Elli replied: "All this stuff is copied in Iran or Pakistan. But goods coming from *kharej* are something else [*ye chiz-e digan*]"

One young man in Golestan put the difference between Iranian and *khareji* goods this way: "*Khareji* is original, Irani is parody [*badal*]." Moreover, many Iranian companies choose their brand names as close to the famous international brands as possible, such as Nik ("nice" in Persian, recalling Nike); or Pumak (recalling Puma). As mentioned above, the concept of *kharej* refers solely to the wealthy, modern West, though it literally means abroad in general. Once I was talking about *kharej* with some youngsters.

Shahram: "Do you know Hamid? The one with a goat beard who is hanging around in the back yard every night? He is going to study medicine abroad [*kharej*] soon."

Amir: "Where?"
Shahram: "Pakistan."
They all laughed: "Pakistan is not *kharej*."

This geographical hierarchization puts its mark not only on commodities but also on the quality of other domains such as education, service, lifestyle, and jobs. For example, Western-educated physicians use the foreignness of their training as a "merit" in advertising themselves. On the signboards of doctors' clinics, under the name and specialty of the physician, the location of his/her education is also mentioned. Graduation from England, the U.S., Switzerland, Italy, France, and Germany brings more credit than graduation from Turkey or Romania. Interestingly, I have never seen a doctor's signboard on which Pakistan or India was mentioned, though a large number of Iranians have studied medicine in these countries. Perhaps mentioning these locations would jeopardize the physicians' standing in the marketplace. The other side of this attachment to *khareji* quality is the disparagement of domestic quality. Iranian products, usually traded in the bazaar, are seen as worthless and short-lived. Even Iranian foodstuffs are considered unhealthy and of poor quality. I was told all the time not to eat Iranian food and snacks. Foreign chocolate, chips, chewing gum, and beverages (smuggled from Dubai) are supposed to be tastier.

A constant comparison with *kharej* has caused widespread "lack of self-respect" among Iranians. Iranians are harsh critics of their society, culture, and individuals. Iran is a country in crisis. Mass poverty, economic corruption, political instability, addiction, and increasing unemployment are just a few examples. In conversations about the current situation, I frequently heard the phrase "People get what they deserve [*khalayeq har che layeq*]." Herzfeld writes about a compatible situation in Greece. He makes an analogy between Greek model of female identity (lack of self-control, illiteracy, deprivation) and the Greek's view of their own national subordination to Europe (1986: 221).

As mentioned, another side of the lack of self-respect is conspiracy reasoning: "What has happened and will happen is planned by foreign powers." Iranians have no power or control over their destiny. "They [foreign powers] brought in this regime and they will take it away in due time." For many Iranians this reasoning is perhaps a way of discharging themselves from guilt for what has happened and responsibility for the future. The fear brings even more respect for foreign powers and disrespect for Iranians.[11] Complaints are frequently heard about how badly everything is carried out in Iran compared with the *kharej*, where everything is correctly managed.

Simon: "Youth in *kharej* at my age have much experience. Here there is nothing to experience. A *khareji* young person has study, sex, and work. We have nothing."

Dara: "I have a cousin who grew up in Canada. He came here recently for a short visit. Can you believe it, I was not able to see him! He had a well-planned life. Today I do this, tomorrow I go there. His life has a plan—not like us, all the time loitering."

Hamid: "In Japan you cannot see a day-old egg in the stores. Every day, eggs from the day before are replaced with fresh ones. Here you should be grateful if you get a month-old egg."

Jens-e irani (Iranian goods or quality) is usually classified as poor and inadequate. High quality goods are generally assumed to be made in the U.S., Germany, England, Japan, or Sweden. Electronic goods made in industrial countries in Southeast Asia, known in Iran as *bazar-e moshtarak* (united market), are also believed to be of good quality. In fashion, clothes, and cosmetics, France and Italy come first. During the 1990s, Turkey too acquired a good reputation for its clothes. *Jens-e turk* (Turkish goods or quality) is a common pledge in the clothing business (see Miller 1997a: 336).

Similar to the case with consumption goods, ideas of *kharej* are mobilized in the discourse on health, aesthetics, and sexuality. When I returned to Iran after eight years in Europe, many of my Bakhtiari relatives were surprised at how thin I was. For Bakhtiaris to be slim is to be sick, and fleshiness is a sign of health. "One who goes to *kharej* becomes fat [*chagh*] and healthy [*sallem*]." Not unexpectedly, every *khareji* is seen, if not as a physician, at least as a medical expert. I was asked for medicine all the time. The most appreciated gift from *kharej* is medicine.

People frequently assert that there is the rule of law in *kharej* (*qanoun dareh*), but in Iran matters follow not regulation (*zabeteh*) but relation (*rabeteh*). There are innumerable jokes about the bad quality of Iranian goods, works, service, and so forth. One, which I heard more than ten times in Tehran, follows below.

A JOKE

A man dies. It is discovered that he will be sent to Hell. Since he has some good deeds in his record, he gets a chance to choose between the Iranian and the *khareji* Hell. The man asks the difference between them. God explains that it is the same kind of torture in both. Hot molten lead will be poured into the man's throat through a funnel. The difference is, while this happens three times a week in the Iranian Hell, it occurs only once a week in the *khareji* Hell. The man without hesitation chooses the *khareji* one and is promptly sent there. After a month he thinks about some friends in the Iranian Hell. He says "Poor things! They suffer two times more than me." He goes to visit them and surprisingly he finds them joyful and delighted. He asks: "How come? Are you not drinking molten lead three times a week? His friends laugh blissfully and say: "You fool. We have not been tortured even once here. In the *khareji* Hell there is discipline and a well-regulated system. The torture is carried out on time. But here is the Iranian hell. One time there is lead and funnel but the torturer does not appear. The other time he comes but forgets the funnel. Next time he comes with the funnel but there is no lead."

*   *   *

The lure of *kharej* is also erotic. European (*farangi*) women have been the locus of erotic fantasy for many Iranian men since the late seventeenth century. While this occidentalist imagination about erotic and exotic *khareji* women was first formed by the seventeenth-century Persian travelers' accounts of Europe, it was promoted by Hollywood films, pornographic movies, TV serials, and sexual icons like Sophia Loren, Marilyn Monroe, and Madonna. European women's "beauty" and "sexual liberty" provided a subtext for an erotic imagination of Europe and Europeans (see Tavakoli-Targhi 2001: 54–76). It was always amazing to meet Arash and hear his imagining about *kharej*, which corresponds to his imagination on eroticism. In his mid-twenties and from the lower middle class, he lives with his parents and a younger brother in central Tehran. His father is a civil servant and his mother a nurse. Arash is unemployed and, like many other Iranian young people wants to start a new life in *kharej*. I met him once when he had followed Simon to Golestan. His curiosity and attachment to *kharej* made me a good informant who could answer his endless questions. Afterward I used to meet him in my apartment or in their house. He says: "I hate Tehran. A healthy life is impossible here. You must be an addict or a thief or a charlatan to enjoy life [*hal koni*] here. Every time I come out, even when I go to the market in our neighborhood to buy something, I get into a quarrel with someone." Arash is always nervous and grumbles about everything Iranian. He even dislikes Iranian girls:

They are hairy like men. They all have a mustache and hair on their arms. Shaggy [*pashmalou*] Iranian girls just can't make me randy. *Khareji* girls do not have hair on their body. Clean and beautiful [*tamiz o qashang*], girls over there are more feminine. Believe me, if you look under an Iranian girl's skirt you will find a large cock. The only Iranian girl I liked had grown up in Los Angeles. She was in Iran for a few years. She was OK. After all, she was like *khareji* girls. But she left Iran to find a blonde cock [*doudoul tala*].

Sofka Zinovieff writes about a similar approach among Greek men who regard North European women as "superior, sophisticated, and clean" (1991: 216). *Khareji* women are seen as "a window to the wide world" (Cohen 1971) for young Iranian men.

Khareji Taste Contra Bazari Taste

"Foreign taste" (*saliqey-e khareji*) dominates Golestan both by putting a mark on space and by characterizing commodities. Among urban middle-class Iranians this "foreign taste" is opposed to what is known as "*bazari* taste" (*bazari pasand*). The latter refers to cheap, low quality, flashy, made-in-Iran commodities. The concept is also used when evaluating films, art, houses, the interior of a restaurant, or home decoration, to name but a few instances. In the popular idiom the term *bazari* means:

- everything that is of bad taste (*bad saliqeh*), badly manufactured (*bad sakht*), and coarse (*faghedeh zerafat*);
- plain (*amiyaneh*) speech or behavior;
- trivial and vulgar (*mobtazal*) things;
- common, usual, repeated things without value.[12]

The conjunction between Islam and the bazaar and the close relations between the bazaar and the present regime in Iran have reinforced anti-*bazari* attitudes among the young people (for the bazaar-Islam alliance see Ashraf 1990). Business, *kasebi*, is considered a job without prestige among the educated middle class in Iran. The stereotype of *kaseb* or *bazari* (businessman) depicts a mean, but affluent, man who earns his money through dishonest dealings. He is usually represented as an overweight, hairy *hajji*, possessing minimal modern "cultural capital." This stereotype of the *bazari* has also been impersonated in modern literature and popular films. It is best embodied in Hajji Agha, the main character of the classic novel with same title by Sadeq Hedayat (1324/1945), who uses this figure to criticize the traditional Iranian society. Terms such as *bazari*, *bazari maslak* (one who has *bazari* style), or *bazari pasand* (taste of the *bazari*) are used as insults by modern middle-class Iranians.

The distinction between "foreign taste" and "*bazari* taste" forms aesthetic preferences among the youth. The imagined "*bazari* taste" relates to the assumed sexual taste for plump, white women with large breasts, like the pre-Revolution actresses of Iranian B-films such as Mahvash, Sepideh or Shahnaz Tehrani. The alleged sexual ideal of the *bazari* is quite different from the ideal young men in Golestan have themselves.

Their erotic preference is for Mariah Carey and the Spice Girls. Once I was talking with a young Sharaki about cars. He said that his favorite car was the BMW. I asked: "How about Mercedes Benz?" He answered: "Not any more. Benz has become a *bazari* car. Every new rich *bazari* has a Benz."

One day I annoyed Amir when I compared Golestan with the bazaar. He was a student at Tehran University who had been running a handicraft shop with his mother on the ground floor since 1996. Obviously irritated, he said:

There is a huge difference between this *passazh* and the bazaar. The atmosphere is different. We are not like *bazaris*. A *bazari* may be rich and live in north Tehran, but he still has his *bazari* character. Most of the shopowners here are educated. Most of us went into business because of the bad economic situation. We began from nothing. Unlike most entrepreneurs here, we had no business experience before. To run a business here is costly. We pay a high rent and monthly charge. This affects the price of our commodities. It is true that Golestan is an expensive *passazh*, but our commodities and service are unique. The clientele of Golestan are special. They are wealthy and pay good money for quality stuff. Most of them have lived or traveled in *kharej* and have experiences of *khareji* services. In the whole of Iran, Golestan is the most similar to Western shopping centers. 90 percent of our clientele are tourists or nonresident Iranians. There are many shops like ours in central Tehran, but they come here because here is classy.

He is right. The Golestan shopping center is a place usually visited by nonresident Iranians.

Two Madres-ye Tatbiqi, adaptation schools catering for children of returnees from the diaspora, are located not far from Golestan. Furthermore, while the presence of foreigners in Tehran is infrequent, encounters with non-Iranians is a daily matter in Golestan. Mr. Afshas, head manager of Golestan, told me that "the reputation of Golestan has even reached the Gulf Emirates. When they travel to Tehran they visit Golestan; it is a tourist attraction." Other Shahrakis proudly reminded me that many diplomats and other foreigners were resident in Shahrak-e Gharb. This was confirmed by the number of cars with diplomat plates I saw parked in the front of the Golestan shopping center every day.

Peyman is a thirty-seven-year-old man who runs a store selling "nomadic" carpets on the second floor. Peyman too was eager to indicate differences between the atmospheres in Golestan and the bazaar:

The majority of entrepreneurs in Golestan are not *bazari*. They are educated and have had other jobs. They have retired and then opened a shop here. Unlike the *bazari*, we have good relations with each other. In the bazaar people are thirsty for each other's blood. They are charlatans and become rich at ordinary people's expense. They could even cheat their own mother. Whatever you do to change a *bazari*, he still has his *bazari* character [*joun be joune bazari bekoni bazam bazari-ye*].

Two years ago Peyman sold his carpet store in central Tehran and opened this one in Golestan. In his old store he sold "ordinary" carpets to "ordinary" Iranian customers; here he has selected aesthetic no-madic *kelims* for another category of customer. Even when "local cul-ture" is objectified in "souvenir" form in handicraft shops, it is adjusted according to the taste of foreigners or nonresident Iranians. Peyman says:

My customers are entirely nonresident Iranians. Parents who go abroad to visit their children also buy *kelims* from us as presents. They pay a higher price here but they get what suits the taste of Westerners [*saliqe-ye khareji*]. I travel myself to the Bakhtiari and the Qashqa'i nomads and select *kelims* which I think will suit my clientele. I wash them with sand several times, so that they look old and match my customers' taste.

Mr. Afshas declared: "In Golestan the economic patterns of the bazaar, such as the practice of bargaining [*chounezani*], or the tradi-tional credit system [*nesiyeh*] do not work. Here transactions are based on cash." An economy based on money contributes to increasing anonymity, individualization, and impersonal social relations. Cus-tomers in Golestan in fact also try to bargain, but it rarely works and the practice is strongly discouraged. Another *passazh* on Mirdammad Av-enue had a policy totally banning it. The owner, a rich German-based Iranian businessman, had strictly forbidden it. One shopkeeper in Golestan associates bargaining with the bazaar:

In the bazaar there is no price-tag on goods. The customer asks the price and the *bazari* doubles it and then the bargaining game begins. Here the customer can see the price of the commodities. The price is fixed here and is fair. There is no place for bargaining over our prices. We could also do like the *bazaris*. Double the price and then bargain.

However, the bazaar is more complex than the picture presented by people in Golestan. To characterize the bazaar as static and "local" and Golestan as stably "global" would be misleading. Many aspects of the bazaar are "global," and Golestan is "local" in many ways.[13] In spite of its lack of local anchorage, Golestan is not entirely "delocalized" even in its forms and symbols. There are attempts to hitch on to a "local" identity. The name of the mall, Golestan, comes from the classic lyric collection by Saadi, a highly respected twelfth-century Persian poet. Tawny bricks, with some features of traditional Iranian architecture, give the building an Iranian form. Mr. Afshas, the manager, proudly stated, "Golestan will be a historic building in the future."

However, for my middle-class young Tehranis with their West-oriented lifestyle, the contemporary bazaar stands out as an emblem of traditional lifestyle (*zendegi sonati*) and reactionary politics (*mortaj'e*). By distinguishing themselves from the people of the bazaar with its connotations of backwardness, Golestan people want to demonstrate that they are "modern."

Shopping, Spectacle, Imagination

Once I asked a researcher at Tehran University how consumption in Golestan differs from consumption in the bazaar. He differentiated between the bazaar as a market for "basic needs" and Golestan as a market for "luxury commodities" and desire. This would agree with the model presented by Campbell (1987: 60), who believes that satisfaction-seeking and pleasure-seeking are two different activities. While the former refers to a lack that needs to be satisfied, the latter is a reaction to stimuli in a certain fashion. And finally, satisfaction-seeking and pleasure-seeking may be different aspects of the same activity. Such notions are ambiguous. A luxury commodity for one person may be a basic necessity for someone else. For instance, while a microwave oven for a single working parent in Tehran is a "basic need," it might be seen as a "luxury" for a rural family. Furthermore, yesterday's luxury can be today's necessity. Apart from that, it is still the bazaar which provides "luxury" for many Iranians from the working class and the provinces.

Shopping at modern malls is as much a matter of leisure as it is a matter of business. It is often associated with holiday time, as something to do when one is free from other burdens. While the bazaar is closed on Fridays, Golestan is more crowded then than on any other day in the week. For a majority of the youth, hanging around in Golestan is thus a case of pleasure-seeking, an "imaginative hedonism" (Campbell 1987), rather than of purchasing. They come to Golestan to have fun "time out of time." Mr. Afshas often lamented the presence of young people, thinking that they damaged the business in Golestan: "80 percent of all visitors come here to ramble." At several meetings of the council of managers, the main debate was on how to solve the problem of young nonpurchaser flâneurs. On different days and at different times Golestan is occupied by varying categories of people who come there for different purposes. In the morning, Golestan is visited mainly by elderly and aged people, who primarily come for shopping. Then the place closes for a siesta between 2 and 5 P.M. In the late afternoon, Golestan is full of young people strolling back and forth. They gather in the yard and spend several hours there till Golestan is closed at 10.30 or 11 P.M.

Choosing to go to the *passazh* or the bazaar is decided by generation-defined taste. Middle-class youth do not go the bazaar for purchasing. None of the Shahraki young people I know have ever been in the bazaar. Even the south Tehrani youths I met prefer to purchase clothes in the *passazh*. Simon and Robert work in the bazaar but come to Golestan to have fun. Shopping at Golestan offers a symbolic value. Elli—perhaps a little enviously—said of her friend: "Leila always shops in the Golestan. She knows that she can buy same jeans or whatever it is much cheaper in ordinary shops on the street. But shopping at Golestan gives status. I think it's stupid. Leila pays twice the price just to boast that she shops at Golestan." Thus shopping is about more than just purchasing a commodity. It is also a matter of pleasure, class, and status.

PERFORMING MODERNITY

Golestan attracts young people from all over Tehran. The majority are daily visitors, "mall-rats" (Kowinski 1985). Some of the them talk about "mall-addiction." The standard answer to my questions about their motives for, and expectations of, their daily visits to Golestan, was "There is nothing to do here in Tehran. There is no entertainment [*tafrih nist*]. We come here to kill the time" or "we come here for loitering [*allafi*]." *Allafi* is the "art of doing nothing." It refers to hanging around, spontaneously deciding what to do next, and accumulating companions as one goes along.[14]

Allafi is regarded by the establishment as meaningless and harmful for young people. The Mani School is a prestigious boys' school a block behind the Golestan shopping center. The principal of the high school, Mr. Modir, was worried about Golestan. His main trouble was

the girls who stroll around inside and outside Golestan and try to mislead boys. Our school has a good reputation for discipline and strict control. We have imposed a green uniform for our students, so that we can have better control over them. If our boys go to Golestan during or after school time, they are easily recognized by their uniform. If they go there wearing the uniform, they will be disciplined and it definitely affects their grades.

Compared with other parts of Tehran, the "moral police" in Golestan showed more "tolerance." This "relative freedom" (*azadiye nesbi*), as my informants from Javadieh and Nazi Abad called it, is in itself one attraction of Golestan. Another attraction of Golestan is being able to obtain illicit cultural products as well as the latest information about what is going on in the pop culture. X shop sells permitted (*mojaz*) films and music, but many young people go to this shop to buy illicit ones "under the counter." Regular clients come in and ask "what recent film or music are there?" According to the owner, Western and Los Angeles-produced Iranian pop music sells best. Pirated copies of the most recent films, sometimes still on screen in Europe or the U.S., are sold.

Golestan as a Sexualized Space

In a city dominated by gender-segregated public spaces, for many Tehrani youths *passazhs* are the only spaces where they have an opportunity to "present themselves" (Goffman 1959) to the other sex. For these young people, shopping is not a backstage activity undertaken in order to prepare for a performance on the stage. Rather it is itself a front-stage act. They dress up and go to *passazhs* to be seen. The other side of loitering in the *passazhs* is watching and being flâneur, a "secret spectator of the spectacle of the spaces and places of the city" (Tester 1994: 7):

flânerie can be understood as the activity of the sovereign spectator going about the city in order to find the things which will occupy his gaze and thus complete his [or her] otherwise incomplete identity, satisfy his [or her] otherwise dissatisfied existence; replace the sense of bereavement with a sense of life. (7)

The gaze of the young flâneurs in Golestan is often erotic. They look for the opposite sex to complete their incomplete selves in a society which is trying to banish young romance. Golestan is indeed a scene for performing what the Islamic state defines as "cultural crimes."

In Golestan, the body movements, gazes, and short verbal comments of boys about girls and vice versa create a sexually loaded atmosphere. Young men come to Golestan for *dokhtar bazi* (flirting with girls) and young girls for *pesar bazi* (flirting with boys). Through the corridors, in the courtyard, in the queue to a public phone, or just standing in front of a shop window, girls and boys flirt with each other. Girls are often subjected to *matallak*, erotic verbal taunt. The "moral police" attempt to separate the sexes, but are rarely successful. Tehrani boys are experts at whispering their phone numbers in a few seconds as they pass by girls, who in turn are skilled in memorizing the numbers. Such interaction takes place under the disguise of doing something else. Boys and girls do not look at each other and "do not talk" to each other. In Golestan I accompanied Simon practicing such a spy-film-like exchange of telephone numbers. I asked him why it did not work in other places but only in the *passazhs*. He answered: "There are many escape routes [*dar-rou*]. Here you can pretend that you are looking at the shop windows. If I pass by the same girl more than twice in a park or on the street, everybody would know what was going on. Here we just go back and forth and pretend to be looking at shops."

In the bazaar, the Islamic order is taken as given. The hegemonic Islamic morality in the bazaar asserts and expects virtuous behavior and dress. An Iranian sociologist told me that the serious atmosphere of the bazaar imposes its morality on its visitors. In Golestan this is the task of the moral police and the *basijis*. Every fifteen minutes a warning is announced by loudspeakers in the mall: "Respected Sisters, observe Islamic veiling" (*khaharan-e mohtaram, hejab-e eslami ra reayat konid*). In restaurants and cafeterias signs announce: "We cannot serve improperly veiled women." Café owners are ordered to post this warning.

Despite the illegality of prostitution and the harsh punishment it might bring, Iranzamin Street in front of Golestan has the reputation of being a red light street. Moreover, runaway girls from the provinces and from southern Tehran hang around in Golestan, offering their bodies for sale. The erotic ambiance in Golestan is also promoted by reproducing heterosexual desire. This is done through the commercialization of sexuality as a form of spectacle for consumption (Öncü 2002). Paradoxically, while women should be totally veiled in public and no parts of the female body should be visible to men, all kinds of exhibitionist women's clothes are displayed on mannequins in the shop windows. This makes shopping a sexual event. The coincidence of shopping and male leisure-seeking makes Golestan a masculine playground.

Carnivalesque Golestan

Sometimes after dark young men go behind the wall of Golestan or to the nearby park to dance. Often there is a kind of dance competition between rival gangs from different parts of Tehran. They come to Golestan to perform the latest dance fashions and thereby to "shame out the rivals" (*ro kam koni*). The dance competitions I witnessed were techno-dance. All such activities were, of course, "cultural crimes" and could result in physical punishment. Conventional crimes also take place around the mall. Fadak Park, 150 meters from Golestan, is a hang-out (*fatouq*) for drug dealers. Young people call the park Fandak (the lighter). All kinds of drugs can be obtained, but the young people are usually after hashish, *bang* or *cigarri* as it called. Marijuana is also available but very expensive. To smoke marijuana or hashish is a class question, but also a question of "global" and "local." Hashish has been in Iran for centuries. The word is Persian and is associated with the medieval Hashashin movement. Marijuana is an emblem of Western youth styles. Many Shahraki youth say that they prefer marijuana because "it is classy [*klass dareh*]."

Every weekend evening the corner of Mahestan and Iranzamin Streets in front of Golestan turns into a battle scene between youths and *basiji* policemen. I used to sit on the stairs of the Iranzamin *passazh* (opposite Golestan), where I had a good view. Innumerable cars full of youngsters from Shahrak-e Gharb and other parts of Tehran drive back and forth. In the early evening the police set up barricades on both sides of Mahestan and Iranzamin Streets to control the situation. Policemen armed with machine guns stop cars, especially modern luxury ones. They ask for licenses and registration cards. If there are girls and boys in a car, the driver and passengers are checked out one by one: Who are they and what kind of relationship do they have? If they cannot prove that they are siblings or a married couple, they are in trouble. Playing illicit music in the car, labeled "sound pollution" (*aloudegi-e souti*), also means trouble. Long lines of cars waiting to be checked cause traffic chaos. Usually the police only warn and threaten the youngsters and tell them to leave Shahrak-e Gharb. Many, however, are arrested accused of various "cultural crimes." Young men who have gotten into trouble run after the police officers and ask for indulgence. Despite all the problems, it seems that the youths enjoy it. From time to time illegal music is played loudly to irritate the policemen. Many young people stand along the street and watch the scene with enjoyment. Golestan has traits of what Bakhtin (1984) has called "the carnivalesque." It offers these youths a celebration of chaos, disorder, and anarchy, the inversion of social norms and codes, a pause from the seriousness of everyday life.

Ethnographic Sketches

I

One late afternoon, I was with Simon and his friends. We were sitting on a stone bench in the courtyard of Golestan. One of the boys, who was wearing a baseball cap with a NY logo, exclaimed: "Look they are coming." I turned my head and saw two *basijis* approaching. They stopped in front of us. One of them had a couple of days beard and was wearing a white shirt hanging over military trousers. He took off the young man's cap and asked: "Why are you wearing this?" The young man was furious but did not answer at first. Finally he said, "I had no intention of doing anything. I was just wearing it. It is old and ragged."

The *basiji*, half grinning, said, "If it is ragged you don't need it" and tore into in two pieces. He dropped the torn cap at the boy's feet and went away.

II

I was drinking coffee with a friend in Rang Café. Two young girls came in and sat at a table close to ours. They spoke in Persian and Armenian. After a while one took a piece of paper from her bag and began to read it to the other girl. It seemed to be a letter in Persian. Suddenly I noticed that two young *basijis* were standing at the door staring at the girls. They approached them. One of them tore the paper violently out of the girl's hand. He probably thought it was a love letter and wanted to stop the girl's "cultural crime." He read through the letter, which apparently was not what the *basijis* had thought. He tossed the letter on the table, insulted her, ordered her to hide a little strand of hair hanging from her forehead under the veil, and went out.

III

I came out from Golestan into Iranzamin Street. I was about to jump into a taxi, when I noticed a crowd near the gate of Golestan that opens into Mahestan Street. I went to the gathering. It was only young men collected around a *basiji* on a Honda motorcycle. He was a young man dressed typically like a *basiji*, in a white shirt hanging over military khaki trousers, and a pair of sports shoes. He was talking into his mobile. When I asked a nearby man what was going on, he pointed at a young man, barely twenty-five, sitting on the ground with bowed head. He was bleeding at the nose. The young man was wearing a T-shirt with a logo of the American flag. I found out that he had been stopped by the patrolling moral police. When he made some gestures of resistance he was beaten up and thrown out of Golestan. The policeman was waiting for a car to take the young man to the police station. The young man was humiliated in public, and would apparently have the T-shirt torn to pieces later at in the police station.

*   *   *

The Golestan phenomenon is seen as an incident of social disorder, which is perhaps the main reason for its attracting both the love of Tehrani youths and the hatred of the moral police.

To my question as to why the circumstances around Golestan were so charged, the *basiji* Bahman replied:

Golestan is a special case. Everybody wants to make a big deal of this place. Foreign journalists come here to show that our young people have lost the revolutionary conviction. One month ago a policeman was badly beaten up here. The
same night the BBC broadcast a radio program about the "anti-state atmosphere" in Golestan.

Apart from the ordinary guards of Golestan, who are all middle-aged
men in gray uniforms, there is a team of four young moral policemen
in civilian clothes whose duty it is to ensure that Islamic morality is not
violated. These men are very unpopular among the young people in
Golestan. I rarely saw them during the daytime. They would appear in
late afternoon and at nightfall, when Golestan was crowded with young
people. They patrolled both inside and in the yards. Every night I witnessed the way they strolled from one corner of the courtyard to another and moralized, threatened, warned, and terrorized young
people.
Mr. Afshas said:

These youngsters are disturbers [*mozahem*]. They do not come here to buy
things, but to make trouble for us and other visitors. They come from southern
Tehran. We cannot stop them. They disturb our business. In addition, the presence of these youngsters has made the authorities hostile towards us. Golestan
is victimized. You see, when the conservatives want to attack Khatami's policy,
they use Golestan as an excuse. They come here and take films. Then they manipulate the film to show the Golestan shopping center as a center for anti-
Revolutionary youngsters. We are tired of this situation. We shall send our
complaint to the Leader's office. We are a commercial locality, what sin
[*gonnah*] have we committed?

In short, Mr. Afshas believes that the Islamic government "needs"
Golestan to demonstrate its power. The authorities need a place like
Golestan in order to *discover* what they themselves have created, namely
cultural crimes.

Javad Is Not Modern

Whether one is labeled *javad* or not is mainly concerned with how one
consumes. From being part of a terminology that refers to urban life
and class, the meaning of *javad* has become incorporated into a way of
talking about consumption. One night in Golestan I asked Dara and his
girlfriend Nahid to show me those they regarded as *javad*.
Nahid: "You can recognize them by their style, by their clothes. They
talk loudly, walk in a specific way, and drive Peykan" (an Iran-made car).
Dara nodded toward a young man walking in front of us: "Look at
him. You can see that it is the first time he is wearing jeans. His shirt

does not fit him. *Javad* means somebody who has rural style [*tip-e de-hati*]. *Javad* people are also criminal [*khalaf*]."

Nahid added: "The boys who are behind are *javad*."

I asked: "Behind in what?"

Nahid: "Behind in behavior, clothes, appearance. They have another character [*shakhsiyat*]"

Dara: "*Javad* people dress tastelessly. They are often uneducated and come from the provinces [*shahrestan*]. *Javad* might also refer to new-rich people. They have money and consume expensive goods. Yet it is obvious that they are *javad*. They have a *bazari* style and *bazari* culture. You know, for instance, the color combination, the designs, they just don't fit. They just are a disaster! Besides, the behavior of *javad* people, how they walk and how they talk expresses their *javad* style. They don't know how to shop. They imitate us. Nowadays Shahrak-e Gharb is in vogue. They come here and copy Shahraki style to gain higher status."

Campbell (1987), in the footsteps of Max Weber, has shown how the development of modern consumption was dialectically related to the emergence of Romantic art and literature. He explores how the connection between romantic love in literature, art, music, and popular culture in eighteenth-century England and modern patterns of consumption. His argument is based on a distinction between "traditional" and "modern" hedonism. He argues that modern hedonism is self-illusory: "individuals employ their imaginative and creative powers to construct mental images which they consume for the intrinsic pleasure they provide, a practice best described as day-dreaming or fantasizing" (Campbell 1987: 77). While traditional hedonism tries to control objects in order to gain pleasure from them, modern hedonism finds pleasure in control over the meanings of things. Control is achieved through the power of the imagination. The importance of imagination is revealed by the significant role of the representation of products rather than the products themselves (92).

One contemporary mode of consumption is "window shopping," going around the mall, looking at commodities but not purchasing because of lack of money or intention. Maybe that is why shopping malls have been associated with the "democratization of luxury" (Williams 1982). Most of the young people from south Tehran cannot afford even a cup of coffee in Rang Café, let alone anything else. However, they visit Golestan every day, stroll around, look at commodities, imagine, and talk about consumption. As Miller (1997a) has described for his Trinidadian "limers" in malls, shopping often becomes an extension of verbal banter. As one of my informants said once, "talking about pleasure is the half of it" (*vasvol eysh, nesvol eysh*). It is perhaps the pleasure of the imagined possession. It might be a way for these youth to show their control over the meanings of things they cannot afford. This aspect of consumption, the appropriation of meanings and significances, is the main activity I have seen among young people in Golestan. The *passazh* is a place for communication as much as for purchasing things. Young people in Golestan acquire knowledge about what is "in" now. They in fact acquire "subcultural capital," objectified in particular "trendy" manners, in knowledge about the meanings of things, and in being "in the know" (Thornton 1995).

This power over the meanings of things gives authority to distinguish between who is "modern" and who is *javad*. To be *javad* actually not a matter of possession of objects but a matter of knowledge about them. Thus even wealthy people can be classified as *javad*. My Shahraki youth were agitated about the "new rich *bazari* people" who have moved to Shahrak-e Gharb. These "new rich" people with "*bazari* taste" live in luxury houses and drive foreign cars. They have all the means of a "modern" lifestyle. Yet they still lack power over the meanings of these means. Countless times I heard my Shahraki young people make jokes about the ignorance shown by these "new rich" people over the meanings of the objects they possessed. One afternoon I was with five young Shahraki men in Rang Café and we were talking about such people.

Tina: "A new family moved into the apartment next to us, some months ago. After a while they invited us for dinner. I saw myself how they used the fireplace in the sitting room for a barbecue."

Taraneh: "Foolish people. They serve beer on ice."

Tina: "Our neighbors have the latest equipment in their kitchen but they can't distinguish Michel Stroganof [a popular meal among the middle class] from *Michel Strogoff* [a novel by Jules Verne]."

Ramin: "What a waste of money. Look what type of people can afford these things."

Nima: "Many have jacuzzis and saunas in their luxury houses but they have no idea what they are for. These new rich *bazaris* live in modern apartments but know nothing about *farhang-e aparteman neshni* [the culture of living in an apartment]."

Anni is a Shahraki girl in her early twenties whose real name is Ammenh (an Arabic name)—also the name of the Prophet Muhammad's mother. Anni does not like her name and introduces herself as Anni: "It sounds more modern." I had heard from her friends that she had refused a rich man who had proposed to her "because he had taken off his shoes at the doorway when he came for the proposal ceremony." I asked Anni if this was true. She said: "Our apartment has parquet floors. Any idiot knows that people do not take off their shoes where there is parquet. It was *javad*-esque. Who cares if he was rich? When he does not grasp such simple things, he cannot do anything good with his money."

Knowledge about the meanings of things brings status and the power to present yourself as modern, whether you are rich or poor. It covers knowledge of a broad range of fields, from the BMW Z8 model, to the original name of recent films and personal information about Ricky Martin, to the meanings of foreign words such as "lesbian," to name but a few instances.

Once Farhad asked me about a performer in the Eminem. I did not know him and acknowledged that I was rather ignorant about this kind of music. Farhad gave me a lecture on the pop group and asked other questions I could not answer either. Disappointed, he said: "What then do you do over there, in *kharej*?" Everyone laughed. In that sort of situation they enjoyed their control over the subject. I had no access to, or control over, the meanings of modern music. They did have, and used it to tease me and make me *javad*. It was not the last time I became *javad*. In conversations about cars, mobile phones, Hollywood, or Irangelesi culture, I was the most *javad* in the group.

One late afternoon Dara and I went to Café Shooka to meet Bahar, one of his friends. Café Shooka, in a corner of the Gandhi shopping center on Gandhi Street, is a "cool joint" for Tehrani café-goers. Opened by a writer in the early 1980s, Café Shooka seems very plain among all the glittering coffeeshops in the Gandhi shopping center, but it is a hang-out (*patouq*) for young writers, journalists, and artists. In Dara's words, "it is a meeting place for intellectuals like Parisian cafés." Bahar is a young girl working as a freelance journalist for film journals. She is a regular visitor of the café and usually writes her essays there. Her favorite theme is postwar Hollywood cinema. Since she had come of age only in the late 1990s, her proficiency on American movies surprised me. Bahar can talk for hours about Billy Wilder, Elia Kazan, or David Lynch. But that afternoon we talked mainly about Café Shooka and its customers:

Here in Shooka, intellectualism is about performance [*namayesh*]. To be counted here hinges on being aware of what is "in." For instance, the time of Pink Floyd and the Beatles has passed. Now in Shooka it is the time of The Doors and Nirvana. It is just the same with the cinema, nobody listens to you if you talk about Bergman or Tarkovsky. They were on top until last year. Nowadays there is a crush on Jim Jarmush and Wim Wenders.

To be and perform "modern" is about access. Only a small number of young people enjoy first-hand access to the West, through the media or personal relationships with Iranian expatriates. For instance, Bahar's brother in London regularly sends her *Film Comment* and *Sight & Sound* magazines.

Knowledge about the latest fashions and the "correct way" to consume is spread through personal networks. Thus to know the "right" people is crucial in order to enter the category of "cool" Tehranis. It is about having a kind of "subcultural capital" and the right "attitude," recognized as modern, and about distinguishing oneself from traditionally minded individuals.

Golestan, besides being a site for consumption, is also a stage where individuals present themselves as "modern" both for an audience and for themselves. Even if the majority of the young people in Golestan cannot afford the costly imported commodities in the shops, they can consume the "concept" Golestan represents, being middle-class global citizens. The hegemonic ideology in Iran promotes a revolutionary/ascetic aesthetic of modesty and invites self-abasement. That there exists such a place as Golestan, where individuals can assert themselves and show themselves off according to quite another system of values is a challenge for the "aesthetics of modesty" promoted by the Islamic regime. For the Tehrani youths at Golestan, flânerie is not only a way of leisure. It is also a struggle for subjectivity. It is a challenge that "constantly transforms places into spaces or spaces into place" (de Certeau 1984: 118). Golestan is also a site of pleasure and agency. Where there is consumption, there is pleasure, and where there is pleasure there is agency (Appadurai 1996: 7). However, we can also approach the field from a class perspective. The rich, modern space of Golestan offers a sense of belonging to the upper class. The performances by south Tehrani youngsters are perhaps an attempt to dissociate themselves from their poor working-class neighborhood. They come to Golestan to imagine being part of a "better" life than their own. Golestan represents a dream of economic and cultural capital.

Walter Benjamin believed that there was a revolutionary power in mass culture as it was presented in the Paris arcades. The power he meant is perhaps the power Appadurai sees in "imagination" (1996). Benjamin saw the arcades as a site where the mass culture materializes in a collective energy, by which the "antiquarian effect of the father on his son" could be overcome. Such a generation break is also an aspect of what is happening at Golestan. The young Iranian *allaf*s at Golestan are seen by the authorities as juveniles who imperil not only Islamic values and norms but also their parents' world. The mass culture represented at Golestan is considered to be a "cultural invasion." The Golestan shopping center is a window on the West, a scene for performing/consuming/learning "modern being." It functions as a center of information, vision, and imagination for young people. It is also a site where the knowledge of "how to be modern" is communicated. As I have shown, people in Golestan want to demonstrate that they are modern by dissociating themselves from "tradition" as it is embodied in the *javad* and *bazari*. The stereotypes of *bazari* and *javad* are produced by the discourse of modernization. These "local" and "traditional" types are forged by the "globalized" modern Shahrakis.

Chapter 5
The Third Generation

On the eve of the Revolution we were called the dispossessed, then after the war and under the "Construction era" [doran-e sazandegi] we were renamed a "vulnerable group" [ghesh-re asib pazir]. Now they call us riff-raff and vulgar [arazel o obash] and assault us.

—*Simon*

We never forgive our parents for the disaster they call revolution.

—*Reza*

The Third Generation

Iran has a bomb. No, no. Not that bomb. This bomb is hiding in plain sight— in high schools, universities, and coffee houses. It is a bomb that is ticking away under Iranian society. . . . It's called here the Third Generation.

With these initial remarks *New York Times* journalist Thomas Friedman began his article in June 2002.[1] The article, which resulted in Friedman being barred from Iran, was about the increasing conflict between the state and the young generation. The article was translated into Persian and reprinted in whole or in part in some Iranian dailies. Although "the Third Generation" had been used as a term in public debate since late 2001, it became a celebrated motto thanks to Friedman's article. The term has quickly become recognized inside Iran. A large number of youth websites and magazines appeared, introducing themselves as "by the third generation for the third generation," such as Chelcher-agh, Golestan-e Iran, or the website of www.nasle3.com, to name but a few.

The website nasle3 (the third generation) is used as a forum for political and social debates about the situation of contemporary youth. One of its sections is "What the Third Generation Says" (*nasl-e sevoum che migoyad*), where letters, poems, and features are published. The following lines are from one of them:

Third Generation, a Confused Generation

I label the third generation a confused generation [*nasl-e motahayer*]. A generation who were newborn at the Revolution and today are the youth of this country. They became reluctantly involved in the Revolution. They had neither
information on events nor power to affect them. After the Revolution this generation suffered from the war, bombardment, sacrifice, martyrdom. This generation is puzzled. This generation has experienced social restrictions in
childhood, in schools, and at universities. They have constantly been criticized.
They revolt. They question and require answers. I am one of the third generation. I do not know what I ought to do to take my rights. Struggle against or sub-
mit to circumstances? And what shall I do with the next generation? Where is
this generation going?[2]

There is a general idea among people that the young generation's
confusion is in large part the consequence of being split between two
oppositional social roles, one indoor and the other outdoor. The Third
Generation has grown up in a dual society with dual norms and values.

Public and Private Selves

The most conspicuous aspect of social life in post-revolutionary Iran is
certainly its cultural duality between life in private and in public. The
spatial division between the "veiled" private and the "unveiled" public
(explored in Chapter 2) offers space for performing an illicit lifestyle.
In private spaces the hegemony of the Islamic social order disappears.
Thus, how selves are presented differs radically between indoors and
outdoors. A female university professor, for instance, who appears
wrapped in a black *chador* at work, joins a family party in a sexy décol-
leté dress at night. The most illustrative scene of such adaptation of self-
representation can be found on international flights arriving at Tehran
airport. Half an hour before landing, female passengers, usually unveiled and covered with make-up, line up for the lavatory. When they
come out they are veiled and the make-up has become much paler. By
contrast, as soon as the "fasten your seat belt" sign switches off on flights
leaving Iran, veiled women line up for the lavatory to come out in much
lighter clothing and with different hairstyles.

The majority of Iranians have led double lives since the Revolution.
One life indoors, in a pre-Revolutionary atmosphere, and one life outdoors in accordance with the Islamic social order. For more than two
decades, Iranians have lived with two different, and sometimes opposite, norms and cultures: one official "front stage" and one outlaw "back
stage" (Goffman 1959). Everybody knows the rules of the game. They
know where and when they should switch from one to the other. The
youth of today have grown up in this between-ness. They have received
harsh Islamic tuition from school, the authorities, the mass media, and

the moral police, but a totally different education in the domestic sphere. Parents too teach their children the dichotomy between indoor and outdoor cultures, their different roles, and how to keep the distance between them. In the parents' view, this dichotomy makes the young people "confused." The parents believe that children are *dou shakhsiati*, have dual characters. As Dara put it: "the whole nation is involved in a theater without an audience." His use of the word "theater" struck me. It evoked the classic description of life in Eastern Europe by Czeslaw Milosz (1990).[3]

Shaheen, Dara's elder brother, complains that the failure in his life is that he never followed the "rules of the game":

Sirous and Ali were my classmates in my last year in high school. While Ali and I systematically neglected the rules and codes imposed by the high school authorities, Sirous followed the rules. We two consciously risked being excluded from university and an academic career. Sirous created a hell for himself, split between two ways of life. He adopted a new way of dressing in the high school and started babbling revolutionary jargon. He attended the school's daily assemblies and rallies and listened to revolutionary addresses. Outside school he was the same guy as us. We attended illegal parties, listened to music, and watched movies frowned on by the authorities. Ironically he was the pioneer for punk-style in our group. Not unexpectedly, Ali and I got no chance of an academic education, while Sirous received the fruit he had suffered for. He is now a successful dentist in town. I made a mistake. I destroyed my life. Now, I tell Dara, you have to know what you can do where and vice versa. Otherwise, there is no future for you here. It is simple. Before the Revolution, we prayed at home and drank liquor outdoors. Now we pray outdoors and drink at home.

The Third Generation, however, shows less tolerance towards the duality between indoor and outdoor lifestyles. Young people complain that their parents are forced to be "dishonest" (*dou rang*, two-colored). They say and do something in private and the opposite in public. The young assert that their parents do not dare to face up to problems and instead try to ignore them. Dara complains:

They [the parental generation] are scared to be themselves. To be different. They still believe "If you don't want to be disgraced you have to be like the masses" [*khahi nashavi rousva hamrang-e jamm'at shou*, a well-known Persian expression].

A survey conducted by the Ministry of Culture and Islamic Guidance among 700 Tehrani youngsters between fifteen and twenty-five years of age in 1996 indicates that 95 percent of them believe that "hypocrisy," "deceitfulness," and "falsehood" dominate Iranian society (quoted in Shirali 2001: 146). Having to follow different lifestyles in private and in public has caused "confusion" in the youths' sense of self and identity.

The dichotomization of lifestyle into indoor and outdoor involves more than just playing different roles in different circumstances and has formed a new ethos among young Iranians.

A Bad Generation

As elaborated on before, Islam views the time of youth (*javani*) as a divine gift. It is a time of opportunities, of health, and of endowment. However, it is also a dangerous period of one's life, when one is most vulnerable and exposed to immorality and vice. Like women, young people are seen to be more oriented toward passion (*nafs*) than toward intellect (*aql*), caught in the "storm of instincts."[4] Young people are exposed to "toxins of adolescence" (*afat-e dore-ye javani*). The theocracy sees the "vulnerable youths" as the foremost target of the "cultural invasion" and as an instrument in the hands of counter-revolutionaries. As a young woman writes on the "Third Generation" website: "Adolescence today means crime. A young person is seen as a criminal. When the mass media talk about social corruption [*mafased-e ejtem'ai*] illustrations of young people appear. Accordingly, the majority of our population are criminals."[5] In the view of the authorities, youths are taken to be law-breakers unless the reverse is proved.

Since backstage culture is officially stigmatized as "cultural crime," a large part of young people's everyday life becomes unlawful. Attorney Kambiz Nourozi believes that "the majority of Iranian youth are in a mental state of considering themselves as 'criminal.' Consequently, notions like 'illegality' and 'criminal behavior' do not carry the same meaning for Iranian youngsters as they might do elsewhere."[6] Iranian youths are branded as law-breakers in their trivial everyday life. A large part of their daily practices are classified as unlawful: wearing a T-shirt or a shirt of a color inappropriate for the occasion (e.g., a red one during Moharram), eating ice-cream on the street during Ramadan, playing illicit music in the car, showing more hair or skin than is allowed, or just being in the wrong place at the wrong time (e.g., in front of a girls' high school at 4 P.M. when the girls stream out).[7] I heard frequently from parents that, since the youths are ascribed this social role, they just play it. Recognized as law-breakers, the young generation are deviants and see heroism in their illicitness.

ETHNOGRAPHIC VIGNETTE

Please, whip me. Khosrow, a guy in our neighborhood, was whipped in the square for flirting. Now he walks differently, not because he is injured, but because he walks proudly. Everybody says hello to him. Low-ranking Khosrow

[Khosrow *khaki*] today is called Mr. Khosrow [*agha* Khosrow]. Elders in our quarter take him seriously. He is invited to take tea or juice when he passes shops in the neighborhood. Girls look at him admiringly. I am jealous. Please whip me too.[8]

*   *   *

Proud of their "cultural criminality," today's generation is perhaps the most rebellious generation in the modern history of Iran. They are believed to show disrespect for social and ethical norms, particularly sexual ones (*nasl-e biband o bar*). Having grown up with Islamic mass media and been educated in Islamic schools, they criticize and reject not only political Islam but also Islamic traditions in general, which were unquestionable for their parents' generation. In the summer of 2000, Mohammad Ali Zam, head of Tehran's cultural and artistic affairs, published a report that publicly acknowledged the growth of areligiosity among the young people. According to the report, 75 percent of the total population and 86 percent of the students do not practice Islam.[9] The "epidemic of abandoning faith [*din-gorizi*]" has caused anxiety among representatives of the clergy, such as Ayatollah Montazeri, Ayatollah Taheri, and Mohsen Kadivar. I was frequently told in Iran that even those who used to say their daily prayers (*namaz*) before the Revolution have now stopped doing it. A sociological survey (Abdi and Goudarzi 1378/1999) on "public culture" (*farhang-e 'omoumi*) shows that "religious activities" have decreased in the country, if measured in terms of variables such as paying religious taxes, making pilgrimages, visiting mosques, and attending religious rituals such as *rowze-khani* and *d'oua-ye komeil*. Young and highly educated people show lower rates of religious activity than other categories (44–48). Another survey conducted among students at Tehran University in 1995 indicates a trend of depoliticization and a tendency toward areligiosity. This survey indicates that more than 81 percent of the students believe that young people have a low inclination toward religion. A nationwide survey of more than 15,000 young persons in 2004 shows similar results; 46 percent of them never or rarely go to mosque.[10] In reply to a question on behavioral models for students, about 61 percent referred to Western artists; only 17 percent cited the country's officials as their personal behavioral model.[11]

Moreover, in contrast to the "First Generation," which launched an anti-Western Revolution, a conspicuous feature of the "Third Generation" is their curiosity about the West in general and the U.S. in particular. In Abdi's and Goudarzi's survey, the inclination to the West is shown to have increased dramatically among high-school students during the 1990s (1378/1999: 118–23). More than half the interviewees believe that young people choose their models (*oulgo*) from among Western artists; 75 percent declared that youths are admirers of Western music (122). According to an opinion poll carried out by the National Society of Public Opinion Studies (Moasese-ye Meli-e Pazhohesh-e Afkar-e 'Omoumi) in late September 2002, 74.4 percent of Iranians favor a dialogue with the United States. The society was ordered to be closed by the judiciary, which is dominated by conservative forces, and legal proceedings were launched against the news agencies that published the results of the poll.[12] After the suicide attack on the World Trade Center in New York on September 11, 2001, several hundred young people spontaneously gathered at Mohseni Square in north Tehran. With candles in their hands they demonstrated their sympathy for the American people.

Once I asked Dara for the reason for such a fascination with the U.S. He answered: "It is because the mullahs shout all the time about how awful America is. A thing which is awful in their eyes must be a wonderful thing." Antagonism to the Islamic regime projects an idyllic image onto a country that their parental generation identified as the Great Satan (*sheytan-e bozorg*). The editor of the influential political monthly *Gozaresh* wrote in the June 2002 issue that the younger generation in Iran is the most Americanized generation in the whole region. The systematic anti-American propaganda, particularly by IRIB, over the past two decades has backfired and converted Iranian youngsters into America fans.[13] As I mentioned earlier, to forbid is to create desire. Nevertheless this pattern was changed in 2007 by more hostile American policies toward Iran and the threat of a military attack. Appealing to young Iranians' nationalism and their pride over Iran's nuclear program, according to many political analysts, President Ahmadinejad could weaken U.S. popularity among young Iranians.

New York-based Iranian scholar Hamid Dabashi (2000) asserts that a feature of the young generation is its post-ideological character. In its social movements, such as the student uprising in July 1999, this generation has refused to be associated with any ideology. The ideological preparations which started in the 1960s and resulted in the 1979 Revolution, and in the hegemony of the Islamic ideology during the following two decades, have been counterproductive. Dabashi announces the "death of ideology" in post-Revolutionary Iran (see also Basmenji 2005: 26). In his view, the character of the youth movement makes not only Islamic ideology but any form of ideological metanarrative irrelevant. The material force of the young people's defiance exceeds and post-dates the necessity of any ideological conviction.

Thus, in the discourse of the authorities, the *bidard* Third Generation is also called *biarman* (without ideology). Such an absence of commitment to any ideology is, in the view of many Iranians, a warning sign. Hiva, Dara's mother, is among those who worry:

> This abandoned generation believes in nothing. They have no specific aim [*hadaf-e moshakhas*]. No political appeal, only social ones. They voted for Khatami because he had promised them a more liberal policy with regard to the veil and less pressure on young people. They will vote for anyone who gives them more social freedom [*azadi-ye ejtemma'i*]. If this regime tomorrow liberalizes the relationship between girls and boys, all will become quiet. So this is just a play. The clergy feel the nation's pulse [*nabz-e melat ra daran*]. When they see that young people's frustration is increasing, they liberalize this or that.

Youths seek more individual autonomy rather than political freedom. Dara agrees with his mother: "My generation has no political aspirations [*khaste-haye siasi*]. The only thing they worry about is <u>social freedom</u>."

Since, in today's Iranian society, no single feature of life is apolitical, there is also no "social appeal" which is apolitical in Iran. However, to separate social issues from political ones is a tactic of survival under a repressive regime (I come back to this later). At the same time, what the Third Generation is seeking is vital cultural changes and not simply political ones. Their demand for "individual autonomy" (*azadiha-ye fardi*) goes far beyond the political domain, into the cultural one. Their demand will change the Iranian culture more than any political reform.

Moral Panics

Since the end of the 1990s, the threat of the deviant behavior of young people expressed through moral panics has become a major issue in public debates. According to Stanley Cohen, moral panic occurs when a "condition, episode, person or group of persons emerges to become defined as a threat to societal values and interest; its nature is presented in a stylized and stereotypical fashion by the mass media and politicians" (Cohen 1972: 9). Many social critics warn that a "social collapse" (*fouroupashi-ye ejtemma'i*) is in the making. Dailies and journals publish one alarming report after another on the "ethical collapse" (*fouroupashi-ye akhlaqi*) and "ethical crisis" (*bouhran-e akhlaqi*) among young people. Their distrust of the institution of the family, and their rejection of social norms and roles, are seen as pushing society toward a "social catastrophe" (*fajye-e ejtema'i*).

Caught between parental tutelage and governmental discipline, young people seize any opportunity for self-gratification. Parents complain that, due to lack of entertainment (*tafrih*), unemployment, and an uncertain future, depression is high among the youth, who tend toward delinquency. *Khane khali* (empty house) is a concept among Iranian youth. "Empty house" is an opportunity (for instance, when parents are traveling) to do what is unacceptable to parents and "public chastity." It could be having an "innocent" date, taking drugs, watching pornographic films, or buying sex from a prostitute.

For girls, escaping the boundaries of traditional morality is considerably more complicated than for their brothers. They are caught between the "protective" patriarchal family and a society "hostile to women" (*zansetiz*). This caused a drastic increase in runaway girls during the late 1990s. Taking the risk of rape, delinquency, or perversion, many girls, or, as they are called in Tehran, *karton khab* (sleeping in cartons, homeless), prefer a relatively autonomous life in the streets to a "safe" life under an authoritarian patriarch.[14] The break between the "Third Generation" and their parental generation widens more and more. This generational break is well illustrated in the new cinematic vogue.

Cinematic Representation of Youth

People ask me, is Iran the kind of place where two 12-year-old girls couldn't come out and see the world? Or is it a place where a girl who is 18 could make a film about them?

Samira Makhmalbaf, an internationally celebrated film-maker and one of the Third Generation, spoke these words in an interview in *Newsweek* (October 26, 1998) when she attended the New York film festival. Her answer to the question was "Iran is a place for both of them." She was eighteen when she shot her first feature film, *The Apple* (1998). The film has been praised as the manifesto of the generation to which she belongs. Based on a true story, *The Apple* is about two girls, ages eleven and twelve, who have been imprisoned by their father since their birth. The despotic father attempts to "protect" his beloved daughters from the "outside world." For Makhmalbaf, this is the story of the whole nation—a story of the "protective" parental tyranny exercised over the younger generation (see Dabashi 2001: 262–71).

Contemporary cinema in Iran is more than entertainment. It has been an issue at stake in political life since the Revolution (Devictor 2002: 73). In the absence of press freedom, the cinema has been used as an arena for speaking out about political and social issues which otherwise would been neglected. Film critic Hoshang Golmakani believes that the difference between the cinema and the press in Iran is one of timing. While the press responds instantly, for the cinema it takes some time to do so.[15] Another prominent film critic, Noushabeh Amiri, sees a "major difference between the social function of the cinema in Iran and its function in Western countries. . . . In Iran its function in many cases is to provide social and political commentary, due to the lack of traditional political parties."[16] In contrast to IRIB, Iranian cinema is, in many ways, the mirror of social changes in the society. Since social liberalization was achieved through the election of President Mohammad Khatami on May 23, 1997, a new film genre has emerged, called "Cinema of 23 May" (*sinema-ye dovoum-e khordadi*). This new genre has dominated the Iranian cinema since then and deals with "issues of youth" (*masa'el-e javannan*). It aims to shed light on taboo subjects, such as love, teenage crisis, generational conflicts, drugs, and youth culture. Whereas the patriarchal family and family values are the central core in the politics of representation by IRIB, the avant-garde cinema has courageously challenged their validity.[17] One of the first films to challenge sacred notions such as that of the family was *The Girl in the Sneakers*, by Rasoul Sadrameli. Screened in autumn 1999, this film was a pioneering experiment in displaying a number of problems of young people in Iranian society, and drawing attention to a taboo topic, their cry for comprehension and tolerance.

CINEMATIC VIGNETTE

The Girl in the Sneakers

   Taddai is a fifteen-year-old girl from an affluent family and in childish love with a teenaged boy. One day when she and her boyfriend are strolling around in a park and planning their future, moral police arrest them. They are accused of violating the rules for behavior between related and nonrelated people (*mahram/namahram*). Their parents are called to the police station and the girl is sent for an examination to check her virginity. A policeman takes her to the medico-legal center, where such examinations take place and which is more like a mortuary. In a moving scene following the examination, when the physician has affirmed that she is still a virgin (read pure, chaste, and modest), we face a frightened, perplexed, and humiliated soul. In protest against her living conditions, the system, and her parents, she runs away from home and begins a dangerous and mysterious journey around Tehran, during which she encounters different kinds of people. None of those she turns to understand her scream for help. Her teacher, the old woman in the shop, and the police all preach the same model of purity and chastity. Finally, paradoxically, an "immoral, law-breaker" gypsy woman helps her back to "relative" safety, back to her parents.

* * *

The name of the girl, Taddai, in Persian means "reminder." The girl is supposed to recall all young girls who live under harsh pressure from parents and patron institutions, such as the police and the school. She embodies the victims of the hegemonic discourse of mutual discipline, *amr-e be m'arouf va nahi az monkar*. She is turned into a "criminal" because she was strolling around with an "unrelated" man. Nevertheless, she is defiant. We see her wandering through the city in a pair of sneakers: symbols of rebellion since the 1960s and 1970s, when leftist activists wore sneakers to signal their position. *The Girl in the Sneakers* is a protest against the current situation. Her escape from the most holy institution in Iranian society, the family, is depicted as heroic, albeit unsuccessful. The "happy" ending (in a patriarchal view) of the film—her return to the family—was demanded by the Ministry of Islamic Culture and Guidance to give screen permission. She returns home not because it is "sweet home" but because returning is a choice between "bad" and "worse."

The Girl in the Sneakers was followed by another controversial film, *Siavash*, by Saman Moghadam (1999). *Siavash* is also a bold transgression of the "red line" (*khat-e qermz*, referring to the limit of allowable expression). The film illustrates the generation gap between a *hezbollahi* war veteran and his son, who is a young composer and musician in a rock band. The film showed behaviors that are technically forbidden in real life: playing rock and having an open relationship with a girl, a photojournalist who leads an independent life. Popular among young people and praised as "courageous," these films provoked the conservative forces, who regarded them as "deceptive" and "immoral." *Siavash* for the first time drew a parallel between generational conflict and the political conflict between youth and the state. Since the success of these movies, a series of films about generational conflicts in contemporary Iran have been produced, such as *Sohrab* (Said Soheyli, 2000), *Bad Kids* (Alireza Davoudnezhad, 2001), *The Burned Generation* (Rasool Molagholipour, 1999), *Sweet Agonies* (Alireza Davoudnezhad, 1999), *I, Taraneh, Am Fifteen* (Rasool Sadrameli, 2001), *Party* (Saman Moghadam 2001), *Deep Breath* (Parviz Shahbazi, 2003), *Maxx* (Saman Moghadam 2005), *Offside* (Jafar Panahi 2005), *In the Name of Father* (Ebrahime Hatami Kia 2005). The hero in these films is a "cultural criminal," and the common theme is an appeal for individual autonomy. *Deep Breath* (*Nafas-e amigh*), known as the first Iranian rock movie, is a noir film about two young men from different class backgrounds in Tehran. In a nihilistic ambience, their aim is self-destruction.

If they steal cars or stop eating until they die or let go of the wheel in the middle of a dangerous road, and laugh it all off, there are no reasons whatsoever. They just do it for the heck of it. Actually that's the movie's strategy. Many scenes in the movie have nothing to do with what precedes or follows them. They just are. Isn't that familiar to you? Do you know people like this? . . . [*Deep Breath*] is the first rock movie of Iranian cinema; Rock as a subculture and not as a music style. Characters do as they wish—they steal, break windows, and many other things. The line that separates a cry from a scream has been crossed. Characters scream in this movie (without raising their voices, of course) and, well, that's what Rock is all about.[18]

Not only "Westernized" youngsters but also young *basijis* are also pictured as victims of the current situation. In two celeberated movies, *Crimson Gold* (Jafar Panahi, 2003), and *Gilane* (Rakhash Bani-Etemad, 2005), *basiji* are illustrated as outsider young men who lost their health and future in the war. The society does not recognize their heroic efforts and excludes them as a social burden.

Dead Wave (Ebrahim Hatami Kia, 2001) offers one of the best illustrations of the "generational conflict." Ten years after the war, a veteran officer is still in a war state of mind. He is a *hezbollahi* Don Quixote. Possessed by a deep hatred of the U.S., he is incapable of communicating with his young son. His wife accuses him of living in the past and ignoring their son. The rebellious son and his girlfriend plan to escape to the West to join the festivities for the third millennium (a global imagination). The wife chooses to stand by her son. They attempt to leave Iran on a boat to the other side of the Persian Gulf, but there is an accident and their boat sinks. In the last scenes of the film the son and his mother are rescued by an American helicopter. The officer carries out a suicide attack on an American ship in the Persian Gulf.

The film is based on the triangular relationship of an authoritarian father, an empathetic mother, and a defiant son. The father symbolizes the past, war, and insecurity; the mother embodies safety and kindness. The son is seeking safety in his mother, and the father is a barrier between them. The contest between father and son for mother/wife—the Freudian Oedipus complex—is the core of the story. Iranian "normative modesty" replaces the erotic lure of the mother with the sense of safety and comfort the mother represents. According to the reviewers, an explicit reference to Freud is present in the scene when, after being punished by the father, the son asks the mother to choose between him and her husband.[19] Ebrahim Hatami Kia, the director, illustrates the widening gap between the two generations. On one side there is a "generation without ideology" (*nasl-e biarman*) which is making its own world by modern means (satellite, Internet, or film). On the other there are fragments left over from a generation infatuated with ideological dogmatism. The latter are Don Quixotes who go to war against enemies more imagined than real. The younger generation, in contrast, are a post-ideology generation. They did not make the Revolution, they did not start or end the war. For this generation, the U.S. is not the "Great Satan."

Dead Wave was banned for a long time, partly because the film resembles the real case of General Rezai and his son, perhaps a symbolic facet of the generational conflict in Iran. In June 1998, Ahmad Rezai, twenty-two-year-old son of Mohsen Rezai, former commander-in-chief of the Revolutionary Guards and secretary of the Expediency Council, asked for political asylum from the U.S. embassy in Dubai.

Clashes of Generations

Since the student uprising in July 1999 in Tehran, the generational conflict has become a dominant topic in public debate. An interesting discussion among intellectuals, artists, and even students examines the "father-son conflict" or the "killing of the son" (*pesar koshi*) as the deep-rooted feature of Iranian culture. The generational conflict is ubiquitous in Iranian mythology. Prominent among the myths in *Shahnameh* (Book of Kings) is the epic story of Sohrab. It is a story of the brief life and tragic death of a young hero, Sohrab, at the hands of his own father, Rostam, who is Iran's greatest warrior. Sohrab has never met his father. Raised in a foreign land, he too has become a great warrior and decides to go to Iran to overthrow the Shah Kay Kavus. Being an enemy of the Shah makes him an enemy both of Iran and of God. His rebellion against the authorities puts him at war with his own father Rostam, who is Iran's only chance to defeat Sohrab. Unaware of each other's identities, they fight and Rostam kills Sohrab (see Clinton 1987).

Some Iranian writers reinterpret Freud's Oedipus complex and adapt it to Iranian mythologies. The expert on *Shahnameh*, Mostafa Rahimi, argues there is a "son-killing complex" (*ouqdeh-ye pesar koshi*) in the Iranian culture (see also Davis 1999). In his analysis of the myth, Sohrab seeks a "new order" (*nazm-e nou*), whereas Rostam is the hero of the ancien régime. For Rahimi, "Sohrab's war with Rostam is a battle between modernity [*nouavari*] and conservatism [*mohafezekari*]" (Rahimi 1369/1990: 245). Hence, the confrontation is inevitable. "Sohrab revolts not only against the political and social system but also against the family system" (243). Rostam must either kill Sohrab or abandon power. He chooses the first option. He denies that Sohrab is his son. For him Sohrab is just an enemy from a "foreign land," who must be eliminated.

The story of Siavash is another "son-killing" myth in *Shahnameh.*
Siavash is a young warrior who is indirectly sent to his death by his father. Two Iranian films dealing with father-son conflict are named after
these legends, *Sohrab* (by Said Soheyli, 2000) and *Siavash* (by Saman
Moghadam, 1999). Interestingly, in the movies, unlike the legends, it is
the father who is indirectly sent to death by the son.

The father/son conflict is also reflected in the numerous Persian expressions that praise the "father" and disparage the "son." The harsh
patriarchal attitude in Iranian society glorifies the "manliness" of
mardha-ye qadimi (the men of olden times) as against young men. For instance, expressions such as "no son takes his father's place" (*hich pesari
jay-e pedarash ra nemigirad*) or "smoke rises from the log" (*doud az konde
boland mishe*) refer to the superiority of the father over the son. Although this superiority is also meant to be intellectual, the emphasis is
on physical masculinity. In the expression "smoke rises from the log,"
the log is a metaphor for the physical strength of old men. The young
people are labeled "vegetable oil kids" (*bacheha-ye roghan nabati*) to refer
to the weaker body of youths. The older men are supposed to have con-
sumed "animal oil" (*roghan-e heyvani*) and therefore to be stronger.
There is a criticism of young bodies that implies that gender distinctions are becoming blurred, and this also concerns young females. A
frequently heard comment about young girls in Iran is that "due to hor-
monal meat coming onto the Iranian market after the Revolution
young girls are hairy and less fertile."

Adult rhetoric about young people is often biased and associates
them with frivolity, idleness, stupidity, and carelessness, but the interpretations of what is causing the decline vary. The most striking account
of the younger generation I heard from Masoud, an affluent middle-
aged father of three teenagers. He owned a restaurant in Golestan. In
the summer of 2001, he was arranging for the emigration of his wife
and children to Canada:

The situation is extremely bad for young people here. Today's youth are a wild
generation. They were born in the Revolution, and grew up under Saddam's
bombardment. As teenagers, they were affronted by *basijis*. This generation is
insulted and injured. They have a complex [*ouqdeh*] and want to let off steam.
Today's generation are uncultivated [*bi farhang*, without culture], lazy, stupid,
rude, and arrogant. They have no principles. They are the outcome of twenty
years of humiliation and ill-treatment of youth. Look at how they talk, how they
drive, how they study, how they work. It is a strange generation. They do not accept help or advice. They do not recognize anybody but themselves. In the
whole of Tehran you cannot find a virgin girl any more. I do not want to see my
children becoming like this. I have attempted to make them well brought-up as
"kids-with-family" [*bach-e khanevadedar*]. I am sending them out to experience
real life.

Once at the dinner table I asked Dara's mother, Hiva, about the post-Revolutionary generation.

Hiva: "The generation after the Revolution are intolerable. Their way of thinking is totally materialistic. They go their own way. They have no respect for tradition and values. They have been let loose [*vel shode*]. They do things we cannot even imagine. They have an entirely different attitude toward relationships with the opposite sex."

Shahram: "How could this generation be so 'loosened' as you say?"

Hiva: "I do not know. Maybe due to all these satellite TV channels. Young people watch God knows what and imitate what they see on the TV screen."

Shahram: "How about Dara?"

Hiva: "Dara is brought up within the family [*tou khon-e bozorg shode*, lit. brought up in house]. Those we talk about are brought up in society [*tou jamme-e*]."

After dinner we watched a videotape interview with a Heavy Metal Tehrani. I had borrowed the film from an old friend who worked as a freelance journalist. In the film the young man—dressed in leather and chains, with long hair and black make-up—declared that he had no link with Iranian culture and saw himself as a global person. This statement started a hot debate. While Dara defended the Heavy Metal kid, his mother was upset. She argued that the youth was alienated from his identity.

Hiva: "This is the result of being brought up in two opposite cultures. Young people are torn between informal and formal norms. They are confused and emptied of character and identity. Parents cannot control their children any more. Before the Revolution young people dated in public spaces. They went to the cinema or the discothèque. Now the only entertainment they have is private parties. The girls and boys gather together inside houses. God knows what they do. Corruption is increasing drastically. Drug addiction is going down in age. But the moral police are hunting the ones who have a picture of an actor on their T-shirt. The problem is more serious than you can imagine. The material damage to the country is nothing compared to what the regime has done to people's minds. Ethics and conscience [*voujdan*] do not mean anything to the younger generation. The compassion [*mohabat*] and warmth [*garmi*] we experienced are gone. All these are replaced by a *bazari* ethos [*akhlaq-e bazari va dallali*]."

The generational break was recurrently discussed by young people in the local association in Shahrak-e Gharb. Each time I attended the meetings I was surprised by the bold ways these young peoplr expressed themselves. Patriarchy (*pedarsalari*) and parental authority within the family were criticized. The disjunction with the former generation was explicitly formulated in rejection of their parents' lifestyle, experiences, and norms. The Third Generation are disappointed in their elders, who have, in Dara's words, been "defeated in everything, in the Revolution, in the war, in the building up of a civil society [*jamm'e-ye madani*]." As Simon put it in his street jargon, "The former generation have ruined the country with their Revolution and we must pay the costs."

At the weekly meetings of the management council, younger members freely criticized senior members. Once, during the annual election of members of the council, Dara got into conflict with Dr. Aghasi over the procedure for the voting. Dr. Aghasi had attempted to make an alliance with Dara to vote out another member of the council, whom both of them disliked, but Dara openly criticized Dr. Aghasi for his undemocratic methods. He later told me that "Dr. Aghasi belongs to the past. He is from a generation of despotism [*nasl-e estebdadi*]. He just cannot comprehend the tolerance that we [younger generation] show toward our opponents."

The cultural emancipation of the Third Generation takes place through the rejection of their parents' "generational objects," "those phenomena that we use to form a sense of generational identity" (Bollas 1993: 255). This refers to persons, places, things, and events which have particular meaning for the identity of a generation (259). The Revolution, the "Holy Defense" (*Defa-e Moqadas*) against Iraq's invasion, political Islam, and nativism, are all parts of the parents' "generational objects." During the student movements in the late autumn of 2002, a student monthly called *Rah-e Nou* (New Way) began to publish a series of essays criticizing the "myth of culture." The first essay, in an exceptionally daring style, called in question sacred notions such as "cultural identity" (*hoviyat-e farhangi*), "cultural authenticity" (*esalat-e farhangi*), and "Weststruckness." The essay attacked "cultural-centric thinking" (*tafakor-e farhangmehvar*) as the authoritarian generation's way of ruling.

Culture is a means of power: the fable of culture is over. Yet cultural fundamentalists [*farhangbavaran*] intend to force us to carry forward our parental culture. For them we are only bearers of culture [*hamal-e farhangi*].[20]

The second essay targeted the holy institution of the family. Entitled "Being a Bachelor: This Is the Crime" (Mojarad Bodan: Jorm in Ast), the essay deals with how the norm is based on a "tribalism" (*qabileh-parasti*) ideology, and the single person is the "Other" (*digari*):

In Iranian society the individual is legitimated only as married. The bachelor must be segregated from normal people. S/he is seen as a creature possessing bestial instincts and uncontrollable hedonism.

The most striking accusation in the essay is that the traditional institution of the family is described as a "boutique where women are traded and a shut-in space where sexual complexes expand."[21]

The younger generation's cultural defiance does not mean that they are a romantic democratic "MTV generation." Their malicious sexist and homophobic attitude places them in the same line as their parental generation. For Dara, Simon, and a majority of Iranian young men, the virginity of the girl they want to marry is an indisputable value. Putting the younger generation in a dichotomy with the traditional norms might risk sketching a black-and-white picture of the situation in Iran. For all their interest in sex, young persons in Tehran display ambivalent feelings toward it. Likewise, in spite of their opposition to the cultural puritanism of the regime, they recreate their own cultural puritanism.

Iranian society is experiencing two processes: in Alain Touraine's (1997) terms, of "deinstitutionalization" and "desocialization." Among the Third Generation identity is becoming fragmented, due to globalization and to the fading of the patriarchal "national" model. Institutions are sets of cultural rules that regulate social activities in a patterned way, defining norms of what is right and wrong. The feeling that their generation has been "sacrificed" for a revolution their parental generation made has induced bitterness and deep cynicism. The legitimacy of institutions such as family, school, and religion in Iran has withered away in the eyes of the Third Generation. Such deinstitutionalization is followed by desocialization, "the disappearing of roles, norms, and values through which the life world is constructed" (Touraine 1997: 57). The school and the family often transmit contradictory norms. The interpretation of Islam by parents is quite different from the official one presented by the media and the school. Hence, the validity and authority of the main educational institutions are questioned by the younger generation. The young, in contrast to their parents, are not locked into specific identities and social roles, and their lives still contain a promise of choice and change. Whereas the conventional model of transmission of norms is weakened, new media, such as the Internet and satellite TV channels, transmit alternative modes of socialization. While the whole of Iranian society is going through structural changes (demographic, economic, and sociopolitical), the Iranian youth are experiencing a period of redefinitions: of changing relationships between public and private, between local and global, between self and other, and of redefinition of sexual and bodily experiences (see McDonald 1999).

Chapter 6
Culture of Defiance

The next revolution in Iran will be a sex-revolution

—A journalist in Iran

In each room of this house there is a storm.
When they are raging, we all will be gone

—Federico García Lorca

The second quotation above is from *The House of Bernarda Alba*, the famous play by Federico García Lorca. In February 2002, during the Fajr Festival, *Khaney-e Bernarda Alba* was played in Tehran. This short play is set in rural Spain at the turn of the twentieth century. The characters, all women, live in a cloistered household managed by a newly widowed mother with five daughters. Under the shadow of the Church and the tyranny bred from a need to protect the chastity of the family, the matron (Bernarda Alba) represses her daughters by enforcing an eight-year mourning period. She allows no sign of joy or self-assertion, such as wearing make-up and bright-colored dresses, or contact with the opposite sex. Tension in the family increases and a tragedy is inevitable. Eventually, the youngest daughter revolts against the mother, but the result is violence and her suicide. As it was performed, the play reflected the current situation in Iran rather than that of early twentieth-century Spain. Many young women I talked to about the play recognized themselves in Lorca's tragedy. The hopelessness and anxiety, but also the potential forces of rebellion in the play created a connection between Lorca's imagination and the reality lived by the Iranians. The above citation from the play recalls what Dara in a bitter and prophetical tone once said:

A short time after the Revolution, suddenly there was a severe scarcity of gruel, baby food, and diapers. Ayatollah Khomeini disliked contraceptives and commanded the nation to bear children. The Revolution needed young people. In Ayatollah Khomeini's words "an army of 20 millions." There was a baby boom.

When these babies grew up and started school there was a "school crisis." There were not enough schools. The state changed the school system to get them all in. After school the boys were called to do military service. Again, there were not enough places. After the war, the state changed the system and started to sell exemptions from military service [*moafi*]. The youth then wanted to go to university. Islamic Free Universities mushroomed everywhere. Today the first wave of the "army of 20 million" is out in the labor market. There are no jobs, no future for them. The younger generation see themselves as a "burned generation" [*nasl-e sokhte*], a generation with little to lose. The crisis is here. This generation is like an inundation [*seil*] coming toward us. It is approaching, too late to stop it coming and it destroys everything on its way. Scary but true.

Dara's words echo the voice of a social change in the making. The Third Generation have created their own space, ways of communication, and "tactics" in de Certeau's sense (1984) to subvert the meanings of the adult culture. They have developed several rituals of performative "defiance." In the following pages I present some ethnographic illustrations.

Football as Politics

Jafar Panahi's satirical comedy *Offside* (2005) is a film about female fans who are refused entrance to watch the national team play a World Cup qualifier against Bahrain. They disguise themselves as men in order to go through police control. The movie shows the anguish of several young girls who are captured and wait to be punished for their "cultural crime." Women are not allowed to enter the stadium because male players wear shorts and the audience shout "indecent" slogans. The film shows how "pastoral power" excludes women from the public space with a "caring" and "saving" argument. Nevertheless, on November 29, 1997, many women forced their way inside the stadium to join the celebration and welcome the national team returning from Australia. A few days earlier, the Iranian team had won beaten Australia and qualified for the 1998 World Cup in France. That night the post-Revolutionary generation took over Tehran's streets, squares, and parks. They rejoiced and danced until long after midnight. The representatives of the state were shocked and paralyzed by the immensity of the spontaneous happenings. They avoided confrontation with the people. The joyous tumult was reviewed by the media and the intellectuals as a "social happening" (*hadese-ye ejtema'i*). This "social happening" has later been repeated several times, for instance, at the victory of Iran over the United States in soccer in June 1998, and on October 12, 2001, after a 2–1 win against Iraq in another qualifying match for the 2002 World Cup.

On such occasions, the uncontrollable masses have challenged the
state in two ways. On the one hand, the imposed puritanical rule of
"modesty and chastity" was ignored. On the other hand, the notion of
an *ummat* based on Islamic identity was confronted with nationalistic
sentiments. Many had painted the Iranian flag on their faces. Others
waved large Iranian flags and sang the national anthem. Ten days after
the victory over Iraq, on October 22, Iran was beaten 3–1 by Bahrain in
the final qualifying match, and lost its place at the head of Asian Group
A. Not even an hour after the match, a rumor spread around Tehran
that the Iranian team had deliberately lost the game under pressure
from the officials. The teams' "unusually weak performance" was referred to as proof of this by the young people, and used as an argument
to reinforce the rumor. One rumor had it that the authorities were
frightened of another mass festivity. Another had it that the Iranian
state had made a deal with Saudi Arabia, which would win qualification
for the World Cap if Iran lost the match. The deal was that Saudi Arabia would double the number of visas given to Iranian Hajj pilgrims if
Iran lost.

However, tens of thousands of football fans rushed out onto the
streets, ironically shouting "Bahrain, Bahrain" and sarcastically praising
the side that had defeated Iran. A huge number gathered in the main
square in Shahrak-e Gharb, the traditional gathering place for young
people. They danced and rejoiced as before, irrespective of Iran's victory or defeat. The joyful mood soon turned ugly, however. The crowd
chanted anti-regime slogans and vandalized buses and government
buildings. The police struck back brutally. More than 1,000 people were
arrested and more than 50 were hospitalized.[1] President Khatami de-
plored the unrest, which he blamed on "riff-raff and vulgar" (*arazel va
oubash*) persons. He was criticized by reform-minded newspapers, which
argued that football was only an excuse by the young people to demonstrate their anger and discontent. The homogeneous reaction by youths
in different strata of society and from different parts of the country indicates that such unrest is more about political and social protest than
football hooliganism.[2]

The Student Movement

With 1.5 million students nationwide,[3] universities possess the biggest
potential source of political mobilization. Between July 8 and 14, 1999,
student riots in Tehran shook the whole country. On the evening of July
8, a couple of hundred students gathered at a campus in central Tehran
to protest against the new press law and the closure of a reform-oriented
newspaper, *Salaam*. The protest was peaceful, and after a few hours the

students returned to their hostels. Less than an hour after midnight, however, the police, accompanied by *basijis* and plain-clothes members of Ansar-e Hezbollah, broke into the dormitories, battered the students with batons, and destroyed their belongings, and threw some students out windows. According to the newspapers, 800 rooms were damaged. Five people were killed and dozens wounded. Khatami and his government officials apologized to the students for the incident, but thousands of students nationwide were mobilized in protest. The students were joined by nonstudent young people who turned Tehran University and the streets around it into a battlefield. Thousands of students demanded the dismissal of the police chief, the return of the victims' bodies, and finally the identification and punishment of the plain-clothes Ansar-e Hezbollah. The students did not receive any official response and, as they became more frustrated, their slogans became more radical.

Two decades after the Revolution, Tehran was once again a scene of rebellion of the children of the Revolution. The anti-riot forces, *basijis*, and Ansar-e Hezbollah occupied the streets of Tehran. Just being a young person strolling around central Tehran was enough to get beaten or arrested. Several young men I knew from Golestan shopping center had joined the student protests. Farhad's sixteen-year-old brother was one of them. He was in no way a political activist but gladly took advantage of the situation to give vent to his anguish, he told me later. He was arrested and was jailed for five days. On July 12, Ayatollah Khamenei, the Supreme Leader (*vali-ye taqi'n*), condemned the students and called on *basijis* to come to the "scene." He called the protesting students "saboteurs" and "infiltrators" supported by the U.S. and anti-Revolutionary groups in exile. The order to the *basijis* was clear: zero tolerance toward young people. The students were brutally harassed and mass arrests began in Tehran. Although the student movement of July 1999 was defeated, it radicalized the political atmosphere among young people and made the universities in Tehran to the most politicized universities in the world.

In late autumn 2002, Tehran and other cities witnessed intensified student protests not only against conservative forces but also against "powerless" President Khatami. The student movement is still alive and powerful. In December 2006, students burned pictures of President Ahamadinejad and interrupted his speech with "Death to the dictator" at Amir Kabir University in Tehran. Young people have been the victims of repression and discrimination for more than 20 years. The police roundups during parties, the arrests of teenage boys and girls, and daily public insults and whipping have led them to violence. Once in Golestan shopping center two *basijis* humiliated Simon because of his long hair. When they left us, Simon said with anger in his face, that he hated them so much that he could kill them. He explained in detail how he would kill the *basijis* and how afterward he would be sentenced to death. His parents would then pay blood money and he would be released. Then he calculated, with his finger in the air, that his parents could not afford the blood-money of a *basiji*. To me, his description sounded like an enraged young man's empty words. Gradually, however, I witnessed how such "empty words" could turn into raw violence. Dara told me: "Do not regard the Rapi kids as innocent and harmless. They all have knives and iron rods. If they find a *basiji* alone they show no mercy. This is hate and hatred cannot be controlled." Violence against *basijis* has increased in Tehran. In the clashes between young men and *basijis* during the student uproar in the summer of 2003, more than 50 *basijis* were hospitalized. Bahamn, the *basiji*, admitted the increasing hostility against them:

They do not like us because we try to keep them on right direction. Just like children dislike hearing their parents give them advice. But they hate us for it.

Chaharshanbeh Souri: From a Neighborhood Feast to a Political Agenda

Since the early 1990s the eve of Chaharshanbeh souri has been the night the Islamic regime dreads most. This is an ancient Persian festival performed on the night of the last Tuesday of the Iranian year. It is when the ceremonies of Norouz, the Iranian New Year on March 21, begin. Several fires are lit in every neighborhood and people leap over them to "purify" themselves and chase away evil spirits for the year to come. The leaping over fire is followed by the Iranian version of the "Trick or Treat" of Halloween. Hidden by veils, girls go from door to door in their own neighborhood banging a spoon against a metal bowl and asking for treats or money. Another part of the ceremony is *falgoosh* (fortune hearing). To do *falgoosh*, you stand in a dark corner or behind a fence and listen to the conversations of the passersby, trying to interpret their statements or the subject of their dialogue as an answer to your own questions.

Like other pre-Islamic Persian traditions, Chaharshanbeh souri has been criticized by the theocracy as being *a*revolutionary in its emphasis on Persian rather than Islamic identity, and also for its joyfulness. From the outset, the Islamic state has been hostile to the ritual, perhaps because it involves more outdoor enjoyment and festivities than any other ritual in Iran. Each year, a couple of weeks before the date of Chaharshanbeh souri, the authorities start admonishing and indeed threatening people not to perform the ritual. On the eve of the festival, police forces and *basijis* occupy "suspect neighborhoods" as well as the central parts of Tehran and other large cities to prevent festivities. The Iranian youth nevertheless persist in celebrating Chaharshanbeh souri every year, despite all the aggression and brutality it has brought. On the night of the celebration, Tehran's neighborhoods turn into scenes of cat-and-mouse-style battle between youths, on the one hand, and *basijis* and policemen on the other. Police forces and medical staff are on maximum alert during the ritual.

When I was growing up in Iran in the 1970s, Chaharshanbeh souri was an innocent ceremony of youthful entertainment. For us it was merely a neighborhood party. For today's generation it is a political event, pitting national sentiments against the religious identities imposed from above. The ritual has been transformed into a site for defiance toward the social order and "normative modesty." Young people have forged (in the sense both of falsifying and of forming) a new version of the ritual. The new, politicized Chaharshanbeh souri has become a ritual of protest. Although it is forbidden to display fireworks, lots of fireworks are used. Fireworks smuggled into the country, or homemade ones, much more powerful and dangerous than normal ones, make Tehran sound like a battlefield. The fireworks become stronger and stronger each year, sounding more like hand grenades than fireworks. Occasionally slogans are shouted against the authorities and official personalities. On the eve of Chaharshanbeh souri, Shahrak-e Gharb is the hottest place in the whole of Tehran.

The following observation is from Chaharshanbeh souri in 1999. Already in the early afternoon, Tehrani youths began to prepare the feast. Around 5 P.M. I took a taxi from my apartment in eastern Tehran to Shahrak-e Gharb to join Dara and his friends, who had organized a huge fiesta in Shahrak-e Gharb. Despite the large numbers of riot police in the "suspect neighborhoods" and on the highways, wood and thorn bushes were transported on the roofs of cars or in the backs of pick-ups. Many headed for Shahrak-e Gharb where, according to rumor, the best street scenes could be found. In Dara's neighborhood several bonfires were set up. Irangelesi techno-music, produced in Los Angeles, came from car stereos, and girls and boys danced to it and leaped over the fires. Several times patrolling moral police came into view and people rushed inside the houses. On one occasion a *basiji*, apparently irritated by the atmosphere, ordered some young people to go into their houses. When no one obeyed the order, he aggressively pushed and pulled some of them, yelling insulting words at them. Other young men and several parents protested and stopped him. One middle-aged father pushed the *basiji* away. Accidentally a button of the *basiji*'s shirt came loose. He called for help on his cellular phone. A few minutes later, the neighborhood was filled with *basijis* and policemen, who rushed into the house where the middle-aged man had fled. He was severely beaten in front of us and taken to the police station, accused of "violence" against a *basiji*. That night in Shahrak-e Gharb alone 200 young men and women were arrested, charged with "disrupting public order."

Each year the ritual turns into a real tumult, when clashes break out between youths and *basijis*. In 2006, the police fired tear gas and attacked the celebrators with clubs. More than 1,000 young people were arrested and at least 100 people were injured in Tehran.[4]

Charhashanbeh souri 2002 became a manifestation of the gulf between the national (Persian) and religious (Islamic) identities of Iranians. That year, the month of mourning—Moharram—in the Islamic lunar calendar ran from March 16 to April 13 and coincided with both Chaharshanbeh souri and Norouz. President Khatami ordered people to move Chaharshanbeh souri forward a week to prevent the joyful Persian festivity from coinciding with the Islamic mourning ritual. In contrast to my expectations, the young people received the order calmly. To my surprise, Dara smiled and said: "This year we shall celebrate Chaharshanbeh souri twice. Moharram belongs to the Arabs. We are first Iranians and then Muslims." Simon expressed similar views: "We will have two Chaharshanbeh souri this year and this will drive them [the authorities] crazy [*kon-eshon misoze*, their ass will be burned]."

The day after Chaharshanbeh souri, March 18, 2003, I called Dara and asked him how it had been.

Shahram: "I just read on the Internet that there was a clash between young people and *basijis* in Shahrak-e Gharb and 12 persons were arrested. Did it happen around Golestan?"

Dara: "No. It was calm around Golestan. All I heard was that a *basiji* was beaten in Zone 6. It was not as much fun as past years."

Shahram: "Why?"

Dara: "There were not so many *basijis* on the streets this year. So we just jumped over fires. Without *basijis* there was nothing amusing about Chahrshanbe souri."

Only a week earlier Ashura had been celebrated. I heard that in several places in north Tehran the Ashura ritual (involving mourning and self-flagellation) had been turned into a street festivity by young people. I asked Dara whether that was true.

Dara: "It is exaggerated as usual, but there was a real Hossein Party here in Shahrak-e Gharb."

I heard about the "Hossein Party" for the first time in 1999. This issue by now is recognized as a "problem" in public debates by complaints that the youth of today are damaging the virtue of the ritual. The young people in Shahrak-e Gharb and Meydan-e Mohseni (Mohesi Square) have new ways of performing the Ashura ceremony that differ from the ritual performed in other parts of Tehran. For the Shahraki kids the ritual is an expression not of self-abasement, but rather of self-assertion. Dressed in chic black T-shirts, jeans, and sunglasses, baseball caps (with a "Nike" or "NY" emblem), they march along the streets around the Golestan shopping center. Their attitude is not at all mournful (see Basmenji 2005: 305–6; Varzi 2006: 121–22; Moaveni 2005: 59). Dara said with pride in his voice: "Our ceremony is classy and differs from all others in Tehran. We do a chic mourning [*shic azadari*]." The Hossein Party is a symbolic parody of the convention, which annoys not only the authorities but also the parental generation. In March 2004 about 5,000 young Tehranis gathered around Meydan-e Mohseni to perform Hossein Party on Ashura. They clashed with *basijis* and many were arrested and injured. The parental generation's confusion toward Hossein Party is best shown in Mahmoud Dowlatabadi's, a famous Iranian secular writer, words: "I have never witnessed such an Ashura. . . . It's as if we are distant from this generation, we don't understand them" (Alavi 2005: 125).

Both Chaharshanbeh souri and "Hossein Party" have been transformed into symbolic parodies of the conventions. According to Bakhtin, "Parody . . . is especially well suited to the needs of oppositional culture, precisely because it deploys the force of the dominant discourse against itself" (Stam 1992: 173).

Banal Politics

HETEROTOPIAS OF DEVIATION

Heterotopias of deviation are the spaces in which individuals whose behavior is deviant in relation to the norms are placed, such as resthomes, psychiatric hospitals, and prisons. In this text "heterotopias of deviation" are sites of defiance. Heterotopias "are something like counter-sites, a kind of effectively enacted utopia in which the real sites, all the other real sites that can be found within the culture, are simultaneously represented, contested, and inverted" (Foucault 1986: 24). The defiance of Tehrani youth is performed in many ways and at numerous sites. Aside from *passazhs* and private parties in the city itself, young Tehranis can mingle in relatively relaxed spaces outside Tehran: hiking in the mountains on the northern edge of the city, or making excursions to the Caspian Sea or the ski resorts only a few hours drive from town.

I

Mount Alborz, which borders Tehran to the north, is a common haven for the youths of the city. Darake and Darband, with calm weather, old trees, rivers, and coffee houses, attract young people who flee from the heat and pollution of the city as well as from the prying eyes of the moral police or *basijis*. On weekends, thousands of young men and women carrying tape recorders or CD players occupy Mount Alborz. The sight of a huge number of young people hiking in line—similar to a political manifestation—is visually impressive. Many foreign journalists use illustrations of this scene in their documentaries and reports on Iran. Sounds of forbidden music fill the mountain. Those who want a sense of adventure pack a bottle of vodka or some cans of beer in their rucksacks. Mount Alborz is also a perfect place for dating. The mountains offer girls and boys many hidey-holes to indulge in romantic moments.

Wealthier young people look for fun in the skiing resorts of Dizin and Shemshak about two hours drive from Tehran. Ski slopes have been operational at both places since the 1960s. Dizin is equipped with telecabins and chairlifts, and has very high ski slopes, with the mountain peak reaching an altitude of about 3,600 meters. The slopes are usually packed with young people skiing and snowboarding. Opposite sexes mingle openly. Girls enjoy the freedom to replace headscarves and robes with ski caps and jackets. While the restaurants offer nonalcoholic "after-ski" meals with pizza, sausages, hamburgers, and soft drinks, "sinful" parties, in sexes mingle and consume alcoholic beverages, go on in the surrounding rented villas. To prevent "immorality," a mountain police unit, composed of men and women on skis, was set up in 2000 to patrol the ski slopes. The skiing moral police did not stand a chance, however, against the young people on skis and snowboards, and the project was discontinued.

II

There are public spaces in Tehran where sexuality between unrelated people thrives. One of these spaces is provided by the public taxi. Unlike call-taxis (*taxi telefoni*), public taxis in Iran are shared. Five passengers are packed into a medium-sized car (usually an Iran-made Peykan). Women and men who are not related (*mahram*) are sandwiched together during the ride. Two sit on the front seat beside the driver and three on the back seat. If there is no vacant space in the back and there are two unrelated passengers of opposite sex to who want to sit in front, the male passenger should sit between the driver and the woman. Since he sits on a cushion that fills the gap between the driver's seat and the other one, the woman is lower. Lacking enough space, the man in the middle will stretch his right arm around the woman on his right side and lean toward her. Many young people utilize taxis to have a romantic ride through the normally sex-segregated public spaces. I frequently heard stories from young men about how they enjoyed the erotic moments of physical contact with a strange female body that, outside the taxi, would be separated from them and inaccessible.

Taxis are also a site for political debate. Small publics composed of anonymous individuals from different social categories are created in the privacy of cabs. Some people get out and others get in, but the conversation continues. In Tehran there is even a joke about it: Two men standing by a news stand are looking through the newspapers. One of them says to the other, "There's nothing to read about. Let's take a taxi and get some news." Many taxi-drivers put a sticker on the dashboard that says "political discussion is forbidden" (*bahs-e siasi mamnou*).

III

Coffee shops are another scene where youths perform acts of defiance. They make up a relatively a new type of "public space" for young people, who were otherwise excluded from conventional public spaces. The history of coffee shops in Tehran goes back to the 1940s, when the modernization of the urban landscape of Tehran accelerated. But expectations have remained unfulfilled—coffee shops in Tehran have never played the role they once played in the emergence of the "public sphere" in Europe. As Habermas defines the "public sphere," the concept refers to "a realm of our social life in which something approaching public opinion can be formed." For Habermas (1989) the existence of the public sphere is based on two primary conditions. First, access is guaranteed to all citizens. Second, there must be guarantees of freedom of assembly and association and a freedom to express and publish one's opinions. For Habermas, the public sphere is ideally a place of rational and open discussion. As a site for political debate and organizations which are not part of the state, the public sphere can also be host to what is today termed "civil society." Habermas's emphasis is on a sphere where public debates can deal with policies of the state, a sphere which can, in other words, be a medium between society and the state, in which the public organize themselves and create political opinion. Such a public sphere, at least in its bourgeois form, is said to have developed in Europe in the late eighteenth century, a time characterized by the French Revolution and citizenship ideals. Historically the growth of the European public sphere and the rise of urban lifestyle have been interrelated. The public sphere in this idealized form would be made up of those arenas in which public discussions and the transmission of information occur, such as coffee houses, clubs, and the media.

In the harsh political climate of Iran with its intense state control of the media, the potential of a proper public sphere—in the Habermasian meaning—seems to be obscure or unrealizable. Nonetheless, the Iranians enjoy spaces that are in some sense "public," such as *qahvekhane* (traditional coffee houses) and mosques, and have used them to discuss matters that concern them or to exchange information. In these Iranian "public spaces" there is no guarantee of freedom of expression and access for all citizens, two prerequisite conditions for forming a public sphere. These "public spaces" are dominated by middle-aged Muslim men. Although minority groups, including women, young people, and ethnic and religious minorities, have been excluded from these "public spaces" by the spatial dominance of Muslim men and the cultural norms that reinforce it, they nonetheless have their own subpublic spheres even in Iran. Women, for instance, meet and discuss things at events such as a modest "fashion show" in somebody's living room or at religious gatherings such as *jalaseh* (see Torab 1996, 2006).

Since the late 1990s, coffee shops have mushroomed in the wealthy northern parts of Tehran. While these coffee shops do not provide sites where the public tend to organize and form political opinions, young people nevertheless use them for "everyday forms of resistance." They mingle with the opposite sex or exchange their latest rock music or Hollywood films. They also exchange their knowledge about sex, life abroad (*kharej*), hot Internet sites, fashions, cars, or general lifestyle matters that they can only see through the Internet or satellite TV. The most popular coffee shops in Tehran are on Gandhi Street, which is famous not only for the textile shops that line its northern end, but also for a shopping center that over the years has turned into a veritable mall of coffee shops. There are half a dozen cafés lined up one next to one another, such as Shooka and Café de France, all packed with young people.

Rang Café in Golestan is another in place. Eskan, under a high building with the same name on Mirdamad Street, has long been a youth hang-out. Raees coffee shop on Fajr Street attempts to re-create an atmosphere of the American Starbucks. The logo of Raees on the windows and printed on cups and wrappings resembles the Starbucks logo, and the owner claims that he offers real Starbucks coffee. Young Tehranis who like art and discussions about cultural issues prefer Café Shooka and Café Titr. According to many of them, there are coffee shops where live guitar music or illicit foreign or Irangelesi pop music is played. They say that there are also some coffee shops that close their doors late at night and let regular female clients be unveiled. Coffee shops are criticized by the authorities as places for immoral behavior. Many popular ones have been closed down for not "following Islamic values."

In the coffee shops young people, according to what they themselves claim, do not discuss "political aspirations" (*khasteha-ye siasi*) but talk tirelessly about their "social aspirations" (*khasteha-ye ejtema'i*). They make a distinction between "political" issues, that deal with antiregime activities, and "social" ones, that highlight the "unpretentious" anxieties and needs of young people. At stake are issues such as a more liberal attitude toward relations between boys and girls, a more liberal dress code, more moderate policies toward youth culture, or employment. In spite of their tactic of denial of "political" topics in order to avoid any provocation, their "social demands" are definitely very much "political demands." Coffee shops are counter-sites, characterized with an anti-ideology. Coffee shops are anti-political sites (see Azadarmaki 2006: 161).

Just as Drakulič (1987) wrote about Eastern European societies under communism, politics in Iran is not an abstract concept but a powerful force influencing people's everyday lives. Since the Revolution the trivia of everyday life have been political. The Islamic order has striven to penetrate the very bases of people's lives: what they eat and drink, how they dress, whom they sleep with, whom they look at. In such an atmosphere every aspect of daily life takes on a political meaning. An Iranian takes a political position in his/her everyday practices, from patterns of dressing to hairdos. As lifestyle is politicized, coffee shops play a significant role in the creation of political opinion by being arenas for "banal politics."[5]

IV

Zi zamin means both "basement" and "underground" in Persian. The basement in Tehran is another place/space for cultural defiance. A remarkable activity in Tehran basements is rock. There are numerous rock groups that are "both metaphorically and physically underground" (Nooshin 2005: 464). There is also an online music magazine called *Zirzamin* (underground),[6] which is a forum for the new wave of Iranian underground musicians. Started in early 2006, *Zirzamin* aims to be a connection between different bands that otherwise have no contact with each other. The editor of *Zirzamin*, himself a rock musician based nowadays in Sweden, believes that there are nearly a hundred active underground bands in Tehran.[7] The number includes also other illicit music styles such as Heavy Metal, Rap, Techno, Reggae, and Alternative. By summer 2006, ten albums had been distributed through underground channels. O-Hum and Kiosk have released their albums outside Iran. Others who lack capital to give out albums inside the country or contacts in the Iranian diaspora put their music on their homepages. Music styles like Pop and ethnic are more fortunate than rock. Since the late 1990s and after a wave of liberalizations in the field of youth culture, rock musicians are still "underground." I met Kian, one of the most celebrated bassists among rock fans in Tehran, in a coffee shop in Tehran in August 2006.

Rock cannot be overground because of its rebellious nature. Many rock bands do not want to be overground in order to avoid compromising their music with Ministry of Culture. Under the ground you play what your heart wants, but over the ground there are rules, basijis, and like this. They bully us not only for the music we play but for everything. Our hair, clothes or something else.

It is amazing to see how so many bands worked hard "underground" to create an Iranian rock, perhaps for the first time in Iran. Kian says:

We have never had rock here. What they called rock before the Revolution was a copy of bad Western music. There were one or two exceptions like Farhad and Fereydoun Foroughi. But nothing more. Now in Tehran basements you can hear a rock music which is Iranian. Its lyric, its tune, come from Tehran not from Los Angeles.

Laudan Nooshin, a scholar in ethnomusicology, regards rock music as a site of youth empowerment. "Its significance lies in the fact that it offers young people an alternative space in which to express themselves, to assert their personal freedom" (2005: 494). She believes that young people find an alternative discourse in rock with which they negotiate a series of highly contested relationships between individual and society, between modernity and tradition, between local and global, and between secular and religious.

In recent years a powerful Persian rap has emerged. The editor of www.zirzamin.se believes that rap music is a medium for the young generation to express their collective as well as individual concerns against the dominant culture.[8] An example is the rap song in the movie *MAXX* (2005). The young man in the film expresses his anxiety and anger at his mother (read the parental generation) in a rap song. Walking through streets of Tehran he blames and accuses the parental generation for the individual and social crises he and his generation face:

The city you have built is gray and without love. . . .
What do you have for next generation?
Nothing! But a wall.

Using virtual space as an alternative space for the activities which are forbidden in real space has become a commonplace among Tehrani middle-class youth. For instance, in October 2002, several young male rock enthusiasts arranged "The Underground Music Competition" on the Internet. Unable to perform in real space, underground rock bands put their work on the Internet for competition. The vision of the organizers is "to introduce new talents and music trends not recognized in established circles; to promote a community of underground bands that often work in isolation from one another; to initiate a debate about the place of rock music in Iran and its compatibility with native cultures."[9] The competition was followed by another one in 2004 and a Tehran Avenue Music Festival in 2005 (see also Nooshin 2005: 472–74). The most famous band, O-Hum, distributes its album for free on the Net.[10]

Subversive Laughter

Laughter contains something revolutionary...
Voltaire's laughter was more destructive
than Rousseau's weeping. (Alexander Herzen)[11]

Laughter...liberates from the fear
that developed in man during thousands of years:
fears of the sacred, of prohibitions,
of the past, of power. (Mikhail Bakhtin 1984: 94)

To maintain a sense of humor has certainly been one of the ways of carrying on life in Iran. Drakulič (1987) describes how cheerfulness and everyday acts of defiance helped people to survive communism. Iranians have so far survived the Islamic Republic and even laughed. Political jokes are very popular. New jokes about the authorities in charge are made every day. Such jokes circulate in public taxis, on the Internet, at parties, and in schools. Usually they are sexual, or sarcastically depict officials' ignorance and incompetence.

POLITICAL JOKES

I

Hajj Agha X was sent to Paris when he was Foreign Minister. During a visit to the Louvre, the Foreign Minister of France offered a present to him: the "Shoes of Louis the Sixteenth, sir." Hajj Agha X looked at them and said "They are a bit small for me. Please give me Louis the Eighteenth."

II

During the war with Iraq, Hajj Agha X was taken to visit a school which an Iraqi missile had totally destroyed. Hajj Agha X thanked God and said: "What luck that the missile landed on ruins."

* * *

One hot afternoon in July, I jumped into a public taxi to go to Shahrak-e Gharb. I was the only passenger, and I sat on the front seat and complained of the unbearable heat. Tehran is hottest in July. Even taxi drivers take refuge at home from the burning sun, and it is not easy to find a taxi then. There was no sign of the deadly traffic that Tehran is famous for. The driver geared up and pushed the accelerator as hard as he could. Just before turning on to the Hemat highway, we saw a cleric standing at the edge of the street in the shade of some trees. When we approached him, he cried "Azadi." The driver jammed on the brakes and the taxi stopped a bit from him. All in a sweat from the heat and hurrying after the taxi, the cleric got in and sat in the rear seat. He seemed to be around fifty, with a large body that was obviously out of training. The driver pushed down the accelerator again. After quite a long way on the Hemat highway the driver looked in the mirror and asked the cleric: "Excuse me Hajj Agha, where did you want to go?"

The cleric answered: "Azadi Square."

The driver jammed on the brakes, stopped the car, looked back towards the cleric and said: "Forgive me. We are not heading there." The cleric seemed disturbed and got out. The driver put the car in first gear, looked at me and grinned: "Did you enjoy that?"

"What?" I asked.

The driver said "He [the cleric] was standing under trees but now he is standing in the sun. By the way, he is also on a highway. He will stand there for a long time."

Iranians do not lose their sense of humor even in the face of the everyday open and bizarre violence on the part of the police or *basijis*. People often say that after two decades they have gotten used to this ubiquitous violence. Once, during a weekend visit in Isfahan, I was invited to lunch at my sister's home. At the lunch table my nephew said, with a grin on his face, "Mamma, tell the story of Chaharsanbeh souri and our neighbor." My sister told how, at the Chaharsanbeh souri ceremony the year before, their neighbor had gotten into a verbal conflict with the *basijis* and been brutally beaten in front of his house. My sister's husband tried to stop the *basijis* and was beaten himself. My sister's way of retelling the story was humorous; she could illustrate the scenes of the event in a comical tone. Others in the room laughed. I asked how they could make a joke of such brutality, of which they were themselves the victims. My sister, still laughing, said, "You have been away a long time."

One October day I accompanied Dara and his mother Hiva to Golestan shopping center. First we went to a bank where Hiva wanted to pay a bill. While she stood at the counter, Dara and I sat on chairs in the corner of the office. Suddenly a young *basiji* came up to Hiva and shouted aggressively at her. He yelled out, why was she wearing see-through stockings? She replied calmly that he could avert his gaze and not look at her legs. Upset by her answer, he called her a whore (*kharab*). I seized hold of the arm of Dara, who was now furious and eager to intervene. Reddened by embarrassment or anger, Hiva began to laugh loudly. The *basiji* continued to shout slogans against *bad-hejab* women and left the bank. Later, when we were sitting at a table in the coffee shop sipping our cappuccinos, and Dara gone to greet a friend at the other side of the coffee shop, I asked her what made her laugh.

Hiva said: "What could I do? He was younger than Dara. He could have been my son. And he called me a whore in front of Dara. He called me a whore just because I was wearing see-through stockings. The whole thing is so ridiculous that I could only laugh at him."

Due to the nature of the normative modesty, the humor of the youths in Iran is, however, immediately identifiable as a form of defiance. A tangible instance is sporadically demonstrated on the hills of Darakeh and Darband . Thunderous laughter (*qahqahe*), often sounding hysterical, can frequently be heard from young men who go hiking in groups. Signs warn young people to avoid loud laughter and to "show respect to others and the mountain." Loud laughter is seen as "polluting" the peaceful green environment, or as it is called also in the case of illicit music, "sound pollution" (*aloudegi-e soti*). Young people's laughter in the mountain has always appeared very surrealistic to me. Once Dara and I were hiking in the Darband area. On the way back down to an open-air coffee house for a late breakfast, we saw a group of teenagers quarreling with two *basijis*, who had accused them of "disturbing families and elders with their earsplitting laughter." One said furiously that just laughing was not a crime. I told the *basijis* that these were just kids and that they should let them go. After ten minutes or so of negotiations the *basijis* released them. The teens disappeared upward in a moment and we strolled down behind the two *basijis*. In a little while shouts of laughter again filled the valley. The *basijis* turned to us and in an ironic tune said "They are just kids?"

I asked Dara "What are they laughing at?"

He answered, "Them," and nodded toward the *basijis*.

That laughter echoing in the rocks of the mountain was more than laughter in my ears. For Bakhtin, laughter is the main aspect of carnival. It has both a deep philosophical meaning and a revolutionary power (Bakhtin 1984: 66). Like carnival, the mountain in Tehran is a scene for the laughter that is repressed by the official culture.[12] Bakhtin states that folk humor is always marked by "exceptional radicalism, freedom, and ruthlessness," practiced in "unofficial" spaces such as the hills of Darband. The laughter of the kids in the Iranian mountains was subversive. It expressed the social consciousness of the young people and destabilized the normative modesty imposed both by the state and by the parental generation. Although laughter cannot liberate the oppressed, it can force power to contemplate its own pomposity, and can deflate it with laughter. Laughter is also seen as a powerful tool of the oppressed in the postcolonial regime, a sign of insubordination (Mbembe 1992: 12).

The Language of Defiance

During the second half of the 1990s, a new youth jargon emerged on the Tehran streets. Young people have constructed their own coded language on the basis of an old argot known as *zaban-e motrebi*. It is absolutely incomprehensible to the ears of the parental generation. *Zaban-e motrebi* (musicians' language) was used by groups in old Tehran for secret communication. It came originally from the poor parts of the city and was used mainly among wrongdoers. Almost forgotten, it has been revived by middle-class Tehrani youth. The grammar is simple, but the argot drastically changes the pronunciation of words. The initial letter is replaced with â, and å is added at the end of the word. Then the initial letter followed with í is put at the end. For instance, "sigar" is turned into "aigarhsi" or "Shahram" into "Ahahramhsi." Alongside the *zanabn-e motrebi*, there is a complex and imaginative small vocabulary of about 60–70 words, which makes the youths' language distinct from ordinary Persian. The publication of *A Persian Dictionary of the Young People's Vernacular* (Moshiri 1381/2002) in Tehran in 2002 testifies to the prevalence of this youth jargon, at least in Tehran. To make it on Tehran streets you need to know a long list of slang words, with references to Hollywood as well as to classical Persian. Although the argot often contains sexist and homophobic language, it is widely used by both sexes. In the summer of 2002, the new trend was to speak Persian with an American accent. The trend originates from *Irangelesi* TV channels.

monshi (secretary) = pimp

Maikel jam-kon (lit. gatherer of Michaels—referring to Michael
   Jackson) = moral police patrolling the streets who arrest
   "Weststruck" young people

dava (medicine) = Iranian homemade vodka

Miss Marple = nosy woman

katrin = transvestite

typ-e titanic = snobbish

shaficap = Coffee shop

decorazh-e shodan = to be surprised

Kalon = police station

love andakhtan (casting love) = to befriend one of the opposite sex

Yul Brynner = [after the American actor] thick, slow

shostadelo = teacher

esko = cunt

onak = backside

erika = cock

Arnold-e feshordeh (concentrated Arnold referring to Arnold
   Schwarzenegger) = a short thin man

end-e she (lit. it is its end) = top, best

Pink baz = someone crazy about Pink Floyd

davis = Westernization of the term *dayous* = ignoble

pashom o shishe (wool and glass) = Iran's TV channels referring to
   bearded men on screen

dou dare kardan = to deceive; to fool

open = not virgin.

motodayous = a combination of the first part of *motodayen* (believer)
   and *dayous* (ignoble)

tokhmatic = poor quality. A combination of *tokhom* (testicle) and the
   English suffix *tic*

masmalization = doing a job badly; concealing something. A
   combination of *mast* (yoghurt) and the English suffix *zation*

infiniti = that's it

Consuming the Illicit

Since the Revolution the consumption of illicit culture, particularly visual culture, has been widespread among Iranians. Until the late 1990s,
the state-owned TV and radio allowed no scope for entertainment, let
alone youth culture. Alternative media therefore captured the market.
In all large cities 80 percent of households own a videocassette recorder
(VCR).[13] In Tehran, the audience for video is even larger than in other
parts of the country. There is one video set for every seven persons in

Tehran.[14] Tens of thousands of films are rented or exchanged in Tehran alone. Each household has its contact or, *filmi*, a person who comes with films usually in a briefcase and rents them out. In the mid-1990s the black market in video films had a turnover of up to U.S.$90,000,000. In 1997 *Titanic* conquered the hearts of Iran's youth. In the underground market the VHC of the film earned as much as the whole cinema industry in Iran raised during the year (2,500,000,000 toman, almost U.S.$3,000,000).[15] Another best-selling type of video tape is Iranian pop music clips known as *shou*, produced in Irangeles.

Since the early 1990s, the presence of satellite TV channels in Iran has presented the authorities with a problem. A steady stream of uninvited visual waves enters the country. Although the Majlis passed a bill banning satellite dishes in early 1995, the installations have in practice been tolerated for the past several years, except for occasional raids by the moral police. In June 2006 a new wave of raids to seize satellite dishes began. Iranians have continued to circumvent the prohibition and gain access to the airwaves by various means, including keeping an antenna in a wheelbarrow and trundling it out in the evening. More than 30 Irangelesi TV channels and a few radio programs with distinct representations of Iran and Iranians shape an alternative national imagination for people.

Since the late 1990s, installers of dishes have raced round Tehran erecting illegal dishes for between U.S.$400 and 500. Countless installers work only at night so as not to be seen. Each one connects around eight homes a day with different TV satellites.[16] Households with "analog" dishes receive about 20 Turkish and Italian TV channels or, if they turn the dish around, some Arabic and Indian channels. Turkish channels are popular, not least among Turkish-speaking Azaris. The digital system has brought more than 100 TV channels into the homes of Iranians. Music, fashion, and sports channels are the most popular.

American soap operas and TV serials such as *Charmed*, *Baywatch*, and *Beverly Hills 90210* have large audiences. In 2000 Los Angeles-based National Iranian Television (NITV), a 24-hour satellite television, began broadcasting to Iran. Founded by former pop singer Zia, who today lives in exile in Los Angeles, NITV has become a favorite channel among Iranians. Its broadcasts include music clips, talk shows, interviews with exiled pre-Revolutionary personalities, American lifestyle programs, and old nostalgic films. NITV was followed by other Los Angeles-based satellite TV stations broadcasting to Iran, Pars TV, Tapesh, and ITV. By 2006 the numbers of satellite TV stations was over 30. The most popular one among Iranian young people, Persian Music Channel (PMC), headquartered in Dubai, broadcasts Irangelesi Persian and foreign music videos (see Naficy 1993).

Apart from television, there are radio broadcasts to Iran such as Radio Seday-e Iran, also based in Los Angeles.[17] Other non-Iranian radio broadcasting companies such as BBC, VoA, and Radio Farda often have a special entertainment program. A survey indicates that more than 50 percent of the regular audience for these channels are between fifteen and twenty-five years old.[18] The same survey shows that more than 92 percent watch these channels because of their cheerful (*shad*) entertainment programs, which are in total contrast to the domestic TV programs.

VIRTUAL IRAN

The Internet has become an alternative space for Iranian youth (see Graham and Khosravi 2002). Despite all the obstacles, Internet cafés have been mushrooming in Tehran, and the number of Internet companies and courses is growing throughout the country. The regime is concerned about this. The stream of information and subversive messages into the country is more or less uncontrollable. The state is as wary of political propaganda from exiled Iranians as of the impact of pornography on morals.[19] New sites for youth and used by young people appear every day. The Internet has created a "virtual" space where young people can represent themselves. For instance, iranpinkfloyd.8m is constructed by Pink Floyd fans; tehranavenue is a magazine about the popular culture of young Tehranis; cappauccinomag is a site where Tehrani youth publish their reflections about what is happening in their city; noandishan is a forum for "young alternative thinkers of civil society"; and womeniran[20] is a feminist site. A survey of Iranian young people shows that almost 34 percent choose the Internet, foreign radio broadcasting companies, and satellite TV programs as the source of news.[21]

However, the most subversive feature of the cybertechnology for Iranian youth is the new and simple form of homepage known as a blog. There are up to 700,000 blogs in Persian—the fourth most used language among bloggers in the world. These blogs are a free space where Iranian youngsters write mainly personal diaries, but also about a wide range of topics, ranging from pornography to political issues.[22] Hossein Derkhshan, a pioneer in this field, believes that

The popularity of blogs among young Iranians suggests that great changes have happened in Iranian society during the past two decades, at least among the new generations of middle-class residents of big cities. It shows that they are carrying new values and promoting new lifestyles, which is very rare among older generations who were trying to hide their personal feelings and opinions from the others. Individuality, self-expression, and tolerance are new values which are quite obvious through a quick study of the content of Persian blogs.[23]

In the jungle of Iranian bloggers there are all kind of people, from Iranian neo-Nazi Satan worshipers to feminists and *basijis*. Blogging is not a risk-free activity. Many bloggers are jailed and many others have left Iran (see Alavi 2005). In the view of the director of the National Youth Organization, Mr. Akabri, in September 2005, "the virtual world is under control of Satan."[24]

Blogging is subversive because it brings up issues of civil society, sexual equality, and individualism. Blogging is also subversive because it rejects the norms and values of the parental generation. Older generations assert that blogging has a "vulgar spirit" (*roh-e mobtazaal*). The debate on the vulgarity of blogging is reveals the tension of linguistic and cultural authority (Doostdar 2004) between generations. The language of bloggers is sub-standard. They defy the rules of grammar and orthography. Worse, bloggers challenge ethical norms and show no respect for cultural authenticity and purity. This makes blogging an emancipator.

Blog is now an institution for disorder . . . a space for us modern, educated Iranians. . . . We want to talk. Blog is our liberator. It is why we love it. . . . We show we are not like our parents who were silenced and who died in their silence. We are a different people. We are a generation who blog. Through blogging we will reach a new order, a human order, in which we and our wishes will not be rejected.[25]

Nasrin Alvai, author of *We Are Iran*, a book about Iranian bloggers, puts it, "Iranian blogs offer a unique glimpse of the changing consciousness of Iran's younger generation. It is not less than a revolution within the revolution" (Alavi 2005: 361). This proliferating cyberculture among young people is subversive not only because it opposes the state but also because it undermines the phallocratic culture of the parental generation.

Participation in and consumption of the transnational youth culture, which penetrates the country through satellite TV and radio channels, the Internet, connections with the West through the Iranian diaspora, and so on, offer young Tehranis new options for identification and belonging. Perhaps they also get new opportunities for creating an alternative "imagined community."

Seditious Fever

Another aspect of banal politics is, as an Iranian journalist once put it, "the triumph of the pink color of Valentine over the red color of political Shiism." Earthly love has been taboo in post-Revolutionary Iran. Until the late 1990s, the Ministry of Islamic Guidance and Culture sought to banish any sign of love in books, the press, films, and music. The only permitted love was the Divine one. Fictitious love was banned, such as the books by the best-seller R. Etemadi from before the Revolution. However, since the election of Khatami, "love" has gradually returned to the movies and the press. Films like *Sheida* (Kamal Tabrizi, 1999) and *Sweet Agonies* (Alireza Davoudnezhad, 1998) are only two of the increasing number of popular love-story movies in recent years. Innumerable novels and short stories about love fill the bookshops. The books by Farideh Golbou and Fahimeh Rahimi have been the bestsellers in this genre. While Western pop music is officially regarded as corrupting, partly because it "promotes earthly love," books featuring the songs and poems of Elton John, Pink Floyd, Leonard Cohen, the Rolling Stones, or Bob Dylan are sold in tens of thousands.

However, the most conspicuous sign of the return of "love" is the rising interest among romantic young Tehranis in celebrating the Christian patron saint of lovers, Saint Valentine's Day (see Alavi 2005: 329). Just before Valentine's Day the gift, perfume, clothes, and flower shops are crammed with young people. Shopkeepers in Golestan say this holiday has increased in popularity since the late 1990s. They claim sale increases of 100 percent or more during the days before Valentine's Day. Shops in Golestan and other trendy shopping malls decorate their display windows with pink, heart-shaped cushions and chocolate boxes imprinted with "love." On Valentine's evening, chic restaurants in north Tehran are packed with young couples. This recognition of romantic "love" by young people has been followed by a new attitude toward the body and matters of sexuality. The increasing popularity of Valentine among young people has become an anxiety for the authorities. In February 2003, a cultural official of Tehran Municipality suggested that Iran should have an Islamic Valentine's Day, coinciding with the wedding anniversary of Fatima, the Prophet Mohammad's daughter.

Once I went with Dara to visit one of his friends. He handed me a photocopy of an article in English apparently taken from a magazine for men. It was a kind of "sex manual" of three or four pages with a lot of illustrations, and was about "how to give your girlfriend orgasm." The article was informative about women's bodies and how to have better sexual intercourse. I told them what the article was about. A few weeks later I could see photocopies of a Persian translation of it circulating among young Shahraki men. Such concern about giving oneself and one's partner more sexual gratification is new to me in the Iranian context. Along with other experiences during my fieldwork, this struck me as a sign of the growth of reflection over the self and the body among the younger generation (see Moaveni 2005).

New blogs and websites dealing with sexuality appear one after the other. Cyberspace gives Iranian youth a chance to talk about taboo subjects such as sexuality in general and homosexuality or pornography in particular. www.homan.com is a site for Iranian gays and lesbians. Its "practical gay liberation strategy" is one of "raising awareness." Homan acts as a support group in cyberspace and "attracts and helps many individuals who struggle throughout their coming out process, or would like to explore their sexual identity within the boundaries of Iranian society."[26] It also gives sexually explicit information in Persian about HIV and AIDS for Iranians in Iran who do not have ready access to this type of information. It also provides links to 33 other sites, mostly other gay and lesbian sites for Iranians, including Gay Persia, Iran Queer Collective, Khanaye Doost (for Iranian lesbians), and the sites of international organizations like the International Gay and Lesbian Association, and the International Gay and Lesbian Human Rights Commission. www.cekaf.com and www.jeegar.com are two erotic magazines in Persian, perhaps the first ones.[27]

A male doctor living in the U.S. created a site called Sex Doc, "devoted to sex education for Iranian youth."[28] Writing in Persian, the doctor explains his motives for starting the site as follows:

My country, Iran, is invaded by the most stupid and cruel rulers in our great history (3000 years of civilization). The rulers look at the barbarian culture of Arabs and try to impose similar restriction on [Iranian] people's happiness and their love and sex. I am trying to help them to have a better sex and love life. God bless Iran.

The doctor offers detailed information on topics such as intercourse, masturbation, and genital organs.

Apart from these more organized sites, there is a huge number of personal blogs, where Iranian youngsters publish their erotic experiences and sexual fantasies. While the male host of tootfarangi (strawberry) writes about his daily sexual experiences in Tehran, the female hosts of baakereh (virgin) and zirposh[29] (underwear) "attempt to instruct Iranian boys to kiss the right spots on a female body and to suck girls correctly."

The Body Matters, Even in Tehran

Different kinds of therapists have emerged to help middle-class people "feel better." What is called "design-of-mind engineering" (*mohandes-e tarrah-e zehn*) is one of the recently popular genres of expertise in Iran.

Journals and magazines are crammed with the marketing of various forms of such knowledge that assert that the information offered will help one to use the imagination and the power of the mind to produce positive changes. It offers methods and simple techniques to increase one's self-esteem, to obtain better health and greater vitality, to maintain one's prosperity, and to arrive at a deep state of relaxation. Another form of the "expert system" can be found in "feel-good" self-help manuals. Nasl-e nowandish (the New Thinking Generation) is a publishing firm in Tehran that has invested in this niche. On its website it presents its policy in broken English this way: "With all Persian Books on Motivation, Goal setting, Life, and Self-improvement. We pride ourselves on prompt service and attention to detail. Let us put our expertise to work for you."[30] The "self-help" manuals occupy a large part of the book market in Tehran. Best-sellers are those by Catherine Ponder, such as *Open Your Mind to Prosperity, Dynamic Laws of Healing, Dynamic Laws of Prosperity, Secret of Unlimited Prosperity, Dare to Prosper, The 7 Habits of Highly Effective People.* Other popular books are *Powerful Lessons in Personal Change* by Stephen Covey; *I Ching Wisdom: Guidance from the Book of Changes* by Wu Wei; *The Ten Commandments of Self-Esteem* by Catherine Cardinal; and *Creative Visualization* by Gawain Shakti.

Western forms of fitness have spread among young Tehranis during recent years. Centers of physical and mental training such as bodybuilding, aerobics, yoga, and meditation are mushrooming in Tehran. "Institutes of beauty" are opening everywhere. Ironically, because only the faces of girls can be exposed in public, girls are determined to ensure that they look as good as possible. Accordingly, rhinoplasty has recently become trendy. Nose operations have become so fashionable that Iranian women are happy to wear their postsurgical bandages in public. Dara believes that many girls wear plasters without having been operated on. It is a matter of status. One can see young girls wearing plasters daily in trendy places, such as the coffee shops in the Gandhi shopping center or in Golestan.

The new noses are invariably more "Western." The "aestheticization of the body" (Featherstone 1991) is one of the bases of consumer culture. Boutiques in north Tehran are crammed with illicit cosmetic products. Since the importation of "luxury" commodities such as cosmetics is forbidden, these goods are brought in by "suitcase-traders" or "smugglers" in the Persian Gulf. I accompanied such "suitcase-traders" on two occasions, once to Dubai and another time to Kish Island. Cosmetics made up the main part of the commodities. Small size, high cost at home, and great demand by Iranian consumers are characteristics that make such goods the most regular "smuggled" items. Other favored items are chocolates, crackers, and beverages. A large proportion of the "smuggled" objects are associated with *khareji* smells and scents, which convey meaning nonverbally (Hammer 2002).

Ideas of "celebrating the self" clash with the idea of "normative modesty." As has been elaborated in Chapter 3, the latter promotes "self-abasement" through its emphasis on "romantic poverty," "glamorous death" (martyrdom), and effacement (veiling). This order denies individual autonomy, and personal needs and desires are decried. "Self-assertion" has been seen by the authorities as a sign of defiance and insubordination. As I have attempted to show in the first part of this book, "normative modesty" has been constructed on the basis of elements from Sufism, the *morad/morid* relationship, Shiite rituals, the patriarchal structure in the family, and a preference for modesty. The incompatibility of "self-abasement" and "self-assertion" partly represents tensions between a "traditional" lifestyle and the newly available means of "modernity," for example, transnationally traveling mass media messages and commodities (Appadurai 1996: 3–4). "Celebration of self" and "self-assertion," however, have been described as being the main features of modernity (Lasch 1980; Blumenberg 1983). Accordingly, the clash between "normative modesty" and defiant young people is interpreted as a conflict between "tradition" and "modernity." I elaborate this issue below.

Tehrani Modern

Dara said once: "The entire conflict is just about whether to eat pizza or *abghost*" (a traditional Iranian meal). His culinary metaphor pointed to a pervasive issue among Iranian scholars and the general public. In the view of many people, Iran in the "time of the Shah" was on its way toward *tajadud* (modernity), whereas the Islamic Revolution moved the country back to the old *sonats*. The life mission of the Shah was to drive Iran to "the Gate of Civilization" (*darvaze-ye tamadon*) and make it "one of the five most modern countries in the world." In contrast, it is frequently said that "the Islamic regime has put Iran 1,400 years [the age of Islam] back in history."

The history of Iran in the twentieth century is usually discussed by Iranians in terms of the dichotomy *sonat/tajadud*. The relationship between the two poles has played a crucial role in the configuration of contemporary socio-cultural patterns in Iran. The clergy have consistently opposed *tajadud*.[31] By their "antimodern" politics they were able to manoeuver the discontent with the Shah's modernization program. In the 1960s and 1970s, an extended range of secular intellectuals shared the clergy's antagonism to the modernization policies of the Shah. The rhetoric of "Weststruckness" managed to attract secular

groups who believed that the Shah's project of modernization was stripping Iran of its cultural identity.

For young Tehranis the present order of things is associated with the
Islamic tradition. Not to identify with this tradition is interpreted by
young people and authorities alike as a sign of rejection of the present
order of things. When, in the late 1990s, reformists attempted to present Khatami as a mediator between clergy and young people, he was
characterized as the "connecting point of tradition and modernity."[32]

The young taxi driver said in a prophetic tone: "We are lost between
tradition and modernity." In his ramshackle old Iranian-made Peykan
he was driving me to Shahrak-e Gharb on a September day in 1999. A
book beside the gear lever caught my eye. It was a recent book by
Ramin Jahanbagloo, a well-known Iranian intellectual who has written
several books on modernity. *Iran and the Problem of Modernity* (Jahanbagloo 1379/2000) was a collection of interviews about the confrontation
of Iran with the "modern world." My question about the driver's opinion of the book initiated such a interesting conversation about modernity and tradition in Iran that he parked the car to continue our talk on
the grass along the Hemat highway. The taxi driver turned out to be a
student of history at Tehran University. He believed that "the problem
is that we are neither traditional nor modern. We left one, but have not
yet reached the other. We are lost." Back in the car driving toward
Shahrak-e Gharb, I took the Iranian traffic system as an example. I
pointed to the cars rushing from left and right, not respecting traffic
lines and signals: "We make cars and we use them. But we do not know
about the rules and do not respect others. Nobody drives between two
lines. Nobody flashes their indicator when they change lanes." The
driver agreed with me and attempted to "drive correctly" the rest of the
way, strictly between the lines and flashing when turning. However, he
said,

There is no point in being modern among these people. Now I am driving the
car correctly. But this makes the traffic worse when everybody drives so chaoti-
cally. Driving a car means thinking about the lines and about respecting the
space of other cars. Iranians cannot see lines and directions. Their minds are
chaotic. Traffic should mean collective collaboration but we want only to do
zerangbazi, defend our individual advantage. We Iranians are individualists
when we should be collectivists and we are collectivists when we should be individualists.

In the view of Iranian intellectuals, Iranian society is torn between an
insufficient tradition and a modernity that is not yet internalized. For
an anthropologist, it is difficult to define the border between "tradition" and "modernity." As I briefly sketched above, there has been,

rather, a *tradition of modernity* in Iran.[33] In our discussion "self-abasement" represents *sonat* and self-assertion *tajadud*, but, as I show below with the help of ethnographical vignettes, the values of *sonat* and *tajadud* are not necessarily contradictory and might overlap each other in everyday life.

Sufi Chic

Shideh, mother of an informant, was the leader of a Sufi group in Shahrak-e Gharb. She was a sophisticated pretty woman in her early forties, an educated middle-class widow who lived in her two-story house in Zone 1. Shideh moved to Shahrak-e Gharb in the early 1980s, when she and her family escaped from their hometown, Abadan, which was in the middle of a war zone. Abadan was a tropical, oil-refinery boomtown, located at the Iran-Iraq border. Modern Abadan was built by the British after World War II, but during the Iran-Iraq war (1980–1988) this beautiful city was almost destroyed. Migrants from different parts of Iran as well as India and Britain had joined the native Arabs in transforming Abadan into a transnational semicolonial city. Living there Shideh had enjoyed a "modern" lifestyle, full of "Western" activities such as horseback riding, dancing, and cocktail parties. The Islamic state put an end to that epoch of Abadan. War broke out, and along with other Abadanis Shideh and her family sought refuge in other cities. Thanks to their good economic circumstances, they were able to reconstruct a comfortable life in Tehran. Some years later her husband died of cancer and her son moved out. Life in the new city was not easy for her. She found Tehranis very *sonati* (traditionalist). Displaced from her Abadani lifestyle, and alienated from the new milieu, she felt totally paralyzed and could not even drive a car in the chaotic traffic of Tehran. In Abadan, people drove like Europeans. However, after some years, she found comfort in Sufism. She began reading classic Sufi literature and practicing its order. Nowadays, she does not drink liquor any more. She is veiled in public, albeit loosely and fashionably.

Many of our common acquaintances thought that she had taken a backward step, toward "tradition," but I found her new lifestyle very "modern" in many ways. She attends Sufi gatherings and rituals in the *khaneqah* (the Sufi house of worship) once a week. She has built up a small Sufi group, which includes many young people. Alongside hypnosis classes, yoga, and Jungian study circles, Sufism has become very trendy among middle-class young people in Tehran (see Varzi 2006: 10). On Mondays, the group gathers at Shideh's house. Usually no outsider is admitted to meetings, but Shideh made an exception for me.

Shahraki young people's Sufi activity is an Iranian version of New Age

rather than the Sufism I knew. Many young Tehranis see this "chic Sufism" as a cool religiosity. The chic, well-dressed members would arrive
around 6 p.m. The ritual begins at 7 p.m. First they read and interpret Sufi
texts. Later they pray and chant sacred phrases, followed by singing Sufi
poetry accompanied by *daf* (a large-frame drum with one or more rows
of internal metal rings, which is widely used in Sufi music). The ritual
is always performed in the same room, on the first floor. A nomadic
kelim, a traditional tea set, and pictures of holy Sufis give the room a
plain and "Iranian" atmosphere. This room differs from the rest of the
house, which is filled with English furniture, souvenirs from the
Abadan epoch. Members change their clothes to a simple white dress.
Then they sit on the floor in a circle. There are plentiful amounts of
candy and fruit in the room. Around 10 o'clock it is time for dinner,
which is usually ordered from one of the most famous restaurants in
Tehran, or prepared by a cook Shideh calls in. Contrary to the Sufi
principle of simplicity, the dinner is always fancy and exclusive, served
on a beautiful and expensive English table.

One night after dinner one of the women came into the dining room
holding a cake with burning candles. Everybody began to sing *tavalodet
mobarak* (Persian "Happy Birthday to You"). It was Shideh's birthday.
Celebrating a birthday for adults is not common in Iran. On other
nights I was surprised to find that after the ritual they listened and
danced to Iranian disco music.

Shideh's weekly schedule is divided between aerobics, yoga courses,
massage, and private fashion shows.[34] When I told her I was going to
Dubai for a short visit, she gave me a shopping list of special skin
creams and famous brands of perfume. Shideh was concerned about
her body and wanted to feel good. Such self-celebration contradicts the
conventional Sufi emphasis on self-denial.

I asked Shideh "Isn't this against the Sufi order?"

Shideh: "If your heart is pure, it does not matter what you do. Who
said to care for the self [*be khod residan*] is sin? Be yourself and be comfortable with yourself."

Similar to the "Hossein Party" performed by Shahraki youth,
Shideh's chic Sufism has brought together "self-abasement" and "self-
assertion." Shideh praises transcendental values at the same time that
she celebrates herself. Like Shahraki youth, she oscillates between *sonat*
and *tajadud*. They might think and behave *sonati* in some circumstances
and *motajaded* in other circumstances on the very same afternoon. In
the case of Shideh, we can see not only how *sonat* and *tajadud* mingle,
and appear inseparable, but also how *sonat*-ness is used as a means of
becoming *motajaded*. A chic Sufism is per se a sign of "being modern" in
the sense that it connotes a disassociation from official Islam, repre-

sented by the theocracy. For many Iranian young people, *tajadud* means disassociation from the present order in society. To be *motajaded* might be to dissociate oneself from the dominant "Arabic/Islamic narrative form of representation" of Iran and Iranians. In Chapters 4 and 5 I have attempted to show how Tehrani youth distance themselves from the present norms and social order by the "consumption of modernity." For these young people, the consumption of certain items is a tangible way to "objectify the nature of modernity" (Miller 1995a: 282). For them the entry into the consumption of *khareji* commodities is also seen as an entry into "modernity."

Nevertheless, to be modern, to dissociate oneself from the current situation, does not necessarily entail identifying oneself with *kharej* and the West. Iranian young people use parts of the Iranian culture, such as the pre-Islamic Persian cultural heritage, to construct their own native modernity. I shall briefly depict how "being modern" is performed and experienced as defiance. Other sources of defiance toward the "Arabic/Islamic narrative form of representation" are ethnic cultures, which have been relatively untouched by the official culture. Tribal cultures have recently become popular among Iranians. The clothes, music, signs, and patterns of tribal groups such as the Bakhtiari, whose culture is claimed to be "real Iranian and free from Arab influence," do not evoke the typical Iranian Muslim identity that officials represent.

Defiant Memories

The increasing interest in pre-Islamic culture among the youth indicates a conscious dissociation from Islam and Arabs. Identifying the present situation in Iran with Islam, Iranians usually blame the Arabs for bringing Islam to Iran in the eighth century. It is believed that Arabs put an end to a glorious Persian civilization. Although anti-Arab Persian chauvinism goes back a long way in history (see Tavakoli-Targhi 2001: 75–134), today it has a domestic political significance, demonstrated among middle-class Tehrani young people in the de-Arabization of everyday jargon. They avoid using common Arabic words and expressions, such as *salaam* (hello), which is replaced with Persian *doroud*. Giving ancient Persian names to children is another de-Arabization of Iranian identity. The conflict between parents who choose a non-Islamic name and the national registration bureau (*sabt-e ahval*) has become a common matter. Since the early 1990s, the state has published booklets of "permissible" names. High school students frankly express their aversion to Arabic lessons, which are enforced by the Revolution curriculum. I heard from many that they were proud to have their lowest grade in Arabic.

The fascination with non-Islamic Iranian culture among young Tehranis is articulated in different forms. One of them is the growing appeal of Zoroastrianism. Asserting that the "real" religion of Iranians is Zoroastrianism, young people identify themselves with that religion rather than with "Arab" Islam." The lure of the pre-Islamic Persian identity is also demonstrated in "pilgrimages" to sites of antiquity. One of these recently emerged sites is the village of Abyaneh. Located at the heart of Mount Karkas on the outskirts of Natanz, only 50 kilometers from Kashan, Abyaneh claims to have "remained intact" ever since the Sassanid (pre-Islamic) era, while the rest of the country has lost its authentic cultural identity under one kind of foreign occupation or another. The ancient architectural style and traditional costumes are seen to confirm the "authenticity" of Abyaneh as a pre-Islamic site. The local dialect is claimed to be similar to the Pahlavi language spoken in the Parthian (Arsacide) era (250 b.c.–224 a.d.). Two Zoroastrian fire temples complete the picture. The romantic myth of Abyaneh also emphasizes "the high intelligence" of the people of Abyaneh. One-day tours to Abyaneh offer young people an experience of pre-Islamic Iran. Moreover, small figurines of Ahouramazda, the Zoroastrian God, have become a popular necklace pendant among young people.

Another site of non-Islamic Iranian heritage is Babak Castle, an impressive castle on the top of a mountain in northwestern Iran, about 2,500 meters high. Babak Khoramdin (798–838) was leader of a resistance movement against Arab/Muslim invasion. Since the mid-1990s a new tradition has emerged. Every July 10, thousands of young (mainly Azari) Iranians visit the castle to commemorate him as a national hero. The authorities have shown intolerance toward the annual gathering, and clashes between young people and the police are repeated every year. The non-Islamic, or rather anti-Islamic (Babak fought against the Arabs who wanted to make Iran Muslim) character of the gathering annoys the authorities.

Another example of "faking authenticity" is the Mehr-e Atash (Love of the Fire) Festival, which is arranged by the local association in Shahrak-e Gharb in late April each year in order to revive Iranian identity. In a similar way *Lotous*, "the first Persian fashion journal," uses patterns and styles from the Achaemenian era in order to design clothes for "modern" Iranian women.[35]

As "the invention of tradition" (Hobsbawm and Ranger 1983) has been a means of constructing the modern European nation-state, for Tehrani youths *sonat* has ironically been a resource for becoming *motajaded*. For a young person, being "modern" is an attempt to "invent him/herself and to produce a new and distinctive self." This is the work of the imagination; a constitutive feature of modern subjectivity (Appadurai 1996: 3). For young people in my field, modernity as a lifestyle means to be "*a*-present," to be distinct from "now" in Iran, a break from the present rather than from the past or "tradition." By representing themselves as "modern," they dissociate themselves from the current predicament existing in the Islamic Republic.

Everyday life for young Tehranis is a space where discipline is deflected and resisted. Through a multitude of tactics (de Certeau 1984) articulated in the details of everyday life, Tehrani youngsters challenge the hegemonic social order. Rarely engaging in organized and planned "resistance," young people attempt to avoid subordination to power by using spontaneous and opportunistic practices. As this chapter has ethnographically illustrated, the tactics they use range from violent battles to consumption of illegal commodities, bodily pleasure, and defiant hilarity. It is a performance of defiance rather than political resistance. As we have seen in Chaharshanbeh souri, football riots, student movements, coffee shops, shopping malls, ski slopes, hiking areas, and taxis, this defiance is performed in public locations. Used deliberately or accidentally, these sites are exploited as scenes for challenging dominant meanings. Real public spaces, as well as virtual ones either on the Internet or in the cinema, serve as sites for the collective challenges directed at the authorities.

Conclusion

I have a recurring fantasy that one more article has been added to the Bill of Rights: the right to free access to imagination.
—Azar Nafisi

This is not the real Iran. The real Iran you find in Los Angeles.
—Elli

In the first two chapters, I sought to describe the cultural politics in post-Revolutionary Iran. Besides being based on a machinery of surveillance, authority in Iran is primarily produced through a network of institutions (schools and rituals), social relations (parent/children relations), ideas (normative modesty), and aesthetics (the celebration of austerity). The power of theocracy is forged with the help of cultural institutions such as Sufism (rejecting worldly life), the omnipresence of the Karbala tragedy, and the phallocentric organization of space.

The state has created an official regime of "display" and also of "consumption" (for example, the *basiji* style and Karbala rituals). It has also created and encouraged officially sanctioned and channeled desires, including an unending stream of sacrificial desires (for example, in the form of willing martyrdom). Alongside this official regime the younger generation has developed its own oppositional order of "display" (Chapter 3), including consumption (Chapter 4), that generates a carnivalesque "desire," which is individualistic, sexualized, and to a large extent Western-inspired.

The first two chapters also showed how the Islamic Republic in Iran imposes its will in the form of the strategic control of place. The younger generation's tactics exploit opportunities to transform place into space. They do this through "improper" behavior, veiling, language, humor, "incorrect" colors, consumption in the Golestan shopping center, and Chaharshanbeh souri (the emphasis on a Persian identity rather than an Islamic one), at a "Hossein Party" (parodying convention), during a ride in a taxi (when having an erotic moment or a passionate political discussion), in coffee shops (imagining *kharej*), in basements (and playing Rock), and even hiking in the mountains, young Tehranis defy the imposed social order, albeit in short-lived and place-specific ways (see de Certeau 1984: 37). Public spaces in post-Revolutionary Iran have been a stage for contestation between the official regime of display and the oppositional ones of the younger generation. The Third Generation has created its own carnivalesque rituals. Their ritual is not a moment of antistructure in a dialectical process of structure-making, nor is it a place of nonstructure. It is, rather, the limit and opponent of *official* structure. It displays through parody and distortion the limitations and ineffectiveness of the hegemonized order (Kelly and Kaplan 1990: 137).

The theocracy opposes what it regards as the defining feature of *tajadud* (modernity) among Iranians, namely self-assertion.[1] "Self-assertion" refers to a social, political, and philosophical emphasis upon the autonomous individual in contrast to collective identity.

During my fieldwork, young people demonstrated this self-assertion socially and politically through individual autonomy Young people assert themselves through consumption, humor, and more multifaceted identity building. In these practices of self-construction, consumption of illicit commodities plays a significant role. Contrary to academic opinions that regard consumption in terms of the global dictatorship of capitalism, fetishization, and loss of agency, consumption for many young people in Tehran is a way of displaying their *own* constructed self and rejecting the subject position ordained from above.

However, much of their consumption is possible because of the class position—socioeconomic status—they occupy. I have focused largely on "middle-class" consumers, given the nature of my fieldwork site. But middle-class consumption is also implicated in subcultural styles among young people which are also simultaneously regarded as forms of defiance by the authorities. Research into middle-class culture in non-Western societies usually concludes that participation in transnational cultural projects is not only about "Westernization" but also often about the making of local middle-class culture (Liechty 2003; O'Dougherty 2002). Though there is often a correlation between subcultural capital and economic resources, they can sometimes be in conflict. For example, young Tehranis mock the flashy lifestyle of the nouveaux riches who possess money but not "modern" cultural capital.

It is important to note that within the middle class there are divisions that do not coincide with the division between youth and the authorities. Young Tehranis distinguish themselves from "others": *javad* in contrast to trendy globalized youngsters in Shahrak-e Gharb; *bazari* in contrast to shopping mall loiterers; provincial people from the Tehranis; the traditional (*sonati*) from modern (*motajaded*); and southern Tehranis from northern Tehranis. Although class affiliation is present in this distinction-making, for the young the whole idea of distinction primarily relates to the normative social order imposed by the state and the parental generation.

For many young people in Tehran, *kharej* involves the personal and immediate experience of modernity, from reading *Lolita* to acting in a play by Lorca to arranging an underground rock concert, stressing individual autonomy through participation in political movements, parodying conventional traditions, or simply searching for more sensuous pleasure. This is the paradox of the Islamic Republic: it has been counterproductive. The Islamic Republic has indeed produced what it aimed to eradicate, a self-assertive mode of being, one central theme of modernity.

Expectations of Modernity

One summer morning in 1987, Karachi, Pakistan. I was drinking a *doudpati* (milk-tea) with a young police officer. I was then at the end of my teenage years, the age of most of my informants today. Having fled Iran early that year to avoid military service during the Iran-Iraq war, I was a refugee just like many other tens of thousands of Iranian, Iraqi, and Afghan refugees in Karachi. The young police officer in civilian clothes was stationed in Cantt Station neighborhood, where a large number of refugees were concentrated. He was there to keep an eye on us. He had a room in Sun Shine Hotel at the opposite side of Hotel Shalamar where I lived. Shortly after his arrival in the neighborhood, we became good companions at our common early morning habit of drinking *doudpati* with small crisp "British" biscuits at the small restaurant beneath Sun Shine Hotel. That summer morning, our conversation was about the Iranian and Pakistani national airline companies, Iran Air and PIA (Pakistan International Airlines). We talked about airplane models, international flight routes, and destinations. In a way, we competed with our national airlines by asserting them as the more "advanced" and more "modern" airline. The destinations were, of course, almost limited to the European and North American cities. We did not even consider each other's countries "international" destinations. For us, *kharej* was synonymous with the Western world. Over our *doudpati* cups, me, a persecuted and undocumented refugee together with a low grade police officer from a village in north Pakistan, in a deplorable and dreadful place of indescribable poverty—packed with refugees and human/narcotic smugglers—"traveled in the West"—to use Amitav

Ghosh's words. Ghosh, an Indian anthropologist who later became a celebrated novelist in San Francisco, impressively describes his conversation with an Egyptian imam about the military capacity of India and Egypt as they discussed which one was more "advanced" (1986). In the discussion between the Pakistani police officer and me, our countries' links to *kharej* (the West) through the national airlines (see Ferguson 1999: 235), were used as hallmarks of the modern world. This was my own and my generation's idea of modernity.

19 years later, July 2006. At a funeral ceremony in my village in Bakhtiari (southwestern Iran), under a hot sun in the early afternoon, a sorrowful tribal ritual was performed. During the ceremony, Sepehr joined me. He was only twenty-three years old and the youngest teacher in the village's school. I had not met him since he was a child. Since he came from a poor family and had managed to become a teacher, Sepehr gained everybody's respect in the village. I asked him about his parents and sisters and whether he was married. He answered my question very politely with a question about Jürgen Habermas's view on civil society. I did not have a satisfactory answer to his question. Yet it launched a good discussion on civil society in general. While we watched the ritual, we talked about freedom of speech, women's rights, and secularism. It was amazing to listen to his reflections and witness his fascination with political issues in a village that was remotely connected to Tehran and other large cities and did not even have a library. Sepehr and his generation's intellectual curiosity and their intense participation in the local debates on modernity were striking. In Tehran, the Iranian Artists' Forum (Khaneye Honarmandan-e Iran)[2] is the best location to observe the curiosity of the youth. Weekly courses or lectures are usually packed with young people who come to listen and discuss art and philosophy as well as other cultural and social issues. Moreover, statistics show a considerable number of translations of modern philosophy. For instance, all the books of Friedrich Nietzsche have been translated into Persian and have gone into multiple printings since the 1990s. The same holds for many other philosophers of modernity. There have been more Persian translations of Kant in the past decade than in any other language.[3] This is Sepehr's and a part of his generation's expectation of modernity.

*   *   *

Being modern, as in the case of class, is also a spatial process. The performance of modernity requires a place where difference or distinction is manifested. Shahrak-e Gharb, the Golestan shopping center, coffee shops, Abyaneh, and Babak Castle are some of the stages on which Tehrani young people perform their modernity as well as obtaining new imaginative resources. That these locations are also consumer settings indicates the significance of consumption in the cultural practice of being modern. Chapters 3 and 4 noted how cultural practices by young people in Tehran remap urban space into modern and nonmodern.

As we have seen, the sources of their modernity are multiple. For young people, modernity has not only one center but a range of centers, from Tokyo, Dubai, Moscow, or Stockholm to Los Angeles, and the sources of inspiration range from Zen Buddhism to Nietzsche, local tribal culture, and Zoroaster. They enjoy and imagine a multicentered youth culture that is the result of access to alternative modernities. Consumption of *kharej* (in form of ideas, fashion, visions, or commodities) does not make Iranians Westernized or "mimic-(wo)men." This ethnography shows that young Tehranis' consumption of *kharej* is a process of identity-making in the Iranian context. Their consumption of global youth culture is given meaning in relation to local debates and struggles.

Iran: Whose Imagination?

[I]magine us the way we sometimes didn't dare to imagine ourselves: in our most private and secret moments, in the most extraordinarily ordinary instances of life, listening to music, walking down the shady streets or reading *Lolita* in Tehran. (Nafisi 2003: 6)

With these words Azar Nafisi, a former university teacher in English literature at Tehran University, begins her book, *Reading Lolita in Tehran* (2003). In the mid-1990s, she gathered together seven young women at her apartment every Thursday morning to read and discuss forbidden works of Western literature. Written in a semi-autobiographical and social history style, her book is about these meetings and how these young women attempted to create "another world" for themselves and pretend to be "somewhere else" (Nafisi 2003: 329). At the beginning of *Reading Lolita in Tehran*, Nafisi tells about two pictures she had taken with her seven young female students. "In the first photograph, standing in our black robes and scarves, we are as we had been shaped by someone else's dreams. In the second [unveiled], we appear as we imagine ourselves" (24). "Which one is real?" she asks. "Which of those two worlds was more real, and to which did we really belong?" (26). As she herself asserts, we no longer know the answer.

In this book I tell a similar story about the way young people in Tehran use their imaginations in the cultural practices of everyday life to make sense of their lives. In particular, the way they make sense of their lives by being "modern" (*motajaded*). The popular culture industry in the diaspora, with its concentration in Irangeles, has constructed an image of Iran as it was prior to the Revolution, rather than of contemporary Iran under Islamic rule. How young Tehranis imagine themselves and their nation is influenced by their access to the media. While ignoring entirely Iranian state media products, they are avid consumers of alternative media—satellite TV channels and radio programs, the Internet, and video—in which they can find alternative representations of what it means to be Iranian.

Being "modern" among young Tehranis seems to be a state of mind, rather than a matter of materiality. It is about what one wants or wishes to be: it is imagined. And as we have seen, it is also invented oppositionally; it is about what one does not wish to be. As Appadurai states, "imagination is now central to all forms of agency, is itself a social fact, and is the key component of the new global order" (1996: 31). Imagination is a social practice, a constitutive feature of modern subjectivity. In contrast to fantasy (which implies passivity), imagination is the prelude to expression and, especially when collective, can fuel actions such as nationalist movements (7).

The powerful imaginations produced in the Golestan shopping center, in the Iranian cinema, in coffee shops, in the hills north of Tehran, in the little group who read *Lolita*, or in Irangeles, suggest that the contemporary Iran is not the only possible reality for the nation. For many Iranians, the "reality" found on Tehran's streets is a fake. There is not only one single imagined community but several imagined communities simultaneously at work in the lives of Iranians. Iranians have created an alternative national imagination, a simulacrum—to simulate, to feign, to have what one does not have (Baudrillard 1996: 167). Nevertheless, the alternative national imagination is not a false representation of reality, but it indicates that the "real" Iran does not feel authentic for many Iranians. For many Iranians the "authentic" Iran comes, ironically, from Los Angeles.

For them the "authentic" Iran exists in heterotopias inside the country and in Irangeles, cyberspace, satellite TV channels, and so on. Their alternative national imagination is re/produced in the carnivalesque rituals of the Third Generation. Can a political situation be changed by a carnival? (Kelly and Kaplan 1990: 141). Perhaps not, but imaginations of young people may yet act as a site for social change in the future.

Coda

In September 1999, tired of my fieldwork, I flew to Isfahan to join my family for a weekend. My parents and the rest of my family were at my father's country house, 300 kilometers south of Isfahan. I arrived in Isfahan at nightfall. I would join my family the day after. Nobody expected me in Isfahan, and I had no intention of visiting acquaintances or relatives. That night my home town became a "transit" for me. I left my hotel in downtown Isfahan to walk in Chahar Bagh (Isfahan's Champs Elysées). It was a warm night, and Isfahanis, a people of faithful flâneurs, had taken over the streets and parks. After 12 years absence, Isfahan was not the same familiar city I once knew. Isfahan was not a "foreign land" for me. Rather, it was I who was alien there, or at least it felt like that. Isfahan is a "religious city" (*shahr-e mazhabi*), and its people are known to be culturally conservative and religiously fanatical. Compared with Isfahan—in my informants' terminology—Tehran is "Paris." After several hours wandering on familiar streets but among unfamiliar crowds, I went to Siyose Pol, a bridge over the Zayandehroud River, which divides the city into two parts). It is a 400–year-old bridge built of tawny bricks. This architectural masterpiece has two levels. On the bridge (which is only for pedestrians) you see the surface of the society; virtuous, modest, asexual, and veiled people strolling in large family flocks, while under the bridge (a shady vaulted passageway almost at the level of the river) is a known meeting place for homosexual Isfahanis. However, in the middle of the bridge I saw a familiar face— my English teacher from high school in the early 1980s. Between two tall walls of the bridge, lit by a pale yellow light, almost like a fog lamp, surrounded by black veiled women and somberly dressed men, in a melancholic atmosphere, full of loneliness, I met the man who had opened my teenage eyes to the forbidden *kharej*.

He had been very special to me during high school. We lived in the same neighborhood, and I often accompanied him to or from the school. He was *different*. Always dressed elegantly, in a dark suit, white shirt, colorful tie, and well-polished black shoes, he walked to the school with a *khareji* magazine in his hand. Moreover, his shaven face annoyed the *basijis* in the high school, who did not miss a chance to tease and mock him. Being in his mid-forties and still single in the patriarchal society of Isfahan made him a deviant figure. He was called a pedophile (*bachebaz*) and gay (*hamjensbaz*). He was also marginalized among the staff, who did not want to jeopardize their careers by mixing with him. He was in fact a highly sophisticated man, an exceptional person in Isfahan. Besides English he had a good knowledge of French and German. His great hobbies were collecting stamps, postcards, and coins. His idol was Frank Sinatra, and he loved Gary Cooper—particularly in *High Noon*. He lent me his old issues of *National Geographic* and *Life* (which were of course illegal), and *khareji* LPs (valuable stuff in Isfahan). Despite oppression from school authorities and the harassments, he did not change himself and never gave up his tie. He was finally fired, without a pension.

That night on the bridge, he seemed aged and tired, even if still in his old dark suit and tie. After fifteen years, I had a short but pleasant talk with him that night. This time, contrary to the old days, he asked and I, a returnee with fresh news from *kharej*, answered. That night, on the ancient bridge, under a fog-light, surrounded by unknown masses and in the somewhat overwhelming "traditional" order of things, he once again opened up a parenthesis of cosmopolitanism—curiosity to know the Other—for me. On that ancient bridge—a solid monument of our cultural heritage—we, one exiled and the other outcast, "traveled to the world of the imagination." He might be called a Westernized person. Yet his love for *khareji* music and literature did not make him less Iranian than any other person on that bridge. He had his own way of being Iranian. Different but real.

Why did he choose to disobey orders and risk his career for a necktie or for Frank Sinatra? Why are young people today in Tehran prepared to do the same? Why do they put up with harassment, brutality, and punishment for "trivial" things like dancing, kissing, a *Playboy* magazine, a receiver for satellite TV channels, a pair of Nike sneakers, or a bottle of homemade vodka? Is it a way of survival? Is it to build an imagined world alongside the cruel real one? Why didn't the girl in the telephone booth just push the strands of hair under her scarf and save her life?

Notes

Introduction

1. In the eighteenth century, Jeremy Bentham devised a new structure for prisons, which would allow guards to watch prisoners continuously. From a tower in the center of a ring of cells, one or two guards could constantly monitor those inside the cells. This also meant that those in the cells were always aware of being watched by those in the tower. Bentham believed that the prospect of being constantly under scrutiny would discourage bad behavior. His vision, the Panopticon, would fundamentally alter the function and efficiency of prisons and similar institutions and eventually became a metaphor for society.

2. What Scott calls the hidden resistance of "foot dragging, dissimulation, false compliance, pilfering, feigned ignorance, slander, arson, sabotage, and so forth" (1985: 29), de Certeau terms the practice of *la perruque*, the misuse of work time for personal activity (1984: 25–26). For a critical reading of Scott, see Gutmann (1993).

3. This criticism can be made of de Certeau's own theories of "everyday life resistance," as they contain no detailed ethnography of how people actually carry out resistance. This has partly caused the gender blindness in his theories (de Certeau 1984). In post-Revolutionary Iran, a gender perspective may be particularly pertinent, as women have been especially prominent in challenging the authorities through individual acts of resistance (see Afkhami and Friedle 1994; Moghissi 1993; Esfandiari 1997; Shahidian 2002).

4. For me, reading Foucault's analysis of power always evokes post-Revolutionary Iran. Not surprisingly, he has become very popular in Iran since the late 1990s. Most of his works are translated into Persian and top the best-seller list.

5. For a detailed history of the Birmingham School see Lave et al. (1992).

6. Iran's Youth Employment Organization indicates 60 percent in 2003 (IRNA [Islamic Republic News Agency], April 26, 2003) and the Statistical Center of Iran indicates 50 percent in 1996.

7. *Iran Financial News,* January 19, 2002.

8. *Eghtesad-e Iran* (Iran Economics) 27 (2001).

9. *Newsletter of Chamber of Commerce, Industry, and Mines* 1 (March 2000).

10. Economic Intelligence Unit (2002), 23.

11. *Peyk-e Sanjesh* (Informative Periodical of the Country's Evaluation & Training Organization) 6 (25) (2001).

12. For instance, 8,000 physicians in 2002 were jobless; see *Gofteman* 3 (3) (Winter 2002): 202–7.

13. *Norouz*, October 24, 2001, www.undcp.org/iran, accessed December 2006.

14. *Jaam-e Jam* 3 (603) (June 16, 2002).

15. *Hamshari*, 25 Aban 1379/2000.

16. *Reform and Rectification; Social, Cultural & Training* 1 (8) (Nov. 2002): 46–47.

17. World Population Data Sheet 2006, www.prb.org, accessed December 2006.

18. A disproportionate emphasis on nomadism at the expense of other domains of society is not specific to Iran alone. The anthropology of the whole Middle East suffers from such a shortcoming (see Eickelman 1989: 75). The romantic attraction of nomads was perhaps an effect of *Grass: A Nation's Battle for Life*, a film made by Merian C. Cooper and Ernest Schodsack in 1925. The film documented the heroic migration of 50,000 Bakhtiari nomads over the hazardous Zagros Mountains in search of grass for their herds. *Grass* caused a great sensation in the West and attracted a large number of Western as well as Iranian anthropologists to explore nomadic groups throughout the country, particularly around the Zagros Mountains. In Iran anthropology (*mardomshenasi*) is still taken as synonymous with nomadic studies. In April 1997 I visited the anthropological section of the Department of Social Sciences at Tehran University, to seek advice about planning fieldwork in the bazaar of Tehran (the field I was first interested in). I was advised to do research in Sweden (where I lived). When I asked them to be more specific in their interests within the anthropology of Sweden, they answered, "the Lapps, the Swedish nomads." Brian Street (1990: 247) had a similar experience during his fieldwork in Iran. He was frequently asked by anthropologists which tribe he was studying, not *whether* he was studying "tribes." There are several exceptions, such as Loeb (1977) on the Jewish minority in Shiraz; Beeman (1986) on power in the Persian language; Good (1977) and Good et al. (1985) on medical anthropology; Fischer (1980), Fischer and Abedi (1990), Loeffler (1988), and Thaiss (1973) on Islam as a social institution; Rotblad (1972) on the bazaar; Haeri (1989) on the institution and practice of temporary marriage, *mut'a*, among poor women in the religious cities of Qom and Mashhad; Mir-Hosseini (1993) on Islamic law and women's situation; Adelkhah (1991), Torab (1996 and 2006), and Kamalkhani (1996), on women's situation in urban milieus.

19. Fischer (1980), Good et al. (1985), and Good and Good (1988), however, initiated a new anthropological analysis of the sociopolitical situation in Iran. In his impressive fieldwork in the holy city of Qom, Fischer illuminates the social organization of the clergy and the religious framework of the Revolution. Looking at Shiite symbolism in everyday life, he developed the notion of the "Karbala paradigm" to explore the cultural basis of the political changes. Good and Good (1988) developed the concept of the "Karbala paradigm" and studied emotional discourse in post-Revolutionary Iran by analyzing the Shiite ritual of Ashura. They explored how the state defines the meaning and legitimacy of emotions in the field of politics. The ideas of these anthropologists are obvious in my exploration of the cultural foundation of the Islamic order of things, particularly in Chapter 3. Another anthropological study, which provided me with a new angle for looking at the Iranian society, is William Beeman's study

on the hierarchical structure of the Persian language (1986). He illustrates how tacit power relations, particularly between generations, are embedded in the Persian language.

20. For more on the dilemma of being a native anthropologist in Iran, see Khosravi (1996).

Chapter 1. Cultural Crimes

1. For a general overview of flogging and cultural crime see Amnesty International (1987), *Iran Violations of Human Rights*, 59–60.

2. For some instances see Reuters, December 25, 1999; March 22, 2000; and AFP January 22, 2000; September 7, 2001; September 11, 2002.

3. The pre-revolutionary public law, institutionalized in 1907, represented a compromise between secular constitutionalism and Shiism. Features of the constitutional law that were against *sharia* were modified (see Hairi 1977).

4. Ayatollah Ahmad Jannati, Friday Sermon, August 31, 2001.

5. Islamic Penal Law (Qanon-e Mojazat-e Eslami) (1377/1998), 135–36.

6. However, the cinema and the media industry were rescued from total eradication by Ayatollah Khomeini's speech on February 2, 1979: "We are not opposed to cinema, or radio, nor to television; what we are opposed to is vice and the use of the media to keep our young people in a state of backwardness and dissipate their energies" (Khomeini 1981: 258). Eastern European, Chinese, and later Japanese films replaced Western ones. The Ministry of Islamic Culture and Guidance clearly announced the desirable attributes of an Islamic cinema: a cinema that focuses on themes of the Islamic Revolution; the war between Iran and Iraq, national unity, the victories and self-sacrifices of Iranians," "resistance against cultural invasion," "the family as a social unit," "women as the central axis of the family," and "cultural values of Islam" (Sadr 1379/2000: 44–45). For cinema in post-revolutionary Iran see Naficy (1992, 2000); Dabashi (2001); Tapper (2002); Fischer (2004).

7. www.anasronline.com, accessed April 12, 2001.

8. *Iran News*, February 2, 1995. The postwar Vietnamese state used similar notions in anti-West propaganda, such as "cultural poisons," "spiritual pollution," or "U.S. cultural invasion" (Taylor 2001: 132–33).

9. *Ya Letharat* 9 (186) (July 24, 2002).

10. "Indigestion" is a term Ramin Jahanbagloo used to address the condition at the nineteenth annual Center for Iranian Research and Analysis (CIRA) conference, Toronto, April 29, 2001. For more on this topic see Boroujerdi (1996); Gheissar (1998); Mirsepassi (2000).

11. IRNA, December 15, 1999.

12. *Majlis and Research* 1994: 8–14.

13. *Gozaresh-e Film*. 63 (1995).

14. Ayatollah Emami Kashani, Friday Sermon, September 16, 1994.

15. Minister of the Interior Basharati, *Keyhan*, April 5, 1994.

16. *Majlis and Research* 1994.

17. Agence France Presse, November 10, 2001.

18. For a review of IRIB policy see Mohamadi (1377/1998).

19. Quotations are from the official homepage of IRIB, www.irib.com

20. Constitution of the Islamic Republic, General Principles. Chapter I, Article 8.

21. During this week, *basijis* are praised for their efforts. Representatives of *basij* in other cities are summoned to Tehran. Speeches are delivered by clerics and workshops are organized. However, in order to reproduce the ethos, the regime constantly voices its significance. In mosques, schools, radio, and TV the practice of "requiring what is beneficial and forbidding what is evil" is publicly praised by the authorities. The message is also spread by graffiti on walls. In several places in Shahrak-e Gharb, graffiti proclaim the words of Imam Ali: "Compared to the principle of mutual discipline, all good deeds, even Jihad for God, is like a drop in the sea."

22. "It is basic to Islamic law that the father, the grandfather, the guardian, and the instructor, be he a teacher or a master of a trade, have the authority to discipline a minor. If the father or the guardian beats a boy and he dies, jurists disagree as to the responsibility of the father or guardian. . . . If the instructor beats the boy and the boy dies, then, if the father or guardian had not granted permission for the beating, the instructor is liable as an aggressor. If the permission had been granted for the beating, then he is not liable" (Bahnassi 1982: 183).

23. *Iran Daily*, August 18, 2001

24. Muhammad Ghazali, *Ehya ul-Ulom*, quoted in Panahi (1378/1999: 175).

25. During his period of learning, lasting usually from his teens to his late twenties, the disciple renounces earthly life to give complete allegiance to the master. As a disciple, he has no home, no job, no family, no property, and even no sexual relations. Not surprisingly, the disciple is also called *khadem*, servant. There are several obligations on the disciple. (1) The master owns the life and property of the disciple. (2) Total loyalty and compassion to the master is required from the disciple. (3) Never is he allowed to question the master. (4) He should serve the master. There are several other rules commanding a respectful demeanor, such as not talking loudly, not laughing, not sitting, not eating in the master's presence. Nor should the disciple look into the eyes of the master. The position of disciple results from a long period of being a "servant," and expressing this status in demonstrations of humility in the master's presence. Total obedience is the core of *morad/morid* relations. They are demonstrated in various rituals, such as hand kissing, and the gift-giving that symbolically acts out a "feminization" of the disciple. Moroccan anthropologist Abdellah Hammoudi in an excellent study of Sufism in his country has observed how the bodily practices of the master/disciple relationship reproduce inequalities of power. While the disciple's body should be humiliated, the master's body is seen as blessed and holy. His body has healing power. A sick disciple may suck the master's tongue or swallow his spit or defilement from his body in the hope of being cured. This body contact may also be sexual. "Sexual intercourse with a saintly person is considered beneficial" (Hammoudi 1997: 139). A similar pattern can be found in the *morad/morid* relation. Through the *morid*'s abdication of virility in sexual intercourse and by carrying out "feminine" domestic tasks (cooking, sewing, cleaning, etc.) the *morid* structurally becomes a woman during his education. In order to produce charisma, the *morad* feminizes his *morid*, who becomes like a woman in a patriarchal society to serve his male *morad*. Thus the process of feminization strengthens the master's hegemony over the disciple. Mystical and familial ethics appear as replicas of one another, each reinforcing the other. Exchanges of gifts, rituals, rites of passage, and feminization within the master/disciple relationship, all mirror the political structure in Iran.

26. IRNA, November 29, 1995.
27. *Tehran Times*, November 22, 1995.

Chapter 2. The Aesthetics of Authority

Epigraphs: Nabokov (2001: 42); Shamloo (1991: 518).

1. *Ta'arof* is defined by Beeman (1986: 56) as "the active, ritualized realization of differential perceptions of superiority and inferiority in interaction. It underscores and preserves the integrity of culturally defined roles as it is carried out in the life of every Iranian, every day, in thousands of different ways." One expression of *ta'arof* is the rituals of courtesy that are determined by social distance. See also Asdjodi (2001).

2. Al-e Ahmad's "cultural puritanism" is demonstrated by his xenophobia, which covers all who are not Shiite Muslim Persian-speaking men. When he wants to condemn the nineteenth-century secular intellectuals Mulkum Khan and Tabalof, he emphasizes their respective "Christian" and "Caucasian" identities (1982: 33). Later on, when he refers to another writer he does not forget to caution that "he is Bahai" (33n72).

3. Shariati, *Modernization and Civilization*, www.shariati.com, accessed May 2001; see also Shariati (1979).

4. Slavenka Drakulić, in her impressive description of everyday life in societies under communist regimes in Eastern Europe, describes similar patterns. Trivial acts such as eating pizza or wearing a fur coat or even using make-up were perceived as "bourgeois manners." "A nicely dressed woman was subject to suspicion, sometimes even investigation" (Drakulić 1987: 23).

5. For the illustration see Chelkowski and Dabashi (1999: 130–31).

6. Even American war films, particularly the Rambo series, were shown to the revolutionary militias in order to increase their military morale.

7. Secular political organizations praised poverty as a sign of the dignity of the individual and disciplined their members into complete self-sacrificing. Medhi Rezai, a legendary leader of the Mojaheddin-e Khalq, in his defense speech at the military court before the revolution announced proudly that he had lived on bread and cheese.

8. Czeslaw Milosz, in his classic essay on Stalinist totalitarianism, asserts how fear paralyzes people and makes them adjust themselves to the average type in their style, body movement, and facial expression: "Cities become filled with the racial type well-regarded by the rulers: short, square men and women with short legs and wide hips. This is the proletarian type, cultivated to an extreme, thanks to binding aesthetic standards" (1990: 66).

9. For a detailed study of temporary marriage in Iran see Haeri (1989).

10. A fear of sexuality has also been evident among secular forces. The Iranian left's political morality of puritanism and self-sacrifice denied individual desires of activists in favor of "something bigger." Calling a woman "comrade" (*rafiq*) among leftists and "sister" among Islamists places women in a "sexually forbidden" category (Milani 1992: 27). For further discussion on the issue of sexuality among leftist groups see Shahidian (1996). The leftist organizations were even against sexual intercourse between their members (see Nafisi 1371/1992: 226).

11. Graybill and Arthur (1991: 21) illustrate a similar situation in their study of the Mennonites of the United States, showing how female bodies are con-

trolled. As it is impossible to know a person's commitment to the faith, symbolic forms of self-expression are closely monitored.

12. A 1998 survey on the representation of women in Persian textbooks shows that a woman is recognized only in her role of mother, doing housework (see Kar 1380/2001: 74–77).

13. http://movaghat.blogsky.com, accessed July 2006.

14. *Taqvim-e Zanashoui* (Marriage Calendar), 2nd ed. (Qom: Ateragin).

15. National Youth Organization (2006).

16. Foucault describes how the power techniques of Christianity made individuals into religious subjects. Religious ideas in terms of disciplining the body, sexuality, confession, and a correct relationship to the self turned individuals into subjects over whom the church could exercise power. Foucault believes that the most salient feature of this form of power, as it is exercised in Catholicism, is that it cannot be exercised without knowing the inside of people's minds, without exploring their souls, without making them reveal their innermost secrets. It implies knowledge of the conscience and an ability to direct it (Foucault 1983: 214). By opening oneself, by making confession and acknowledging one's sins, the individual becomes an object of the pastoral power. Pastoral power does not look after just the whole community, but each individual in particular, during his or her entire life.

17. Veiling and unveiling are not new political symbols. Since the early twentieth century, the history of the veil has been interwoven with the history of the Iranian state. Reza Shah's modernization policy started with forced "mass unveiling" (*kashf-e hejab*) in 1936. Inspired by Ataturk's advances in building modern Turkey, Reza Shah sought to change Iran into a Westernized nation-state. Veiling, as a traditional dress code, was abolished in favor of Western dress. The new dress policy included men having to wear a cap called the Pahlavi Cap. All Iranian women were ordered to be unveiled in public. Veiled women were not allowed in cinemas or public baths. Taxi and bus drivers were liable to a fine if they accepted veiled women as passengers (see Savory 1978: 98). This "mass unveiling" in the name of modernization was brutally implemented by the police. Less than a half-century later, women's veiling was once again a top political issue, only this time women were terrorized into being veiled in the name of a "back to the roots" ideology.

18. For detailed documentation on the violence against women accused of *bad-hejabi*, see Kar (1380/2001: 126–33, 239–48).

19. *Kalam-e Emam*, vol. 21, quoted in Nafisi (1992: 177).

20. Cf. Orhan Pamuk's (2006) *huzn* in the Turkish culture.

21. Following the death of the Prophet, the young Islamic community had undergone an intense conflict between Imam Ali and his children on one side and the Caliphs in power on the other—a conflict that underlies the Sunni and Shiite division. At the time of the event, Imam Hossein, his family, and about 70 men had left Medina for Kufa in response to a call from the people of Kufa in southern Iraq, who were oppressed by Yazid, a tyrant Caliph who showed no respect for Islamic rules and values. Stopped by Yazid's army, they camped in the desert of Karbala. Abandoned by the people of Kufa, surrounded by Yazid's forces of about 4,000 men, and cut off from water, Hossein foresaw his failure. After fruitless negotiations, a bloody battle took place, on the 10th day of Moharram, known as Ashura. Imam Hossein and 72 men were killed.

22. For a detailed history of the development of ritual, see Ayoub (1978). For an interesting account of how the ritual of Ashura has traveled from Iraq via

Persia and the Indian subcontinent to the Caribbean Basin see Chelkowski (1993). For a description of the ritual on Trinidad see Thaiss (1999). See also Korom (2002).

23. I was surprised to see how an Armenian in my neighborhood arranged a *rowzeh-khani* ritual in his house. He told me that he is committed (*eradat dashtan*) to Imam Hossein, for his courage and nobility.

24. Saadr ud-Din Vaiz Qazvini, *Riyad al-quds*, vol. 2, 113–14, quoted in Enayat (1982: 182).

25. For the significant effect of the Karbala tragedy on the secular movements see Dorraj (1999).

26. This is a citation of the fifth Imam Jaafar Sadiq.

27. Young *basijis* were sent to the front wearing red headbands with the text "O, Hossein" (*ya Hossein*). As it happened, the Iran-Iraq war went on close to the Karbala desert. Along the roads toward the front signs were posted indicating the distance to Karbala, e.g., "Karbala, 25 kilometers," as a way of inspiring *basijis* and others moving ahead.

28. For further details on the role of Karbala-related symbols in the mobilization of young people in the Iran-Iraq war see Gieling (1999).

29. For this cinema genre, see Varzi (2002).

30. *Zanan* 67, 1379/2000, 2.

31. The political significance of color in the Iranian context resembles the color symbolism of the former Socialist states. Stade shows, in his study of the culture of politics in the GDR, how the West was imagined by the notion *bunt* denoting bright colored, many colored, very varied and chaotic, while the East was identified with *Baukasten*, boxes of toy bricks, associating the color gray with rectangularity and order (see Stade 1993).

32. *AFP*, September 25, 2000; *Zanan* 67, 1379/2000.

33. *Iran*, Sunday, June 2, 2002.

34. Dr. Davar-e Sheykhavandi, Nakhostin Hamayesh-e Mali Asibhay-e Ejtemai (the first national conference on social damages), 11–13 Khordad 1381/2002 in Tehran. See also *Zanan* 88, 1381/2002.

35. *Aftab*, March 2, 2002.

36. See *Hamshahri*, June 28, 2000.

37. Bakhtin in his study of the medieval culture examines how hilarity was suppressed and laughter remained outside all official spheres and all official forms of social relations. Laughter was eliminated from religious as well as non-religious ceremonies. It is striking to read how Bakhtin found similar processes in medieval times. Nevertheless, laughter was "returned" to public life under the shelter of feasts. Every feast, in addition to its official, ecclesiastical part, had another folk carnival part whose organizing principle was laughter: "It was this folklore which inspired both the imagery and the ritual of the popular, humorous part of the feast. . . . The truth of laughter embraced and carried away everyone; nobody could resist it" (1984: 82).

38. *Christian Science Monitor*, October 28, 2005.

39. *ILNA* and *Rooz*, September 14, 2005.

Chapter 3. A Dissident Neighborhood

1. For the significant role of international radio broadcasters in Iranian society, see Seberny-Mohammadi and Mohammadi (1994).

2. 1996 Census of Tehran, *Sarshomari 'Omomi Nofous va Maskan-1375, Tehran (22 Districts)* (Tehran: Statistical Center of Iran, 1999). All statistical information here is from this source.

3. *Bavar*, 1, 2 (November 1998).

4. Tehran Geographic Information Centre (2005: 165).

5. *Hamshahri*, March 9, 2002.

6. Tehran Geographic Information Centre (2005: 132).

7. As Sencer Ayata (2002: 38) discusses in her study of the new suburban middle class in Ankara, in contrast to "high-tempered, ill-mannered uncivilized and communitarian Islamists," "the 'truly civilized' are regarded as individualistic and able to think and act autonomously. They know 'how to behave' in public."

8. See *Bavar* 1 (November 1998); 22 (February 1999).

9. For instance, see *Chicago Tribune*, January 2, 1998.

10. Sidanius and Pratto (1999) discuss how the majority opinion about the status of blacks and other ethnic minorities in American society corresponds with these groups' own notions of their status.

11. Öncü (1999), in her article on urban identity processes in Istanbul, has illustrated a similar "cultural battle" of the highly cultured Istanbulites against the tasteless overconsumption of the rich and the vulgar mass consumption in the lower classes.

12. This Bollywood-influenced Iranian genre found its audience mainly in the working class and the new urban poor, who were often immigrants from rural areas and felt threatened by the unfamiliar modern lifestyle of upper- and middle-class Tehranis.

13. For a further study of the film *Jaheli* see Naficy (1985).

14. AFP, October 13, 2002.

15. *Bavar* 123 (May 1999).

16. Ibid.

17. Ibid.

Chapter 4. A Passage to Modernity: Golestan

Epigraphs: Benjamin (1999: 908); Kowinski (1985: 62).

1. For a discussion of this topic see Miller (1995b, 1997b).

2. Nevertheless, the amount of research that was focused on this significant socio-cultural phenomenon is finite and limited in scope. Except for two anthropological articles (Thaiss 1971; Rotblad 1975—based on unpublished dissertations) almost all research on the bazaar in Iran has studied it in its political context (e.g., Keshavarzian 2007; Ashraf 1359/1980, 1990; Mozaffari 1991).

3. A salient character of Iranian cities is a center formed by three major institutions the royal palace or citadel, the mosque, and the bazaar. The bazaar of Tehran is close to Golestan Palace and the Shah Mosque. The main gate of the mosque opens into the bazaar.

4. Organizational theories distinguish between institution (as a set of cultural rules that may regulate social activities in a patterned way) and organization (as the materialized form of institutions). In the bazaar this distinction is not as clear as it seems. The economic, social and moral arenas are interlocking. Islamic values and ethics permeate the whole socio-economic life of the bazaar. Thus, the bazaar an institutionalized organization.

5. The bazaar is also a sacred place. Ghazali, one of the greatest theologians

of Islam, considered the bazaar to be a proper arena of *jihad*, an internal holy war to maintain one's morality against the temptation to take unfair advantage (Fischer 1995: 207).

6. One way the importance of Islam in the bazaar is explicitly expressed is in its architecture. Unlike modern architecture, with its characteristic straight lines and right angles, the basic shapes of the bazaar and the mosque are arched forms and vaults. The dome-like ceilings, decorated with various plant designs and beautiful brick patterns, recall the space of the mosque. The light that comes in through circular openings in the domes creates a sacred atmosphere. The interpretation made by orientalists of Iranian architecture (manifested primarily in the mosque and the bazaar) usually refers to Sufi spirituality (Ardalan and Bakhtiar 1979; see also Stierling 1976). The physical form of the bazaar is considered to evoke spiritual inwardness (Jabari 1379/2000). In this "exotic gaze" the succession and repetitive style of the bazaar's arcades, circular forms, vaulted ceilings, and *hujrehs* is symbolically interpreted as a continuity of the Islamic tradition. Moreover, the physical enclosed space of the bazaar encompasses a large number of religious buildings. For instance, the bazaar of Isfahan includes 14 mosques, 13 religious schools, and 3 mausoleums. The terminology used in the bazaar points to its integration of religious value and business. The concept *hujreh* refers both to a business office in the bazaar and to a student room in a religious school. A *hajji* is a person who has performed the ritual pilgrimage to the "House of God" in Mecca, but the title is also used for businessmen of the bazaar in order to guarantee the virtue and morality of the *bazaris*.

7. Due to the modernization policy, the guilds lost much of their influence. Extensive import (mostly through state-owned firms) caused a decline in domestic production, especially in certain manufacturing sectors such as the textile industry that were important to the bazaar economy (Ashraf 1359/1980; see also Rotblat 1972, 1975). In the oil nationalization movement in the early 1950s bazaris supported the prime minister, Mohammad Mosaddeq, against the court. His nationalist economic policies were favorable to local industry and the merchants. However, the royal court took power through a coup d'état backed by the U.S.. After the fall of Mosaddeq, the bazaar faced a harsh and repressive period. In the 1970s, due to an intensified modernization of economic arenas, the conflict between the bazaar and the Shah again became intensive. A new capitalist class had emerged, due largely to state-sponsored investments. It consisted of entrepreneurs who, with considerable aid from the state, had become active in the modern sectors of industry and finance (see Parsa 2000: 200–201). The new modern bourgeoisie was more appropriate and reliable for the Shah and his modern Iran than the petty bourgeoisie of the bazaar had been (Ashraf 1990). The state established a Chamber of Guilds with full supervisory power over all bazaar guilds and launched an anti-profiteering campaign against the *bazaris* (Mozaffari 1991). The result was drastic humiliation and persecution of the *bazaris*. By October 1977 more than half (109,800 of 200,000) the shopkeepers in Tehran had been investigated by the price control authorities. 43,000 *bazaris* in the large cities had been jailed or deported to remote areas (Parsa 2000: 206). Nevertheless, the bazaar still dominated trade. It controlled two-thirds of domestic trade and one-third of imports. In the late 1970s, the bazaar of Tehran encompassed 6 square miles with nearly 20,000 shops, and more than 10,0000 persons worked there (201).

8. For the role of *bazaris* in the Revolution see Parsa (2000: 200–216) and Keshavarzian (2007).

9. The entrance of two young women dressed in mini-skirts could cause a huge turbulence in Tehran's bazaar before the Revolution. Once I witnessed a quarrel between a woman covered in a black *chador* and two younger women dressed in dark-blue tunic and headscarf (*mantou va rousari*). They were totally veiled but not well enough for the agitated woman in the *chador*. Pointing at the two women, she complained loudly "old *bazaris* were better. They would not tolerate such shamelessness."

10. In an interesting study, Hammer (2002) examines the role of "border-crossing" truckers in the emergence of Hungarian consumer culture in the 1970s and 1980s. By supplying illicit objects of desire and images of other cultures, truckers, by transporting knowledge and attitudes, contributed to the emergence of a "plurality of social existence" (2002: 84) in socialist Hungary.

11. For conspiracy theory among Iranians, see Ashraf (1374/1995).

12. Shamloo (1377/1998: 1126); see also Moshiri (1381/2002: 31).

13. A popular section of the medieval Iranian bazaar was the Qeysarieh (derived from Caesarea, a town in Asia Minor), where imported luxury goods of the best quality were traded. Today the Qeysarieh in the bazaar is a tourist attraction, where a different kind of "foreign taste" is catered to. Nonresident Iranians and foreign tourists find old stuff here ranging from two- or three-year-old swords to a sixty-year-old door handle. While in Golestan "foreign taste" refers to modern lifestyle, in Qeysarieh "foreign taste" means a search for "authentic" Iranian culture. The bazaar of Tehran still plays a crucial role in foreign trade. Furthermore, historical records give us a softer picture of the bazaar of past times than that conveyed by contemporary Muslim ideals. For instance, we can learn that there were musical groups in the bazaar and that festivities were arranged by *bazaris*. In spite of the hard resistance the *bazari* sector has put up, the modernizing process has also left its mark on the bazaar. A new generation of *bazaris* have grown up in a society very different from that of their fathers. While the older generation had a traditional education from the religious schools and limited insight into modern lifestyles, the new one is educated and influenced by the mass media. Education and expanded professional opportunities have created other options for the *bazaris'* children than the ones that were open to their fathers.

14. See Ericksen (1990) for "liming," a Trinidadian "art of doing nothing"; see also Miller (1994).

Chapter 5. The Third Generation

1. *New York Times*, June 16, 2002.

2. Farzad Hassani, www.nasle3.com, accessed May 2003.

3. In *The Captive Mind* (first published in 1953), Milosz characterized the relationship that prevails between people under Stalinism as acting: "with the exception that one does not perform on the theater stage but in the street, office, factory, meeting hall, or even the room one lives in" (1990 [1953]: 54). Ironically, he in turn was influenced by Joseph-Arthur Gobineau, an orientalist who spent many years in Persia in the mid-nineteenth century. Milosz was struck by the similarities between customs in Eastern European countries and the *ketman* (to conceal) Gobineau had described. *Ketman* is another term for the Shiite tradition of *taqiyeh*, dissimulation of belief.

4. *Javanan Gereftar dar Tofan-e Gharayez*. This is the title of a handbook on

young people published by the center of religious learning in Qom (Hoze-ye Elmiye Qom), n.d.

5. www.nasle3.com, accessed May 3003.

6. *Goft-o-Gu* 19 (1377/1998): 17–27.

7. The similarity with the situation under Stalinist regimes is striking: "A smile that appears at the wrong moment, a glance that is not all it should be can occasion dangerous suspicions and accusations. Even one's gestures, tone of voice, or preference for certain kinds of neckties are interpreted as signs of one's political tendencies" (Milosz 1990 [1953]: 54).

8. Parts of a letter from a young man published on www.gooya.com, accessed November 2001.

9. BBC, June 6, 2000.

10. *Peymayesh-e meli-ye arzeshha-ye javanan* (Tehran: Pazhoheshkade-ye Meli-ye Motaleat-e Javanan [National Center for Youth Studies], 2004).

11. *Asr-e Ma*, April 19, 1995.

12. *Hayat-No*, 1 *mehr*, 1381/2002.

13. *Gozaresh* 136 (1381/2002): 36.

14. The anthropologist Ziba Mir-Hosseini has directed a documentary film about runaway girls in Tehran. Shot in 2000, *Runaway* follows five teenage girls who challenge the former generation's regulations (Mir-Hosseini 2002).

15. *Film Monthly* 18 (249) (2000): 7.

16. *Bulletin of the 10th Festival of Films from Iran*, October 24, 1999.

17. The contest for representation has caused a tension between IRIB and the cinema people. For instance, IRIB has steadfastly refused to use advertisements for films disliked by the conservatives. Ironically IRIB's boycott of a film has usually increased its popularity.

18. www.tehranavenue.com, November 2003.

19. *Film Monthly* 19 (278) (2001): 100–102.

20. *Rah-e Nou* 3 (18) (Aban 1381/November 2002).

21. *Rah-e Nou* 3 (19) (Azar 1381/December 2002).

Chapter 6. Cultures of Defiance

1. AFP, October 23, 2001.

2. *Gozaresh* 128 (1380/2001).

3. For student movements in post-revolutionary Iran see Mahdi (1999).

4. ISNA, March 16, 2006.

5. In his celebrated article on domination and subordination in postcolonial nation-states, Mbembe (1992) examines how power is inherent in the banal routines of obedience and adherence to the innumerable official rituals such as the wearing of uniforms or the hanging of portraits of the despot in one's home or office.

6. www.zirzamin.se, accessed January 2007.

7. Interview with the editor of *Zirzamin*, July 25, 2006, Stockholm.

8. Ibid..

9. www.tehran360.com, accessed October 2002.

10. www.o-hum.com, accessed January 2007.

11. Quoted in Bakhtin (1984: 92 n 37).

12. In his study of Rabelais, Bakhtin (1984) states that folk humor has existed since the Middle Ages and developed outside the official sphere. "Forbidden

laughter" dominated the "unofficial" spheres, the marketplace, feast days, or carnivals (1984: 71–72). Carnivalesque laughter connected bodies of varying age and social class. "This is why festive folk laughter presents an element of victory not only over supernatural awe, over the sacred, over death; it also means the defeat of power, of earthly kings, of the earthly upper classes, of all that oppresses and restricts" (92).

13. *Mehr* 107 (1378/1999).
14. *Naghd-e Sinema* (Cinema Critique) 14 (1377/1998).
15. *Mehr* 107.
16. *Gozaresh-e Film* 180 (1380/2001).
17. I did a short period fieldwork in Los Angeles between January and April 2000 to get an insight into the process of the displaced "culture production." I interviewed artists, musicians, TV producers, and people from music companies. These ethnographies of Irangeles were initially planned to be a part of this book but, due to some changes of focus in the process of analyzing the material, they were taken out.
18. *Gozaresh-e Film* 180.
19. For the role of the Internet in the formation of modern middle-class Tehranis, see Rouhani (2001).
20. www.iranpinkfloyd.8m.com, accessed October 2002; www.tehranavenue.com, accessed October 2003; www.cappauccinomag.com, accessed October 2003; www.noandishan.org, accessed May 2002; www.womeniran.com, accessed September 2003.
21. *Peymayesh-e meli-ye arzehsha-ye javanna-e Iran* (Tehran: Pazhoheshkade-ye Meli-ye Motaleat-e Javanan [National Center for Youth Studies], 2004).
22. For a detailed study of Iranian sites on the Internet, see Graham and Khosravi (2002); Alavi (2005). For an extensive list of Iranian sites visit www.iranian.com.
23. Hossein Derakhshan, "Blogs, an Iranian Perspective," *BlogTalk*—A European Conference on Blogs: Web-based publishing, communication and collaboration tools for professional and private use, May 23–24, 2003.
24. www.emrouz.info/archives/print/2005/09/000490.php.
25. http://sibestaan.malakut.org, accessed July 2006.
26. www.homan.com, accessed November 2002.
27. www.cekaf.com, accessed November 2002; www.jeegar.com, accessed June 2006.
28. http://sexdoc.blogspot.com, accessed November 2002.
29. http://tootfarangi.blogspot.com, accessed November 2002; http://baakereh.blogspot.com, accessed November 2002; http://zirposh.persianblog.com, accessed November 2002.
30. www.naslenowandish.com, accessed December 2002.
31. The popular rhetoric of the Revolution has an "antimodern" ring. The clergy's antagonism to "modernity" (*tajadud*) goes back to the nineteenth century, when their position within education and law was threatened by secularization. There is a common understanding among Iranian scholars that the movement towards modernity in Iran originated in the two severe defeats by Russia in 1804 and 1828. The bitterness of losing a large part of the country in the North, the humiliating conditions imposed by the victorious Russians, and the question of what was to happen to the great Persian kingdom, "awakened" some Iranians both inside and outside the Qajar royal court. Like many other intellectuals, the Crown Prince of the time, Abbas Mirza, was convinced that the

country needed a "New Order" (*nezam-e jadid*), based on *tajadud* (modernity). Modernization was indeed synonymous with Westernization. The only hope was to become like Europeans. By an "unconditional acceptance and promotion of European civilization ... Iran should become Europeanized, in appearance and in essence, physically and spiritually" (Taghizadeh 1339/1960, quoted in Gheissari 1998: 41). The task of modernization began with the system of education, which hitherto had been controlled and conducted by the clergy. Another major reform was implementation of the law (*qanoun*). Reformists advocated *qanoun* as a weapon against religious canons (*shariat*) as well as against the Shah's despotic power. The Constitutionalist Revolution (*mashruteh*) in 1906/7, directed mainly by nationalists and Europe-educated intellectuals, was the first national project for the modernization of Iran. Its main aim was the institutionalization of a civil law, and the first Constitution (*qanoun-e asasi*) was a copy of the Belgian one.

32. *Iran-e Javan* 82 (1999): 26.

33. Regrettably, there have been very few efforts to explore this tradition in Iran. Most historical and sociological studies dealing with modernity in Iran emphasize the dichotomizaton of *sonat* and *tajadud*. An exception is Jamsheed Behnam (1375/1996, 1379/2000) who attempts to map out a native modernity and distinguish it from Westernization.

34. Adelkhah (2000) observes that religious gatherings for women (*jallese*) are indeed meetings where it is legitimate for people, at the same meeting, to pray, make vows, and fix the time for the next body-building session.

35. *Lotous* (first Persian fashion quarterly journal) 2 (no date) (Tehran: Anstitue farhangiye Fakhr).

Conclusion

Epigraph: Nafisi (2003: 338).

1. In his classic, *The Legitimacy of the Modern Age* (originally published in German in 1966), the German philosopher Hans Blumenberg (1983) points to "self-assertion" as the general characteristic of modernity.

2. http://www.iranartists.org/en/, accessed July 2006.

3. *New Republic* 12, June 5, 2006, 27.

Glossary

bad-hejab: improperly veiled
basij: mobilization; refers to voluntary militia
basiji: members of the *basij*
bidard: lit. without pain, painfree; Weststruck; irresponsible; ignorant
gharbzadegi: Weststruckness
haram: unlawful
fokol: Persian version of *faux col* (French for detachable collar)
fokoli: *faux col*-wearer; refers to Iranian dandies who adopted European lifestyle
hejab: veil
Hezbollah: Party of God; refers to pro-government groups
hezbollahi: members of Hezbollah
jahel: ignorant; refers to male chauvinism
javad: nonmodern; local; poor; traditionalist; an Arabic boy's name;
kareji: foreign, from abroad; Western
mahram: related; a legal term denoting a relationship by blood, milk, or marriage
namahram: unrelated; one who is not *mahram*
passazh: shopping arcade, mall
sonat: tradition
tajadud: modernity
toubeh: repentance
ummah: Islamic community
Vali-ye Faqi: The Ruling Jurist; the spiritual leader; today Ayatollah Khamenei.

Bibliography

Abdi, Abbas and Mohsen Goudarzi (1378/1999). *Tahvoulat-e Farhangi dar Iran* (Cultural Changes in Iran). Tehran: Ravesh.

Abrahamian, Ervand (1989). *Iranian Mojahedin*. New Haven, Conn.: Yale University Press.

——— (1993). *Khomenism: Essays on the Islamic Republic of Iran*. Berkeley: University of California Press.

Abu-Lughod, Lila (1986). *Veiled Sentiments: Honor and Poetry in a Bedouin Society*. Berkeley: University of California Press.

Adelkhah, Fariba (1991). *La Révolution sous le voile: femmes islamiques d'Iran*. Paris: Karthala.

——— (2000). *Being Modern in Iran*. New York: Columbia University Press.

Afkhami, Mahnaz and Erika Friedle (1994). *In the Eye of the Storm: Women in Post-Revolutionary Iran*. Syracuse, N.Y.: Syracuse University Press.

Aghaie, Kamran S. (2004). *The Martyrs of Karbala: Shi'i Symbols and Rituals in Modern Iran*. Seattle: University of Washington Press.

Ahmadi, Ali Asghar (1380/2001). *Tahlili Tarbiyati bar Ravabet-e Dokhtar va Pesar dar Iran* (An Educational Analysis of Relationships Between Girls and Boys in Iran). Tehran: Anjoman Ulia va Murabian (Parent-Teacher Association of the Islamic Republic of Iran).

Alavi, Nasrin (2005). *We Are Iran*. London: Portobello Books.

Al-e Ahmad, Jalal (1357/1978). *Dar Khedmat va Khyanat-e Rowshanfekran* (On the Service and Treason of the Intellectuals). Vol. 1. Tehran: Kharazmi.

——— ([1340/1961]/1982). *Plagued by the West (Gharbzadegi)*. Trans. Paul Sprachman. Delmar, N.Y.: Caravan Books.

Amani, Mehdi (1992). *Les effets démographiques de la guerre Iran-Irak sur la population iranienne*. Paris: Institut national d'études démographiques.

Amir-Ebrahimi, Masserrat (1992). L'image socio-géographique de Teheran en 1986. In Hourcade Adle, ed., *Teheran capitale bicentenaire*. Paris-Tehran: IFRI.

——— (1374/1995). Tasir-e Farhang Sara-ye Bahman bar Zendegi-ye Ejtema'i va Farhangi-te Zanan va Javanan-e Tehran (The Impact of Bahamn Cultural Complex on the Social and Cultural Life of Tehran's Women and Youth), *Goft-o-Gu* 9: 17–26.

——— (1999). L'intégration socioculturelle du sud de Tehéran dans la capitale. Ph.D. dissertation, Université Paris X.

——— (1380/2001). Zanan, Tajrobe-ye Shahr va Zohor-e Andarouniha va Birouniha-ye Jadid. *Jens-e Dovom* 10: 4–16.

Amnesty International (1987). *Iran Violations of Human Rights: Documents Sent by Amnesty International to the Government of the Islamic Republic of Iran.* London: Amnesty International.

Anderson, Benedict (1983). *Imagined Communities: Reflections on the Origin and Spread of Nationalism.* London: Verso.

Appadurai, Arjun (1988). Putting Hierarchy in Its Place. *Cultural Anthropology* 3: 36–49.

——— (1996). *Modernity at Large.* Minneapolis: University of Minnesota Press.

Appadurai, Arjun and Carol A. Breckenridge (1995). Public Modernity in India. In Carol A. Breckenridge, ed., *Consuming Modernity: Public Culture in a South Asian World.* Minneapolis: University of Minnesota Press.

Ardalan, Nader and Laleh Bakhtiar (1979). *The Sense of Unity: The Sufi Tradition in Persian Architecture.* Chicago: University of Chicago Press.

Ardebili, Mosavi (1380/2001). *Towzihoule Masael.* Qom: n.p.

Arjomand, Said Amir (1989). Constitution-Making in Islamic Iran: The Impact of Theocracy on the Legal Order of a Nation-State. In June Starr and Jane F. Collier, eds., *History and Power in the Study of Law: New Directions in Legal Anthropology,* Ithaca, N.Y.: Cornell University Press.

Asad, Tala (2000). Agency and Pain: an Exploration. *Culture & Religion* 1 (1): 29–60.

Asdjodi, Minoo (2001). A Comparison Between *ta'arof* in Persian and *limao* in Chinese. *International Journal of the Sociology of Language* 148: 71–92.

Ashraf, Ahmad (1359/1980). *Mavan-e Tarikhy-e Rushde Sarmayedari dar Iran.* Tehran: Zamine.

——— (1990). Bazaar-Mosque Alliance: The Social Basis of Revolts and Revolution. *International Journal of Politics-Cultures and Society* 1 (4): 538–67.

——— (1374/1995). Tavahoum-e Toute-e (Conspiracy Theory). *Goft-o-Gu* 8: 7–46.

Ashuri, Daryoush (1376/1997). *Ma va Moderniyat* (We and Modernity). Tehran: Sarat.

Augé, Mark (1995). *Non-Places: Introduction to an Anthropology of Supermodernity.* London: Verso.

Avini, Sayyed Morteza (1379/2000). *Rastakhiz-e Jan* (Resurrection of the Soul). Tehran: Saqi Publishers.

Ayata, Sencer (2002). The New Middle Class and the Joys of Suburbia. In Deniz Kandiyoti and Ayfle Saktanber, eds., *Fragments of Culture: The Everyday of Modern Turkey.* London: I.B.Tauris.

Ayoub, Mahmoud (1978). *Redemptive Suffering in Islam: A Study of the Devotional Aspects of Ashura in Twelver Shiism,* The Hague: Mouton.

Azadarmaki, Tagi (2006/1385). *Patouq va modernite-ye Irani* (Patouq and Iranian Modernity). Tehran: Loh-e Fekr.

Baghi, Emaduldin (1379/2000). *Jamm'e Shenashi Qiyam-e Emam Hossein* (Sociology of Imam Hossein's Movement). Tehran: Nashre Ney.

Bahnassi, Ahmad Fathi (1982). Criminal Responsibility in Islamic Law. In Cherif Bassiouni, ed., *The Islamic Criminal Justice System.* New York: Oceana.

Bakhtin, Mikhail (1984 [1965]). *Rabelais and His World.* Bloomington: Indiana University Press.

Barth, Fredrik (1969). Introduction. In Fredrik Barth, ed., *Ethnic Groups and Boundaries: The Social Organization of Culture Difference.* Oslo: Universitets Forlaget.

Basmenji, Kaveh (2005). *Tehran Blues: Youth Culture in Iran.* London: Saqi.

Bassiouni, Cherif M. (1982). *The Islamic Criminal Justice System.* London: Oceana.

Baudrillard, Jean (1996). *Selected Writings.* Ed. Mark Poster. Cambridge: Polity Press.
Bayat, Asef (1997). *Street Politics: Poor People's Movements in Iran.* New York: Columbia University Press.
Beck, Ulrich (2002). The Cosmopolitan Society and Its Enemies. *Theory, Culture and Society* 19 (1–2): 17–44.
Beeman, William (1986). *Language, Status, and Power in Iran.* Bloomington: Indiana University Press.
—— (2001). Emotion and Sincerity in Persian Discourse: Accomplishing the Representation of Inner States. *International Journal of the Sociology of Language* 148: 31–57.
Behnam, Jamsheed (1375/1996). *Iraniyan va Andish-ye Tajadud* (Iranians and Ideas of Modernity), Tehran: Farzan.
—— (1379/2000). *Berlaniha: Andishmandan-e Irani dar Berlan* (Iranian Intellectuals in Berlin). Tehran: Farzan.
Benard, Cheryl and Zalmay Khalizad (1984). *The Government of God: Iran's Islamic Republic.* New York: Columbia University Press.
Benjamin, Walter (1999). *The Arcades Project.* Cambridge, Mass.: Belknap Press of Harvard University Press.
Bloch, Maurice (1989). *Ritual, History, and Power: Selected Papers in Anthropology.* London: Athlone.
Blumenberg, Hans (1983 [1966]). *The Legitimacy of the Modern Age.* Cambridge: Mass.: MIT Press.
Bollas, Christopher (1993). *Being a Character: Psychoanalysis and Self Experience,* London: Routledge.
Boroujerdi, Merhdad (1996). *Iranian Intellectuals and the West: The Tormented Triumph of Nativism.* Syracuse, N.Y.: Syracuse University Press.
Borneman, John (1992). *Belonging in the Two Berlins: Kin, State, Nation.* Cambridge: Cambridge University Press.
Briongos, Ana (2000). *Black on Black: Iran Revisited.* London: Lonely Planet.
Brown, Michael F. (1996). On Resisting Resistance. *American Anthropologist* 98 (4): 729–49.
Buck-Morss, Susan (1991). *The Dialectics of Seeing: Walter Benjamin and the Arcades Project.* Cambridge, Mass.: MIT Press
Campbell, Colin (1987). *The Romantic Ethic and the Spirit of Modern Consumerism.* Oxford: Blackwell.
Cheheltan, Amirhasan (1380/2001). *Tehran, Shahr-e Biaseman* (Tehran, the City Without Sky). Tehran: Negah.
Chelkowski, Peter (1991). Popular Entertainment, Media and Social Change in Twentieth-Century Iran. In *The Cambridge History of Iran.* 7 vols. Cambridge: Cambridge University Press, 1968–1991. 7: 765–814.
—— (1993). Traces of Iranian Rituals in the Caribbean Observances of Moharram, *Iranshenasi* 5 (1): 54–71.
Chelkowski, Peter and Hamid Dabashi (1999). *Staging a Revolution: The Art of Persuasion in the Islamic Republic of Iran.* New York: New York University Press.
Clinton, Jerome W. (1987). *The Tragedy of Sohrab and Rostam: From the Persian National Epic, the Shahname of Abol-Qasem Ferdowsi.* Seattle: University of Washington Press.
Cohen, Anthony (1985). *The Symbolic Construction of Community.* London: Tavistock.

196   Bibliography

Cohen, Erik (1971). Arab Boys and Tourist Girls in a Mixed Jewish Arab Community. *International Journal of Comparative Sociology* 12 (4): 217–33.

Cohen, Stanley (1972). *Folk Devils and Moral Panics: The Creation of Mods and Rockers*. London: MacGibbon & Kee.

Dabashi, Hamid (2000). The End of Islamic Ideology. *Social Research* 67 (2): 475–503.

——— (2001). *Close Up: Iranian Cinema, Past, Present, and Future*. New York: Verso.

Davis, Dick (1999). *Epic and Sedition: The Case of Ferdowsi's ShĀhnĀmeh*. Washington, D.C.: Mage.

de Certeau, Michel (1984). *The Practice of Everyday Life*. Berkeley: University of California Press.

Devictor, Agnès (2002). Classic Tools, Original Goals: Cinema and Public Policy in the Islamic Republic of Iran (1979–97). In Richard Tapper, ed., *The New Iranian Cinema: Politics, Representation and Identity*. London: I.B.Tauris.

Dirks, Nicholas B. (1994). Ritual and Resistance: Subversion as a Social Fact. In Nicholas B. Dirks, Geoff Eley, and Sherry B. Ortner, eds., *Culture/Power/History: A Reader in Contemporary Social Theory*. Princeton, N.J.: Princeton University Press.

Dirks, Nicholas B., Geoff Eley, and Sherry B. Ortner (1994). Introduction. In Nicholas B. Dirks, Geoff Eley, and Sherry B. Ortner, eds., *Culture/Power/History: A Reader in Contemporary Social Theory*. Princeton, N.J.: Princeton University Press.

Doostdar, Alireza (2004). "The Vulgar Spirit of Blogging": On Language, Culture, and Power in Persian Weblogestan. *American Anthropologist* 106 (4): 651–62.

Dorraj, Manochehr (1992). Populism and Corporatism in Post-Revolutionary Iranian Political Culture. In Samih K. Farsoun and Mehrdad Mashayekhi, eds., *Iran: Political Culture in the Islamic Republic*. London: Routledge.

——— (1999). Symbolic and Utilitarian Value of a Tradition: Martyrdom in the Iranian Political Culture. In Fred Dallmayr, *Border Crossings: Toward a Comparative Political Theory*. Lanham, Md.: Lexington Books.

Douglas, Mary (1982). *Natural Symbols*. New York: Pantheon.

Drakulić, Slavenka (1987). *How We Survived Communism and Even Laughed*. New York: Vintage.

Dreyfus, Hubert and Paul Rabinow (1983). *Michel Foucault, Beyond Structuralism and Hermeneutics*. Chicago: University of Chicago Press.

Economic Intelligence Unit. *Iran Country Profile*. London: EIU, 2002.

Eickelman, Dale F. (1989). *The Middle East: An Anthropological Approach*. Englewood Cliffs, N.J.: Prentice-Hall.

El Guindi, Fadwa (1999). *Veil: Modesty, Privacy and Resistance*. Oxford: Berg.

Elias, Norbert (1978 [1939]). *The Civilizing Process: The History of Manners*. Oxford: Blackwell.

Enayat, Hamid (1982). *Modern Islamic Political Thought*. London: Macmillan.

Eriksen, Thomas H. (1990). Liming in Trinidad: The Art of Doing Nothing. *Folk* 32: 23–43.

Esfandiari, Haleh (1997). *Reconstructed Lives: Women and Iran's Islamic Revolution*. Baltimore: Johns Hopkins University Press.

Farsoun, Samih K. and Mehrdad Mashayekhi, eds. *Iran: Political Culture in the Islamic Republic*. London: Routledge.

Featherstone, Mike (1991). *Consumer Culture and Postmodernism*. London: Sage.

Ferguson, James (1999). *Expectations of Modernity: Myths and Meanings of Urban Life on the Zambian Copperbelt.* Berkeley: University of California Press.

Fischer, Michael M. (1980). *Iran: From Religious Dispute to Revolution.* Cambridge, Mass.: Harvard University Press.

——— (1995). Bazaar. *The Oxford Encyclopedia of the Modern Islamic World,* vol. 1. Oxford: Oxford University Press.

——— (2004). *Mute Dreams, Blind Owls, and Dispersed Knowledges: Persian Poesis in the Transnational Circuitry.* Durham, N.C.: Duke University Press.

Fischer, Michael M. and Mehdi Abedi (1990). *Debating Muslims: Cultural Dialogues in Postmodernity and Tradition.* Madison: University of Wisconsin Press.

Floor, William (1984). Guilds and Futuvvat in Iran. *ZDMG* 134: 106–14.

Foucault, Michel (1977). *Discipline and Punish: The Birth of the Prison.* London: Allen Lane.

——— (1983). The Subject and Power. Afterword in Herbert Dreyfus and Paul Rabinow, *Michel Foucault, Beyond Structuralism and Hermeneutics.* Chicago: University of Chicago Press.

——— (1986). Of Other Spaces. *Diacritics* 16 (1): 22–27.

——— (1990 [1978]). *The History of Sexuality: An Introduction.* New York: Vintage.

——— (1997 [1982]). Technologies of Self. In Michel Foucault, *Ethics: Subjectivity, and Truth,* ed. Paul Rabinow. New York: New York University Press.

——— (2000 [1978]). Governmentality. In Michel Foucault, *Power,* ed. James Faubion. New York: New Press.

Friedberg, Anne (1994). *Window Shopping: Cinema and the Postmodern.* Berkeley: University of California Press.

Geertz, Clifford (1979). Suq: The Bazaar Economy in Sefrou. In Clifford Geertz, Hildred Geertz, and Lawrence Rosen, *Meaning and Order in Moroccan Society: Three Essays in Cultural Analysis.* Cambridge: Cambridge University Press.

Gheissari, Ali (1998). *Iranian Intellectuals in the 20th Century.* Austin: University of Texas Press.

Ghosh, Amitav (1986). The Imam and the Indian. *Granta* 20 (Winter): 135–46.

Gieling, Saskia (1999). *Religion and War in Revolutionary Iran.* London: I.B.Tauris.

Goffman, Erving (1959). *The Presentation of Self in Everyday Life.* New York: Doubleday.

Good, Byron J. (1977). The Heart of What's the Matter: The Structure of Medical Discourse in a Provincial Iranian Town. Ph.D. dissertation, University of Chicago.

Good, Byron J., Mary-Jo DelVecchio Good, and Robert Moradi (1985). The Interpretation of Iranian Depressive Illness and Dysphoric Affect. In Arthur Kleinman and Byron J. Good, eds., *Culture and Depression: Studies in the Anthropology and Cross-Culture Psychiatry of Affect and Disorder.* Berkeley: University of California Press.

Good, Mary-Jo DelVecchio and Byron J. Good (1988). Ritual, the State, and the Transformation of Emotional Discourse in Iranian Society. *Culture, Medicine and Psychiatry* 12 (1): 43–63.

Graham, Mark and Shahram Khosravi (2002). Reordering Public and Private in Iranian Cyberspace: Identity, Politics, and Mobilization. *Identities* 9 (2): 219–46.

Graybill, Beth and Linda B. Arthur (1999). The Social Control of Women's Bodies in Two Mennonite Communities. In Linda B. Arthur, *Religion, Dress and the Body.* Oxford: Berg.

Gutmann, Matthew (1993). Rituals of Resistance: A Critique of the Theory of Everyday Forms of Resistance. *Latin American Perspectives* 20 (2): 74–92.

Habermas, Jürgen (1989). *The Structural Transformation of the Public Sphere: An In-quiry into a Category of Bourgeois Society*, Cambridge, Mass.: MIT Press.

Haeri, Shahla (1989). *Law of Desire: Temporary Marriage in Iran*, London: I.B.Tauris.

Hairi, Abdul-Hadi (1977). Shi'ism and Constitutionalism in Iran: A Study of the Role Played by the Persian Residents of Iraq in Iranian Politics. Leiden: E.J. Brill.

Hall, Stuart and Tony Jefferson (1983 [1975]). *Resistance Through Rituals: Youth Subcultures in Post-War Britain*. London: Hutchinson.

Hammer, Ferenc (2002). A Gasoline Scented Sinbad: The Truck Driver as a Popular Hero in Socialist Hungary. *Cultural Studies* 16 (1): 80–126.

Hammoudi, Abdellah (1997). *Master and Disciple: The Cultural Foundations of Moroccan Authoritarianism*. Chicago: University of Chicago Press.

Hannerz, Ulf (1987). The World in Creolisation. *Africa* 57: 546–59.

Hedayat, Sadegh (1324/1945). *Hajji Agha*. Tehran: n.p.

Hegland, Mary (1983). Two Images of Hussein: Accommodation and Revolution in an Iranian Village. In Nikki Keddie, ed., *Religion and Politics in Iran: Shi'ism from Quietism to Revolution*. New Haven, Conn.: Yale University Press.

Heidari, Gholam (1379/2001). *Tarikh-e Tahlili-e Sad Sal Sinamay-e Iran* (An Analytical History of One Hundred Years of the Iranian Cinema). Tehran: Cultural Research Bureau.

Herzfeld, Michael (1986). Within and Without: The Category of Female in the Ethnography of Modern Greece. In Jill Dubisch, ed., *Gender and Power in Rural Greece*. Princeton, N.J.: Princeton University Press.

——— (1997). *Cultural Intimacy: Social Poetics in the Nation-State*. New York: Routledge.

Hobsbawm, Eric and Terence Ranger (1983). *The Invention of Tradition*. Cambridge: Cambridge University Press.

Jabari, M (1379/2000). *Hamishe Bazar*. Tehran: Agah.

Jahanbagloo, Ramin (1379/2000). *Iran va Modernite* (Iran and the Problem of Modernity). Tehran: Goftar Publishing Corp.

Kamalkhani, Zahra (1996). *Women's Islam: Religious Practice Among Women in Today's Iran*. Bergen: Bergen University Press.

Kar, Mehrangiz (1378/1999). *Sakhtar-e Hoghoghi-ye Khanevadeh dar Iran* (Legal Structure of the Family System in Iran), Tehran: Roshangaran & Women Studies Publishing.

Kar, Mehrangiz (1380/2001). *Pazhoheshi darbar-e Khoshonat aleihe Zanan dar Iran* (Research About Violence Against Women in Iran). Tehran: Roshangaran & Women Studies Publishing.

Kelley, Ron and Jonathan Friedlander (1993). *Irangeles: Iranians in Los Angeles*. Berkeley: University of California Press.

Kelly, John D. and Martha Kaplan (1990). History, Structure, and Ritual. *Annual Review of Anthropology* 19: 119–50.

Keshavarzian, Arang (2007). *Bazaar and State in Iran: The Politics of Tehran Marketplace*. Cambridge: Cambridge University Press.

Khomeini, Ruhollah (1323/1944). *Kashf al Asrar*. Qom: n.p.

——— (1981). *Islam and Revolution: Writings and Declarations of Imam Khomeini*. Berkeley, Calif.: Mizan Press.

Khosravi, Shahram (1996). Can a Khan Be an Anthropologist? *Antropologiska Studier* 54–55: 71–80.

Khosrokhavar, Farhad (1995). *L'islamisme et la mort: le martyre révolutionnaire en Iran.* Paris: l'Harmattan.

Korom, Frank J. (2002). *Hosay Trinidad: Muharram Performances in an Indo-Caribbean Diaspora.* Philadelphia: University of Pennsylvania Press.

Kowinski, William Severini (1985). *The Malling of America: An Inside Look at the Great Consumer Paradise.* New York: Morrow.

Lamb, Sara (2001). Generation in Anthropology. *International Encyclopedia of the Social Behavioral and Sciences,* vol. 9. Oxford: Elsevier.

Lasch, Christopher (1980). *The Culture of Narcissism: American Life in an Age of Diminishing Expectations.* New York: Warner Books.

Lave, Jean, Paul Duguid, and Nadine Fernandez (1992). Coming of Age in Birmingham: Cultural Studies and Conceptions of Subjectivity. *Annual Review of Anthropology* 21: 257–82.

Lewis, Richard D. (2000). *When Cultures Collide: Managing Successfully Across Cultures.* London: Brealey.

Liechty, Mark (2003). *Suitably Modern: Making Middle-Class Culture in a New Consumer Society.* Princeton, N.J.: Princeton University Press.

Loeb, Laurence (1977). *Outcaste: Jewish Life in Southern Iran.* New York: Gordon & Breach.

Loeffler, Reinhold (1988). *Islam in Practice: Religious Beliefs in a Persian Village.* Albany: State University of New York Press.

Luhrmann, Tanya M. (1996). *The Good Parsi: The Fate of a Colonial Elite in a Postcolonial Society.* Cambridge, Mass.: Harvard University Press.

Madanipour, Ali (1998). *Tehran: The Making of a Metropolis,* New York: John Wiley.

Mahdi, Ali Akbar (1999). The Student Movement in the Islamic Republic of Iran. *Journal of Iranian Research and Analysis* 15 (2): 15–32.

Majlis and Research (1994). (bimonthly publication of the Islamic Consultative Assembly's Center for Research) 12 (Oct.–Nov.).

Mannheim, Karl (1952 [1928]). The Problem of Generations. In Paul Kecskemeti, ed., *Essays on the Sociology of Knowledge.* London: Routledge.

Mbembe, Achille (1992). The Banality of Power and the Aesthetics of Vulgarity in the Postcolony, *Public Culture* 4 (2): 1–30.

McDonald, Kevin (1999). *Struggle for Subjectivity: Identity, Action, and Youth Experience.* Cambridge: Cambridge University Press.

Mernissi, Fatima (1975). *Beyond the Veil: Male-Female Dynamics in a Modern Muslim Society.* New York: Halsted.

Milani, Farzaneh (1992). *Veils and Words: The Emerging Voice of Iranian Women Writers.* Syracuse, N.Y.: Syracuse University Press.

Miller, Daniel (1994). *Modernity: An Ethnographic Approach.* Oxford: Berg.

——— (1995a). Consumption Studies as the Transformation of Anthropology. In Daniel Miller, ed., *Acknowledging Consumption: A Review of New Studies.* London: Routledge.

——— (1995b). Consumption as the Vanguard of History. In Daniel Miller, ed., *Acknowledging Consumption: A Review of New Studies.* London: Routledge

——— (1997a). *Capitalism: An Ethnographic Approach.* Oxford: Berg.

——— (1997b). Could Shopping Ever Really Matter? In Pasi Falk and Colin Campbell, eds., *The Shopping Experience.* London: Sage.

Milosz, Czeslaw (1990 [1953]). *The Captive Mind.* New York: Vintage International.

Mir-Hosseini, Ziba (1993). *Marriage on Trial: A Study of Islamic Family Law.* London: I.B. Tauris.

200   Bibliography

———. (2002). Iran's Runaway Girls Challenge the Old Rules. *ISIM Newsletter* 9: 23.

Mirsepassi, Ali (2000). *Intellectual Discourse and the Politics of Modernization: Negotiating Modernity in Iran*. Cambridge: Cambridge University Press.

Moaveni, Azadeh (2005). *Lipstick Jihad: A Memoir of Growing Up Iranian in America and American in Iran*. New York: Public Affairs.

Moghissi, Haideh (1993). Women in the Resistance Movement in Iran. In Haleh Afshar, ed., *Women in the Middle East: Perceptions, Realities, and Struggles for Liberation*. London: Macmillan.

Mohamadi, Majid (1377/1998). *Daramadi bar Jamme-eshenasi va Eghtesad-e Farhang dar Iran-e Emroz* (An Introduction to the Sociology and Economics of Culture in Today's Iran). Tehran: Ghatreh Publishers.

Moshiri, Mahshid (1381/2002). *Farhang-e Estelahat-e Amiyaneh-ye Javanan* (Dictionary of the Young People's Vernacular). Tehran: Agahan Ide.

Motahari, Morteza (1379/2000). *Hemas-ye Hosseini* (Hossein's Movement). Tehran: Sadra.

Mottahedeh, Roy (1985). *Mantle of the Prophet: Religion and Politics in Iran*. New York: Simon and Schuster.

Mozaffari, Mahmod (1991). Why the Bazaar Rebels. *Journal of Peace Research* 29 (4): 377–91.

Nabokov, Vladimir (2001 [1935]). *Invitation to a Beheading*. London: Penguin

Naficy, Hamid (1985). Iranian Writers, the Iranian Cinema and the Case of Dash Akol. *Iranian Studies* 17 (2–4): 213–50.

——— (1992). Islamizing Film Culture in Iran. In Samih K. Farsoun and Mehrdad Mashayekhi, eds., *Iran: Political Culture in the Islamic Republic*. London: Routledge.

——— (1993). *The Making of Exile Culture: Iranian Television in Los Angeles*. Minneapolis: University of Minnesota Press.

——— (2000). Veiled Voice and Vision in Iranian Cinema: The Evolution of Rakhshan Banietemad's Films. *Social Research* 67 (2): 559–77.

Nafisi, Azar (2003). *Reading Lolita in Tehran*. New York: Random House.

Nafisi, Majid (1371/1992). *Dar Jostojoy-e Shadi*. Stockholm: Baran Bok Förlag.

Nafisi, Rasool (1992). Education and the Culture of Politics in the Islamic Republic of Iran. In Samih K. Farsoun and Mehrdad Mashayekhi, eds., *Iran: Political Culture in the Islamic Republic*. London: Routledge.

Najmabadi, Afsaneh (1991). Hazards of Modernity: Women, State and Ideology in Contemporary Iran. In Deniz Kandiyoti, ed., *Women, Islam and the State*. London: Macmillan.

——— (2005). *Women with Mustaches and Men Without Beards: Gender and Sexual Anxieties of Iranian Modernity*. Berkeley: University of California Press.

National Youth Organization (2006). *Policy and Legislation*. Tehran: National Youth Organization.

Navab-Safavi, Mojtaba (1357/1978). *Jame'e va Hokumat-e Eslami* (Islamic Society and Governance). Qom: Entesharat-e Hejrat.

Newman, Katherine (1996). Ethnography, Biography, and Cultural History: Generational Paradigms in Human Development. In Richard Jessor, Anne Colby, and Richard A. Shweder, eds., *Ethnography and Human Development: Context and Meaning in Social Inquiry*, Chicago: University of Chicago Press.

Nooshin, Laudan (2005). Underground, Overground: Rock Music and Youth Discourses in Iran. *Iranian Studies* 38 (3): 465–94.

O'Dougherty, Maureen (2002). *Consumption Intensified: The Politics of Middle-Class Daily Life in Brazil.* Durham, N.C.: Duke University Press.

Ong, Aihwa (1999). Clash of Civilizations or Asian Liberalism? an Anthropology of the State and Citizenship. In Henrietta L. Moore, ed., *Anthropological Theory Today.* Cambridge: Polity Press.

Ortner, Sherry B. (1995). Resistance and the Problem of Ethnographic Refusal. *Comparative Studies in Society and History* 37 (1): 173–93.

Öncü, Ayfle (1999). Istanbulites and Others: The Cultural Cosmology of Being Middle Class in the Era of Globalism. In Ça lar Keyder, ed., *Istanbul: Between the Global and the Local.* Lanham, Md.: Rowman and littlefield.

——— (2002). Global Consumerism, Sexuality as Public Spectacle, and the Cultural Remapping in the 1990s. In Deniz Kandiyoti and Ayfle Saktanber, eds., *Fragments of Culture: The Everyday of Modern Turkey.* London: I.B. Tauris.

Pamuk, Orhan (2006). *Istanbul: Memories and the City.* London: Vintage.

Pahlavi, Mohammad Reza (1980). *Answer to History.* New York: Stein and Day.

Paidar, Parvin (1995). *Women and the Political Process in Twentieth-Century Iran.* Cambridge: Cambridge University Press.

Pais, José M. (2000). Transitions and Youth Cultures: Forms and Performances. *International Social Science Journal* 52 (164): 219–32.

Pakravan, Emineh (1971). *Téhéran de jadis.* Paris: Negel.

Panahi, Mahin (1378/1999). *Akhlaq-e Arefan* (Sufi Ethics). Tehran: Rouzaneh.

Parsa, Misagh (2000). *States, Ideologies and Social Revolutions: A Comparative Analysis of Iran, Nicaragua, and the Philippines.* Cambridge: Cambridge University Press.

Qanon-e Mojazat-e Eslami (Islamic Penal Law) (1377/1998). Tehran: Ketabkhane-ye Ganj va Danesh.

Rahimi, Mostafa (1369/1990). *Trazhedi va ghodrat dar Shahnameh* (Tragedy and Power in Shahnameh). Tehran: Nilofar.

Rahnema, Ali (1998). *An Islamic Utopian: A Political Biography of Ali Shariati.* London: I.B. Tauris.

Rejali, Darius M. (1994). *Torture and Modernity: Self, Society, and State in Modern Iran,* Boulder, Colo.: Westview Press.

Rose, Nikolas and Peter Miller (1992). Political Power Beyond the State: Problematics of Government. *British Journal of Sociology* 43 (2): 173–205.

Rosen, Lawrence (1989). *The Anthropology of Justice: Law as Culture in Islamic Society.* Cambridge: Cambridge University Press.

Rotblat, Howard J. (1972). Stability and Change in an Iranian Provincial Bazaar. Ph D. dissertation, University of Chicago.

——— (1975). Social Organization and Development in an Iranian Provincial Bazaar. *Economic Development and Cultural Change* 23 (2): 292–305.

Rouhani, Farhang (2001). The Home as a Site of State Formation: The Politics of Transnational Media Consumption in Tehran. Ph.D. dissertation, University of Arizona.

Sadr, Hamid Reza (1379/2000). Sinama-ye M'aser-e Iran va mazamin-e an (The Contemporary Iranian Cinema and Its Themes). In Issa Rose and Sheila Whitaker, eds., *Zendegi va Honar: Sinema-ye Noien-e Iran* (Life and Art: The New Iranian Cinema). Tehran: Ketab Sara.

Sa'edi, Gholam Hossein (1380 [first ed. n.d.]/2001). *Tars va Larz* (Fear and Tremble). Tehran: Nashr-e Mah.

Sanadjina, Manuchehr (1996). A Public Flogging in South-Western Iran. In Olivia Harris, ed., *Inside and Outside the Law: Anthropological Studies of Authority and Ambiguity.* London: Routledge.

Savory, Roger M. (1978). Social Development in Iran During the Pahlavi Era. In George Lenczowski, ed., *Iran Under the Pahlavis*. Stanford, Calif.: Hoover Institution Press.

Scott, James C. (1985). *Weapons of the Weak: Everyday Forms of Peasant Resistance*. New Haven, Conn.: Yale University Press.

Seberny-Mohammadi, Annabelle and Ali Mohammadi (1994). *Small Media, Big Revolution: Communication, Culture, and the Iranian Revolution*. Minneapolis: University of Minnesota Press

Shadman, Fakhr ed-Din (1326/1947). *Taskhir-e Tammadon-e Farangi* (Possessed by Western Culture). Tehran: Majlis.

Shahidian, Hammed (1996). Iranian Exile and Sexual Politics: Issues of Gender Relations and Identity. *Journal of Refugee Studies* 9 (1): 43–72.

—— (2002). *Resistance in the Islamic Republic: Emerging Voices in the Iranian Women's Movement*. Westport, Conn.: Greenwood Press.

Shamloo, Ahmad (1343/1964). *Aida dar Ayeneh*. Tehran: Maziyar.

—— (1991). Dar in Bonbast. Trans. Ahmad Karimi Hakak in Revolutionary Posturing, *International Journal of Middle East Studies* 23 (4): 507–31.

—— (1377/1998). *Ketab-e Koucheh*, vol. 1. Tehran: Maziyar.

Shariati, Ali (1979). *On the Sociology of Islam: Lectures*. Berkeley, Calif.: Mizan.

Shay, Anthony (1999). *Choreophobia: Solo Improvised Dance in the Iranian World*. Costa Mesa, Calif.: Mazda.

Shayegan, Daryush (1992). *Cultural Schizophrenia: Islamic Societies Confronting the West*. Syracuse, N.Y.: Syracuse University Press.

Shields, Rob (1992). *Lifestyle Shopping: The Subject of Consumption*. London: Routledge.

Shirali, Mahnaz (2001). *La jeunesse iranienne: une génération en crise*. Paris: Presses Universitaires de France.

Sidanius, Jim and Felicia Pratto (1999). *Social Dominance: An Intergroup Theory of Social hierarchy and Oppression*. Cambridge: Cambridge University Press.

Stade, Ronald (1993). Designs of Identity: Politics of Aesthetics in the GDR. *Ethnos* 3(4): 241–58.

Stam, Robert (1992). *Subversive Pleasures: Bakhtin, Cultural Criticism, and Film*. Baltimore: Johns Hopkins University Press.

Stephen, Lynn (1995). Women's Rights Are Human Rights: The Merging of Feminine and Feminist Interests Among El Salvador's Mothers of the Disappeared. *American Ethnologist* 22 (4): 807–27.

Stierling, Henri (1976). *Isphahan: image du paradis*. Paris: Lausanne.

Street, Brian (1990). Orientalist Discourses in the Anthropology of Iran, Afghanistan, and Pakistan. In Richard Fardon, *Localizing Strategies: Regional Traditions of Ethnographic Writing*. Washington, D.C.: Smithsonian Institution Press.

Tapper, Richard, ed. (2002). *The New Iranian Cinema: Politics, Representation and Identity*. London: I.B.Tauris.

Tavakoli-Targhi Mohamad (2001). *Refashioning Iran: Orientalism, Occidentalism, and Historiography*. Basingstoke: Palgrave.

Taylor, Philip (2001). *Fragments of the Present: Searching for Modernity in Vietnam's South*. Honolulu: University of Hawai'i Press.

Tehran Geographic Information Centre (2005). *Atlas of Tehran Metropolis*. Tehran: Tehran Geographic Information Centre

Tester, Keith (1994). Introduction. In Keith Tester, ed., *The flâneur*. London: Routledge.

Thaiss, Gustav E. (1971). The Bazaar as a Case Study of Religion and Social Change. In Ehsan Yarshater, ed., *Iran Faces the Seventies.* New York: Praeger.
——— (1973). Religious Symbolism and Social Change: The Drama of Husain. Ph.D. dissertation, Washington University.
——— (1999). Muharram Rituals and the Carnivalesque in Trinidad. *ISIM Newsletter* 3.
Thornton, Sarah (1995). *Club Cultures: Music, Media and Subcultural Capital.* Cambridge: Polity Press.
Torab, Azam (1996). Piety as Gendered Agency: A Study of Jalaseh Ritual Discourse in an Urban Neighbourhood in Iran. *Journal of the Royal Anthropological Association* 2 (2): 235–52.
——— (2006). *Performing Islam: Gender and Ritual in Iran.* Amsterdam: E.J. Brill.
Touraine, Alain (1997). *Pourrons-nous vivre ensemble?* Paris: Fayard.
Udovitch, A. L. (1987). The Constitution of the Traditional Islamic Marketplace: Islamic Law and the Social Context of Exchange. In Shmuel N. Eisenstadt, ed., *Patterns of Modernity,* vol. 2: *Beyond the West.* London: Pinter.
Varzi, Roxanne (2002). A Ghost in the Machine: The Cinema of the Iranian Sacred Defence. In Richard Tapper, *The New Iranian Cinema: Politics, Representation and Identity.* London: I.B.Tauris.
Varzi, Roxanne (2006). *Warring Souls: Youth, Media, and Martyrdom in Post-Revolution Iran.* Durham, N.C.: Duke University Press.
Williams, Rosalind H. (1982). *Dream Worlds: Mass Consumption in Late Nineteenth-Century France.* Berkeley: University of California Press.
Willis, Paul (1977). *Learning to Labour.* Farnborough: Saxon House.
Wilson, Elizabeth (1992). The Invisible Flâneur. *New Left Review* 191: 90–110.
Yaghmaian, Behzad (2002). *Social Change in Iran: An Eyewitness Account of Dissent, Defiance, and New Moments for Rights.* Albany: State University of New York Press.
Zahedi, Dariush (2001). *The Iranian Revolution Then and Now.* Boulder, Colo.: Westview Press.
Zamani, Mustafa (1379/2000). *Javanan Chera?* (Youth Why?). Qom: Bounyad-e Farhangi Payam-e Islam (The Cultural Foundation of Islamic Message).
Zinovieff, Sofka (1991). Hunters and Hunted: Kamaki and the Ambiguities of Sexual Predation in a Greek Town. In Peter Loizos and Papaxiarchis Evthymois, eds., *Contested Identities: Gender and Kinship in Modern Greece.* Princeton, N.J.: Princeton University Press.

Filmography

Agha-ye Gharn-e Bistoum (Siamak Yasami, 1343/1964).
The Apple (*Sib,* Samira Makhmalbaf, 1376/1998).
Bad Kids (*Bache-haye Bad,* Alireza Davoudnezhad, 1380/2001).
The Burned Generation (*Nasl-e Sokhte,* Rasool Molagholipour 1378/1999).
Dead Wave (*Moj-e Morde,* Ebrahim Hatami Kia, 1380/2001).
Deep Breath (*Nafas-e Amigh,* Parviz Shahbazi, 1382/2003).
Divorce, Iranian Style (Kim Longinotto and Ziba Mir Hosseini, 1998).
Gilane (Rakhshan Bai Etemad, 1384/2005).
The Girl in the Sneakers (*Dokhtari ba Kafshha-ye Katani,* Rasol Sadrameli, 1378/1999).
The Glass Agency (*Azhans-e Shishei,* Ebrahim Hatami Kia, 1376/1997).

Grass (Merian C. Cooper and Ernest B. Schoedsak, 1925).
The Greek Ship (*Keshti-ye Yonani,* Naser Taghvai, 1377/1999).
Grimson Gold (Jafar Panahi, 1382/2003).
I, Taraneh, Am Fifteen (*Man, Taraneh Panzdah Sal daram,* Rasol Sadrameli 1380/2001).
Joje Fokoli (Reza Safai, 1353/1974).
MAXX (Saman Moghadam, 1384/2005).
Offside (Jafar Panahi, 1384/2005).
Party (Saman Moghadam, 1380/2001).
Runaway (Ziba Mir Hosseini, 2000).
Siavash (Saman Moghadam, 1378/1999).
Sohrab (Said Soheyli, 1379/2000).
Sweet Agonies (*Masa'b-e Shirin,* Ali Reza Davoudnezhad, 1377/1998).
Sheida (Kamal Tabrizi, 1378/1999).

Index

individual autonomy, 128, 170–71
International Gay and Lesbian Human
Rights Commission, 160
Internet: restrictions on, 98; blogs, 41,
157–58, 160; cyber-ethnography, 12;
cafés, 94, 97–98, 157; phone calls, 98;
primary users, 97–98; and rock music
subculture, 67, 149, 151; sexuality blogs
and websites, 41, 160; as subversive
space of defiance, 157–58; Third
Generation websites, 122–23
In the Name of the Father (film), 131
Iran, "authentic," 174
Iran and the Problem of Modernity
(Jahanbagloo), 163
Iran, demographics, 5–8; birth
rate/population growth, 6; changes,
5–6; economic growth, 7; and
emigration, 8; Shahrak-e Gharb profile,
61–63; and social crises, 5–8; and the
three generations, 5; and
unemployment, 6–7, 62, 177 n.6
Iran Times, xii
Iran-Iraq War (1980–88), 20, 29, 58, 77,
164, 171; and *basijis*, 29, 38, 77, 183
n.27; deaths and martyrdom, 52, 183
n.27
Irangeles and pop culture industry, 19, 68,
88, 112, 156–57, 174; Persian and
foreign videos, 156; radio broadcasts to
Iran, 157; techno-music and
Chaharshanbeh souri, 143; TV
channels and radio stations, 154,
156–57. See also *shou*
Iranian Artists' Forum (Khaneye
Honarmandan-e Iran), 172
Iranian Constitution, 25
Iranzamin Street, 73, 75, 114–15. *See also*
Golestan shopping center
Isfahan, 88–89, 175–76; bazaar of, 185 n.6;
Julfa (Armenian district), 15; "key"
informants in, 11; *passazhs* (shopping
centers), 91; Siyose Pol (bridge),
175–76
Islam: and Arab culture, 166; areligiosity
of Third Generation, 73, 126; differing
interpretations by parents and
media/schools, 137; and
dogs/impurity, 84–85; and post-
ideological character of Third
Generation, 127; and "principle of

mutual discipline," 25–26; self in, 17;
and traditional bazaars, 99, 113, 184
n.5, 185 n.6. *See also* non-Islamic
Iranian culture
Islamic Penal Code, 17–19, 27, 44–45
Islamic Republic of Iran Broadcasting
(IRIB), 22–24, 127, 130, 187 n.17
Islamic Revolution (1979), 99; agenda on
purity and consumption/consumerism,
36; and attack on popular culture,
19–20; and bazaars, 100; and birth rate,
6; discourse and Karbala paradigm, 51;
discourse on tradition and modernity,
8; and romanticization of poverty, 36;
experiences by three generations, 5. *See
also* post-Revolutionary Iran
Islamic Revolutionary Guard Corps, 29
ITV (satellite TV station), 156

Jafarkhan az Farang Amadeh (Jafar Khan Is
Back from Europe) (play), 79–80
Jahanbagloo, Ramin, 163, 179 n.10
jahel (ignorant), 80–81
Jamm'e Shenasi Qiyam-e Emam Hossein
(Sociology of Imam Hossein's
Movement) (Baghi), 50
jargon, youth, and language of defiance,
154–55
Javadieh neighborhood, 39, 60, 62, 70, 71,
74, 84, 88, 90
Javad, javad-ness: consumption patterns,
70–71, 116–20; and construction of
Shahraki identity, 70–75, 170–71;
defining "*javad*-ness," 70–71; dress and
rural style, 116–17; at Golestan, 71, 88;
ideological/cultural differences from
Shahrakis, 73–75, 90; internalization
of," 71, 88; and uncultured masculinity,
70–71, 76; and "new rich" *bazari*, 71,
118–19; Shahrak-e Gharb/Javadieh
dichotomies, 76, 90; and Shahraki
identity, 70–75, 90; status hierarchies
and "attitude"/style, 71–72;
stereotypical comments about bodies
of, 76; and threats to Shahraki purity,
72–73; views of Shahrakis by, 75–76
Javanan, Chera? (Youth, Why?) (religious
handbook), 28, 43
Joje Fokoli (Fokoli, the Chicken) (film), 80
jokes, political, 151–52. *See also* humor
journalists, foreign. *See* media, foreign

Sa'edi, Gholam Hossein, 35
Safai, Reza, 80
Salaam (reform-oriented newspaper), 140–41
"Saqakhaneh School," 50
Sarab (Mirage) (television program), 24
Satan worship: Arvin, the Iranian Satan worshipper, 67, 68, 70, 74; and bloggers, 158
satellite television dishes, 23, 88, 156
Scott, James C., 2, 177 n.2
self-abasement: and aestheticization of modesty, 32–33, 120; in Iranian mythology, 49–53; and Karbala paradigm, 50–51; and normative modesty, 32–33; and Persian language of "self-lowering," 32–33; and self-assertion, 120, 162, 165
self-assertion, 170–71, 189 n.1; and celebration of self, 162, 165; and individual autonomy, 170–71; and modernity, 162, 170, 189 n.1; and normative modesty, 162; and self-abasement, 120, 162, 165
self-help manuals, 160–61
September 11, 2001, attacks, 127
sexism, 137, 154
sex-segregation in public places: Golestan, 98, 112–13; and heterotopias of deviation (public sites of defiance), 146–47; Internet cafés, 98; and Khomeini, 46; and modesty, 44; public taxis, 146–47; ski resorts, 146; and veiling, 46
sexuality: and aestheticization of modesty, 39–40, 41–44; ambivalence and puritanism, 137; Ayatollahs' treatises on, 41–42; and *bazari* taste, 107–8; black color and sexual shame, 54; blogs and websites, 41, 160; commercialization and spectacle, 113; and "cultural crimes," 16–17, 112; and European/*khareji* women, 106–7; extramarital sex, 16–17; flirting, 112; and Golestan, 112–13; and handbooks on moral corruption, 28; homophobia, 137, 154, 176; homosexuality, 160; *kharej* and discourse on, 105; in marriage, 39–40; and National Youth Association, 42–43; new attitudes toward the body, 159–60; and pervasive

sexuality discourse, 41; post-Revolutionary state publications, 41–43; prostitution and red light districts, 7–8, 73, 113; and "public chastity," 40; and public taxis, 146–47; repression (turning into sin), 41–44; and romantic love, 159; and secular leftists, 181 n.10; sex manuals and sex education, 159–60; and sexual crimes/sins (confession/repandance, 43–44, 182 n.16; sexualized comments about bodies, 76; sexualized/erotic gaze of flâneurs, 112; veiling and desexualization of society, 39–40; and virginity, 137
Shadman, Fakhr ed-Din, 78–79
Shahnameh (Book of Kings), 49, 133–34
Shahrak-e Gharb, 57–90; "adaptation schools," 66, 108; anonymity, 64, 184 n.7; apoliticalness, 73; areligiosity, 73; Ashura ritual, 85–86, 145; *basijis*, 57, 73, 76–78; *bidard* youths, 10–11, 78–82, 83–85; center for Westernized youth culture, 87–89; and certain type of youth, 69; Chaharshanbeh souri, 143–44; vs. other Tehran neighborhoods, 61–63; design of original neighborhood, 60–62; and elite, 61; employment, 62; famous people residing in, 63, 64; and first week of Ramadan, 180 n.21; football riots, 140; home decoration styles, 68; household size, 62; and Iranian diaspora, 66–67; and *Javad*, 70–76, 90, 170–71; journalist interest in "global" features, 68, 116; literacy, 62; local associations, 48, 65–66, 73, 86–87, 135–36, 167; local newsletters, 63, 64, 65, 86; media misrepresentation and consequences, 86–87, 90; name, 60; non-/anti-Islamic values, 84, 89–90; nostalgia for traditional lifestyles, 69–70; occupations, 62, 63; physical boundaries, 61; political carnival and pro-Khatami youth, 85–86; political conservatives and anti-Shahrak rhetoric, 85–86; population data, 61; and purity, 72–73, 75, 84–85; "relative freedom," 64, 87–89; Shahraki/non-Shahraki dichotomy, 76, 90; sociological/demographic profile,

Acknowledgments

This book is part of the project *Traveling Modernities: A Transnational Study on the Dilemmas of Being Young,* which began in 1998. During the six-year period of fieldwork and writing I received help from many more people and institutions than I can possibly mention.

I thank Professor Gudrun Dahl, whose intellectual guidance is present on every page of this book. I am also grateful to Professor Ulf Hannerz for his generosity and concern for my academic career. He read the entire manuscript and made insightful remarks. Mark Graham, teacher, colleague, and friend, has challenged and encouraged me since my first year as an undergraduate student in social anthropology at Stockholm University. He made detailed comments on the entire manuscript and helped me to clarify my thoughts. A special debt of gratitude is owed to Professor Charles Westin. During the time that it took me to write this book, I have been the beneficiary of his support and encouragement.

I am deeply indebted to all young Tehranis who shared their thoughts, experiences, and emotions with me. Special thanks to Dara, Simon, Bahman and Elli. I am grateful to Dr. Soheila Shahshahani at Shahid Beheshti University in Tehran, who gave me valuable help and suggestions during the fieldwork and afterward. I have had comments on parts of this book from Helena Wulff, Professor Said Mahmoudi, Karin Norman, Fataneh Farahani, Professor Seteney Shami, Annika Rabo, Victor Alneng, Thaïs Machado-Borges, Anna Hasselström, Eva-Maria Hardtmann, Galina Lindquist, Johan Lindquist, and Reza Arjmand. Their critical suggestions have made this book better. I thank Professor Kirin Narayan (University of Wisconsin) and Professor Paul Stoller (West Chester University), who believed in this book and encouraged me to publish it. My particular thanks go to editors at the University of Pennsylvania Press. First to Peter Agree, Social Sciences editor, for taking a chance on the manuscript, to Chris Hu, who guided me into finishing.

Örjan Bartholson and Paolo Favero are also members of the *Traveling Modernities* project. They have provided intellectual inspiration and solid friendship. Hasse Huss is thanked here for the pleasure of the—almost a decade long—intellectual dialogue we have had over cups of coffee in the various cafés on campus. Many thanks to the Bank of Sweden Tercentenary Foundation for financial support. To my parents, Parvaneh and Nader, I express my deepest love and gratitude. I owe special thanks to Roxane, Maryam, and Kian for their support and tolerance of my absences and absent presences.